FORENSIC DENTISTRY

Edited by
Paul G. Stimson
Curtis A. Mertz

Taylor & Francis
Taylor & Francis Group

Boca Raton   London   New York   Singapore

A CRC title, part of the Taylor & Francis imprint, a member of the
Taylor & Francis Group, the academic division of T&F Informa plc.

Library of Congress Cataloging-in-Publication Data

Catalog Record is Available from the Library of Congress

Visit the CRC Press Web site at www.crcpress.com

© 1997 by CRC Press

No claim to original U.S. Government works
International Standard Book Number 0-8493-8103-7
Printed in the United States of America   4 5 6 7 8 9 0
Printed on acid-free paper

Contents

Preface

Forensic dentistry, like all the forensic sciences, has come a long way since the publication of the last textbook on forensic dentistry. The editors would like to thank the many students and other interested individuals who, over the years, have asked questions that have stimulated some of the answers found in this text. We appreciate the opportunity to share this material and have assembled, we think, an outstanding list of contributors to this topic of forensic dentistry.

We have included a chapter that will be most helpful to those who are faced with a trial date or an aggressive attorney: "Survival Techniques in Another World — The Courtroom". We are indebted to William P. Bobulsky, J.D.; Carol E. Henderson, J.D., Professor of Law, Nova Southeastern University; and Judge Ronald Vettel for their insights which were used to cover this area. We have been told that this is a first in textbooks of this type.

Another chapter that we are excited about is "Buried Crime Scene Evidence: The Application of Forensic Geotaphonomy in Forensic Archaeology". To our knowledge, this is also a first in a textbook on forensic dentistry.

The other chapters by our contributors are all excellent. A big thanks to Judge Haskell Pitluck for permission to include his bite mark case citations — another example of his caring and sharing with the forensic odontology group and the forensic group overall. A hearty thanks also goes out to Dr. Richard R. Souvironfor permission to use the Bundy material .

We owe a debt to the following individuals for information, assistance, ideas, literary contributions, and just for "being there" to help us: Professor Dennis C. Dirkmaat; Senior Development Engineer Nick N. G. Dong, M.D.; Ronald H. Krasney, M.D., for ophthalmological consultation; Mrs. Leah Krevit, one of the most helpful librarians we know; Jeffrey Hoover, D.M.D., who is not only gifted as an endodontist but also in the use and correction of written English as well; and to the members of the Division of Oral Pathology who have allowed us the freedom to pursue this effort.

We recently ran across a quotation from Schopenhauer that may be significant here: *"Every man takes the limits of his own field of vision for the limits of the world."*

Thanks especially to our wives who have graciously given us the time to assemble this text and to the University of Texas Dental Branch for use of the library, photography service, etc.

Finally, we owe a tremendous debt of gratitude for the patience of the publishers of this text.

Paul G. Stimson, D.D.S., M.S.
The University of Texas Health Science Center at Houston,
Dental Branch.

Curtis A. Mertz, D.D.S.
Ashtabula, Ohio.

The Editors

Paul G. Stimson, D.D.S., M.S., is Professor in the Division of Oral and Maxillofacial Pathology in the Department of Stomatology at The University of Texas Health Science Center at Houston Dental Branch. He received his dental degree from Loyola University in Chicago and his Master of Science in General Pathology from the University of Chicago. He is board certified in Forensic Odontology and Oral Pathology. Dr. Stimson has been a faculty member and lectured at the Armed Forces Institute of Pathology in the Forensic Dentistry Course since 1968 and has been on the faculty and served as course consultant for the Southwest Symposium on Forensic Dentistry during their last thirteen symposiums. During the past two symposiums he also served as Course Co-director. He was co-editor, with Dr. S. Miles Standish, of the *Dental Clinics of North America* issue directed to forensic dentistry. Dr. Stimson is a charter member and has served in the offices of the American Society of Forensic Odontology, from secretary-treasurer to president. He has also served the on the board of the American Board of Forensic Odontology (ABFO) as secretary-treasurer, vice-president, president-elect, and president. Until recently, Dr. Stimson was Chairperson of the Civil Litigation Committee for the ABFO. He has served on the Education Committee of the American Academy of Forensic Sciences and is presently the parliamentarian for the ABFO and past parliamentarian for the Houston Society of Clinical Pathology.

Dr. Stimson is an editorial consultant for the *Journal of the American Dental Association,* and has been for many years. Dr. Stimson has many publications and presentations in the field of oral pathology and forensic odontology, lecturing extensively in the United States, Canada, Mexico, England, and the Scandinavian countries. He has both testified and consulted in numerous bite mark homicide cases, personal injury cases, and standard-of-care cases for both the prosecution and the defense. He recently did the necessary dental identifications in the Phillips Refinery explosion and fire in Pasadena, Texas, resulting in the identification of 14 of the 24 deceased victims by dental means. Dr. Stimson is presently a consultant in Oral Pathology to M. D. Anderson Cancer Center Hospital and the Houston Veterans Hospital in Houston. He has been the forensic dental consultant to the Harris

County Medical Examiner's Office since 1968. His honors include: Jurisprudence Section Award, American Academy of Forensic Science (1991); Who's Who in America, Southwest Section; Who's Who in Houston; Who's Who in Health Care, First Edition; Who's Who in Science and Engineering, Second Edition; Omicron Kappa Upsilon (Faculty Member); Fellow American Academy of Oral and Maxillofacial Pathology (by examination); Fellow, American Academy of Forensic Sciences. His most recent award was the Odontology Section Award of the American Academy of Forensic Sciences "In Recognition of Service to the Field of Odontology" at their annual meeting in Nashville, Tennessee in February, 1996.

Curtis A. Mertz, D.D.S., attended the University of Texas in Austin and received his dental degree from Ohio State University in Columbus, Ohio. Dr. Mertz then served as a fellow in Oral Diagnosis and Oral Diagnosis and Oral Surgery at the Cleveland Clinic. He continued his education at Kent State University. Dr. Mertz was Chief Executive Officer and guided a large group of dental specialists in a private practice in Ashtabula, Ohio. This was the first such practice of its kind in the United States at the time of its inception in 1946. Dr. Mertz was instrumental in the founding of the various specialty boards under the auspices of the Law Enforcement Assistance Administration (LEAA) grant from the Federal Government. The first certifying board to be created was the American Board of Forensic Toxicology in 1975, followed by the American Board of Forensic Odontology (ABFO) in 1976, and then the American Boards of Forensic Document Examiners and Forensic Anthropology in 1977. Other specialty certifying boards soon followed. Dr. Mertz was elected as the first president of the ABFO shortly after it was founded and served for two years. He presently sreves as a forensic odontologist on the Disaster Mobilization Operational Readiness Team (DMORT) for Region VII, which was created under the Federal Emergency Management Association (FEMA), U.S. Department of Health and Human Services. He is also a consultant in Forensic Dentistry for the Armed Forces Institute of Pathology, and a contract consultant in Human Factors Group of the Federal Aviation Administration (FAA) and the National Transportation and Safety Board (NTSB). Dr. Mertz is a consultant and postgraduate lecturer in the Department of Forensic Anthropology at Mercyhurst College in Erie, Pennsylvania. He is also a consultant to the Pennsylvania State Police. Dr. Mertz also serves as forensic dental consultant to many state and local law enforcement agencies in Ohio and the surrounding states. He belongs to many professional groups and has multiple hospital affiliations and served on active duty in the Army during World War II. Some honors he has received are: American Academy of Forensic Science Charter Member Award, 1986; American Board of Forensic Odontology President's Award, 1976 and 1979; American Society of Forensic Odontology Founder's and Second Presidential Award, 1970; American Academy of Forensic Sciences, Odontology Section Award in Recognition of Outstanding Contributions to the Forensic Sciences, 1986; Distinguished Faculty Award, Forensic Dentistry Courses, Armed Forces Institute of Pathology, 1989 and the American Academy of Forensic Sciences Jurisprudence Section Award, 1991. He has lectured in Africa, Israel, North and South America, and Asia (People's Republic of China) on forensic dentistry and the handling of mass disaster victims following any type of extreme tragedy. He has published numerous articles on both practice management and forensic dental subjects. His most recent award was the Odontology Section Award of the American Academy of Forensic Sciences "In Recognition of Service to the Field of Odontology" at their annual meeting in New York, in February 1997.

Contributors

Gregory S. Golden, D.D.S.
Diplomate, American Board of
Forensic Odontology

Forensic Dental Consultant
Chief Odontologist
County of San Bernardino
Upland, California

Michael J. Hochrein
Special Agent
Federal Bureau of Investigation
St. Louis, Missouri

William R. Maples, Ph.D.
Distinguished Service Professor
CA Pound Human Identification Laboratory
University of Florida
Gainesville, Florida

Curtis A. Mertz, D.D.S.
Diplomate, American Board of
Forensic Odontology

Forensic Dental Consultant
Armed Forces Institute of Pathology
Washington, D.C.

**William M. Morlang II, D.D.S.,
D.A.B.F.O.**
Forensic Dental Consultant
Armed Forces Medical Examiner
Armed Forces Institute of Pathology

Associate Clinical Professor
School of Medicine
Wright State University

USAF School of Aerospace Medicine
San Antonio, Texas

Haskell M. Pitluck, J.D.
Judge, 19th Judicial Circuit
McHenry County Courthouse
Woodstock, Illinois

Paul G. Stimson, D.D.S., M.S.
Professor of Dental Pathology
Division of Oral and Maxillofacial Pathology
University of Texas Dental Branch
Houston, Texas

Consultant, Harris County Medical Examiner

**Gerald L. Vale, D.D.S., M.D.S.,
M.P.H., J.D.**
Clinical Professor and Associate Dean
University of Southern California School
of Dentistry

Co-Director of Dentistry
Los Angeles County+USC Medical Center

Chief Forensic Dental Consultant
County of Los Angeles Department
of Coroner
Los Angeles, California

Glenn N. Wagner, D.O.
Assistant Armed Forces Medical Examiner
Deputy Director (Navy)
Armed Forces Institute of Pathology
Washington, D.C.

Victor Walter Weedn, M.D., J.D.
Lieutenant Colonel, U.S. Army
Chief Deputy Medical Examiner
DOD DNA Registry
Office of the Armed Forces Medical Examiner
Armed Forces Institute of Pathology
Washington, D.C.

Larry D. Williams, J.D.
AFIP Legal Counsel
Armed Forces Medical Examiner's Office
Office of Legal Counsel
Springfield, Virginia

Franklin D. Wright, D.M.D.
Diplomate, American Board of
Forensic Odontology

Forensic Dental Consultant
Hamilton County Coroner's Office
Cincinnati, Ohio

This book is dedicated to the late William F. Maples, Ph.D. in appreciation of his pioneering work during the formative years of the odontology section in the American Academy of Forensic Sciences and the American Board of Forensic Odontology. We are grateful to Dr. Maples for his devotion and the unselfish amount of time and teaching he gave to forensic dentistry to assist in identification problems.

Others who should also be mentioned are Drs. Ellis Kerley and Clyde Snow. The requests from Drs. Maples, Kerley, and Snow for assistance from qualified forensic dentists helped to alert medical examiners, coroners, prosecutors, defense attorneys, and the judicial bench as a whole to the complexity and need of human identification by dental means. The late Jay Schwartz, as a member of the jurisprudence section, was also a great help in this area.

Scientific Methods of Identification

1

GLENN N. WAGNER

Introduction

Forensic identifications by their nature are multidisciplinary team efforts relying on positive identification methodologies as well as presumptive or exclusionary methodologies. Typically, this effort involves the cooperation and coordination of law enforcement officials, forensic pathologists, forensic odontologists, forensic anthropologists, serologists, criminalists, and other specialists as deemed necessary. In each discipline, there is the need to develop scientific evidence relative to the questions of fact regarding identification in a defensible manner grounded on general rules of acceptance, reliability, and relevance. Most techniques applied are used by all or most of the disciplines, often for slightly different purposes.

In the forensic sciences, a great deal of effort is spent on the identity or confirmation of identity of the victim(s) and perpetrator(s). This labor intensive aspect of a medicolegal investigation focuses on the six major questions asked in any such forensic investigation:

1. Who is the victim?
2. What are the injuries?
3. How were the injuries sustained?
4. Where did the injuries occur?
5. When did the injuries occur?
6. If the injuries were caused by another person, by whom?

Each of the questions are co-related. Most investigations involve several "autopsies", one of the victim(s), one of the scene, and one of the circumstances of injury and/or death. These "autopsies" are designed to discover and preserve evidence, document that evidence, analyze that evidence, and apply that evidence towards reconstructing the events leading to the injury and/or death. Most such investigations focus on physical evidence that is

0-8493-8103-7/97/$0.00+$.50
© 1997 by CRC Press LLC

deposited or transferred from victim to perpetrator and vice versa. This presumed relationship is known as Locard's principle and is the basis for much of what is attempted in the fields of criminalistics and forensic chemistry. The development and application of molecular biology techniques, especially DNA profiling, reflects this principle and the current reliance on technology in medicolegal investigations.

Identification Parameters

Legal certification of an individual's identity is based on a number of parameters most of which are centered about the individual's appearance and personal effects. As such, many persons are buried or cremated based on a visual identification or other presumptive identification methods. Where possible, a positive identification is preferred to a presumptive identification in such medicolegal cases. Positive identifications traditionally involve a comparison of pre- and postmortem data which are considered unique to the individual. These methods include: (1) dental comparisons, (2) fingerprints, palm prints, and footprints, (3) DNA identifications, and (4) radiographic superimpositions (vertebrae, cranial structures including frontal sinuses, pelvic structures, bone trabeculae, and prostheses). Presumptive identifications which include visual recognition, personal effects, serology, anthropometric data, and medical history do not usually identify unique characteristics of the individual but rather present a series of general or class characteristics which may exclude others based on race, sex, build, age, blood group, etc. Most positive identifications today are based on dental examinations and fingerprints and are fundamental procedures in medicolegal death investigations including mass disasters. The development of DNA analysis is providing investigators with yet another very important tool in the identification process.

Forensic Odontology

Forensic odontology has three major areas of utilization: (1) diagnostic and therapeutic examination and evaluation of injuries to jaws, teeth, and oral soft tissues, (2) the identification of individuals, especially casualties in criminal investigations and/or mass disasters, and (3) identification, examination, and evaluation of bite marks which occur with some frequency in sexual assaults, child abuse cases, and in personal defense situations.

The odontological identification examination of a decedent is based on a systematic comparison of the pre- and postmortem dental characteristics of the individual based on the dental record and supporting radiographs (apical films, panographs and medical skull films). A variety of techniques can be used to narrow the search and are based on presumptive identification data which are often sorted with computer assistance. The final identification is based on validation of the premortem data and their comparison with the postmortem data. Any discrepancies between the two records must be explained. Most dental examinations of this nature rely heavily on the presence of restorations as well as the structure and relationship of one dental structure to another. This comparison can be complicated by any attending trauma or by the absence of adequate premortem dental information. It is also noteworthy that many individuals enter adulthood without dental restorations due to the institution of fluoride treatments and better oral hygiene. This increasing circumstance complicates dental identification efforts especially when computerized databases are used such as CAPMI (computerized assisted postmortem identification system) which tabulates restorations and missing teeth as sorting parameters.

In problem cases, a variety of techniques are used to assist in the identification issue. These include (1) amino acid racemization studies, especially aspartic acid, (2) incremental line and other histology studies, (3) scanning electron microscopy with and without energy-dispersive X-ray analysis, (4) metal ratio analysis in bone and teeth, (5) serology studies for blood groups, serum proteins, and polymorphic enzymes, and (6) most recently, DNA analyses. Ideally, any such analyses should not completely destroy the structure(s) since any challenges to the identification may require additional and often independent testing.

Every such identification effort requires an understanding of the available testing methodologies (literature and practical experience), the expected function of such testing, and its limitations.

Ancillary Technologies

Age Determinants

Aspartic acid racemization has been used for age estimation based on its presence in human dentin. This technology applied to dental forensic issues is a spinoff of paleontology studies on fossil bone and shells. Most protein components in the body consist of L-amino acids, whereas D-amino acids have been found in bones, teeth, brain, and the eye's crystalline lens. D-amino acids are believed to have a slower metabolic turnover and subsequently a slower decomposition rate. Aspartic acid has the highest racemization rate of all of the amino acids. In 1976, Helfman and Bada[2] used this information to study age estimation by comparing D/L aspartic acid dental ratios in 20 subjects with good results (r = 0.979). A high coronary D/L ratio was noted in the younger age group, decreasing with age presumptively due to environmental changes. The tooth sectioning was transverse in the Helfman and

Bada study. In 1985, Ogino et al.[3] reported this application in forensic odontology specimens for age determination at the time of death. In 1990, Ritz et al.[4] reported on the extent of aspartic acid racemization in dentin for age determination at the time of death, concluding that this methodology could provide a more accurate determination of age than other aging parameters. This determination was based on a linear regression equation: $\ln (1 + D/L)/(1 - D/L) = 2k$ (Aspartic)t + constant, where k = 1st order kinetics and t = actual age. In 1991, Ohtani and Yamamoto[5] studied this aspartic acid relationship using longitudinal sections, with better results ($r = 0.991$). The teeth used in this study were the lower central incisors and first premolars. Subsequently, they found that better age estimations could be achieved with fractionating the total amino acid fraction (TAA) into an insoluble collagen fraction (IC) and a soluble peptide fraction (SP). As compared to the total amino acid assay or the insoluble collagen fraction, the soluble peptide fraction had higher concentrations of aspartic acid and glutamine, both hydrophilic acids. Ohtani and Yamamoto concluded that there was good correlation between Asp D/L and actual age expressed by a reversible linear equation for IC and SP as well as TAA and that SP appeared to provide the most reliable age estimation because of a high racemization rate — roughly three times that of TAA. The technique requires longitudinal sectioning of the tooth and removal of the dental pulp, washing with 0.2 M hydrochloric acid, distilled water (×3), ethanol, and ether (5 min each) and then powdering in an agate mortar. Fractionation and extraction was accomplished by adding 1 ml of 1 M HCl to 10 mg of powder and then centrifuge at 5000 rpm for 1 hr at 5°C. The ratios were then quantitated by gas chromatography using N-trifluoroacetyl isopropyl ester derivatives and a helium carrier gas. These studies yielded age estimations within three to four years of actual age.

Dental histology has been used for age estimations as well, largely based on the work of Gustafson.[6,7] Maples[8] in 1978 reported on an improved technique of using dental histology for estimation of adult age by using multiple regression analyses based on Gustafson's parameters of attrition, paradontosis, secondary dentin, cementum, root resorption, and root transparency. He concluded that multiple regression analyses allowed improvement of age estimation in adult human teeth with more precision and less variables. He also noted that the second molar (position 7) was the best to use for histological aging techniques and that dental aging can be used in the same way as epiphyseal fusion, osteon aging, cranial sutures, and changes in the pubic symphysis have been used in contemporary and prehistoric populations for aging purposes. Maples and Rice[9] in 1979, however, reported on persistent difficulties in the Gustafson dental age estimations despite relatively accurate and easy ways to determine ages of mineralization, crown completion, eruption and root completion, which are usually complete by age 30. The difficulties appeared to be those of statistical errors in the published articles.

In 1991, Skinner and Anderson[10] reported a case study involving the recovered cranium of a native Indian child in British Columbia, Canada in which individualization and enamel histology was used for identification based on the presence in the dental enamel of the primary and secondary dentition of stress markers, termed striae of Retzius, which could be correlated with known stressors in the life of the presumed missing child. Incremental brown striae in the enamel of teeth were described by Anders Retzius in 1837. Gustafson demonstrated in 1955 the similarity in incremental lines between contralateral pairs of teeth from a single individual. Since 1963, Boyde has been the best-known proponent of the methodology.

Cook[11] described a case in which this technique was used against other estimators of age based on pathological findings at autopsy, radiographical evidence, and anthropological data. She noted that a number of studies had been done using Gustafson's criteria on the six parameters used (attrition, secondary dentin deposition, paradontosis, cementum deposition, root resorption, and root transparency) with each parameter scored from 0 to 4 based on equal weight. The resulting scores were compared against known age by linear regression relative to age variance.[12-17] These studies showed reasonable consistency in confidence levels but an age variance of 7 to 15 years. In summary, incremental line analysis appears to complement these histological studies and could be added to dental eruption data, at least in younger populations, with good results.

The premise for incremental line analysis in identification efforts is based on the fact that these lines have the same pattern in an individual whose enamel formed at the same time in a given dentition. The different teeth developing in one individual give the same pattern of incremental lines which is distinct from that of another individual, in effect creating a "fingerprint" of enamel development specific to the individual.

Incremental line analysis is usually done on ground sections of longitudinally sectioned dentition which results in the destruction of the dental structures. The Skinner and Anderson[10] study is unique in that ground sections were not used. Reconstructed crowns were embedded in crystal clear polyester casting resin with Fiber-tek catalyst and allowed to cure. They were then longitudinally sectioned at 180 to 200 μm with a Buehler-Isomet low-speed saw with a diamond wafering blade. The mounted sections were examined and photographed at ×20 magnification with ordinary and polarized light. Composite photographs were then created showing the entire labial/buccal enamel to homologize striae between teeth.

Limitations in incremental line age determinations appear age dependent. Lipsinic et al.[18] studied the correlation of age and incremental lines in the cementum of human teeth and found that direct predictions of age based on these lines generally underestimated the age of older specimens. There was, however, correlation between the number of lines and age. These authors concluded that such studies would have greater usefulness if a large enough population group was studied and that a computer-generated formula resulted.

As a side note, age can be estimated by histological evaluation of osteons in bones. Kerley[20] in 1965 reported on his success with microscopic age determinations in cortical human bone. In 1978, Kerley and Ubelaker[21] published a revised method based on the same technique. Both involve use of ground sections and osteon counts. This technique is in common use in anthropology laboratories. Singh and Gunberg[22] applied this methodology to mandibular bone sections with good results, suggesting that combining bone section histology with dental histology provides a valuable comparative age determination in unknown remains.

Dental Structure Identification

Scanning electron microscopy with and without energy-dispersive X-ray analysis has been used to identify teeth by dentinal tubules and evidence of previous restorations especially in incinerated remains.

Carr et al.[23] in 1986 reported a case in which the scanning electron microscope was used to confirm dentition in recovered remains from the burned wreckage of a gasoline truck involved in a transportation mishap. Recovered tooth fragments were carbonized and not morphologically recognized as teeth. The desiccated specimens were mounted on aluminum stubs using silver paint, coated with gold-palladium in a sputter-coater, and viewed and photographed on a Joel T-300 SEM at an accelerating voltage of 20 kV. Identification of the specimens as dentition was based on the presence of dentinal tubules. The investigators noted that in addition to dentinal tubules, SEM provided evidence of tool marks and other defects. Use of SEM with EDX provided a profile of elements present which may identify a particular type of dental material. Fairgrieve[24] in 1994 reported a similar case involving SEM on incinerated teeth to evaluate parallel striations in tooth enamel and dentine as evidence of previous dental restorations.

Smith[25] in 1990 reported the application of SEM with EDS (energy-dispersive X-ray fluorescence spectrometry) analysis on MIA remains from southeast Asia based on examination and analysis of proximal facets. The author concluded that this technique had potential for detecting residual restorative materials in facet areas and in determining the existence and composition of unrecovered adjacent restorations. Smith also noted that this preliminary study indicated that it was possible to detect restorative material residue on the proximal surfaces of unrestored teeth and indicate the antemortem existence of a restoration on the adjacent tooth surface. This knowledge could be valuable in presumptive identifications where the teeth with critical restorations were not recovered with the primary remains, but teeth proximal to those with restorations were present.

Sorting by Metal Ratios

In 1986, Fulton et al.[26] reported on the use of metal ratios in the reassociation of scattered and mixed human bones. This work, conducted at Kansas State University, relied on published work on trace elements present in bone in archaeological materials, especially the work of Lambert et al.,[27] who attempted to relate bone metal ratios with diet. A total of 11,958 individual element determinations were made by atomic absorption and neutron activation. Concentrations of 21 elements sampled at 54 places in 30 human bones in each of 5 human skeletons indicated that there were sufficiently consistent metal ratios in bone specimens within an individual to reassociate fragmented remains yet they varied with sufficient discrimination from other individuals to be a useful sorting tool. The magnesium/zinc ratio was the most reliable, with zinc/sodium, magnesium/sodium, and chromium/sodium ratios useful supplemental comparative studies. Furthermore, individual trace elements such as arsenic complement this sorting process effort. The authors concluded, however, that this ancillary procedure did not provide sufficient individuality to be used alone, but was a valuable adjunct to standard anthropological techniques typically used for sorting commingled remains.

Serological Parameters

Forensic serology has been applied to odontological investigations with reasonable success. In dental pulps, ABO blood groups and serum proteins Gm, Km, and Gc are present as well as eight polymorphic enzymes (PGM, PGD, ADA, AK, EsD, Fuc, DiA3, and transferrin).

Kido et al.[29] in 1993 reported on the use of transferrin C subtyping by isoelectric focusing electrophoresis in dental pulps. Sensitive immunoblotting techniques had previously identified transferrin subtypes in urine, blood stains and semen. The Kido et al. study showed good correlation between serum and dental pulp specimens.

In 1993, Lopez-Abadia and Ruiz de la Cuesta[30] reported a simplified method for phenotyping alpha-2-HS glycoprotein in serum, bloodstains, and dental pulp using isoelectric focusing electrophoresis on neuramidase-treated specimens, with excellent results.

Although DNA studies are replacing many of the serological techniques applied to identification efforts, these techniques provide useful sorting data in relatively short periods. Serology continues to play an important role in reassociation efforts in mass disasters, transportation mishaps and explosions when DNA analysis is not readily available or involves a lengthy delay, often up to several months. Serology studies are especially useful when joined with anthropological and odontological methodologies. To get access to the dental pulp, if this is the primary source of the serological material, the tooth must be crushed or sectioned. Many of the techniques used have their basis in similar studies on bone specimens.

Lee et al.[31] in a series of articles reported on their successes in determining genetic markers in human bone including ABO and IGH grouping using a combination of absorption-elution and two-dimensional absorption-inhibition methodologies. In these studies, bone was cleaned, powdered, then extracted with PBS (phosphate buffered saline) at pH 7.2. They found that the combination of methodologies was more successful than either technique alone.

Like dental histology techniques for aging, a combination of dental and bone serological studies would prove complementary if needed, especially in reassociations. DNA profiling methodologies, like restriction fragment length polymorphism (RFLP) analysis offer similar opportunities but because of DNA degradation often require PCR (polymerase chain reaction) analysis for amplification of allele-specific areas and subsequent study.

Odontoanthropology

For a number of practical reasons, many forensic odontologists have resisted pressures to characterize an unknown dentition by age, race, or sex except in general terms. Lasker and Lee[33] and Aitchison,[34] often referenced, both described racial traits in the human dentition. Even aging methodologies appear equally shared among forensic odontologists, anthropologists, pathologists, and often radiologists. Both anthropologists and radiologists rely heavily on radiographic evidence of aging, dental eruption patterns, and changes in the facial structures with age such as the angle of the mandible, zygomatic arches, and lateral pterygoid plates. Harris and McKee[35] in 1990, studied tooth mineralization characteristics in blacks and whites from the southern U.S. in individuals ranging in age from 3.5 to 13 years. They found that females develop more rapidly than males, and that blacks are nearly twice as sexually dimorphic (7.2%) as whites (3.7%). Within each sex, blacks achieved mineralization stages significantly earlier, by approximately 5%, than whites. Anthropologists also appear more eager to use a variety of observations to assist them in obtaining a dental age with a skeletal age for comparison. Sexing parameters generally in use involve classical anthropometric measurements.

Rogers[36] in the *Testimony of Teeth: Forensic Aspects of Human Dentition*, reviewed the efforts of many authors to use the human dentition for determinations of age, sex, race, and individualization. He focused on several useful categories: (1) heredity — size and genetic peculiarities, (2) wear characteristics, (3) pathology — caries and periodontitis, and (4) restorations — dental fillings and prostheses such as crowns, bridges, and dentures. This approach represents a composite analysis of general features and is useful for presumptive sorting of unknown remains.

In 1976, Burns and Maples[37] reported on three parameters of dental aging: formative, degenerative, and histological. The formative parameter includes tooth mineralization, crown completion, eruption of the crown, and complementary roots. Degenerative measurements include tooth wear, tooth color, and periodontal attachments. Histological assessments include the degree of secondary dentin deposition, cementum apposition, root resorption, and root transparency. The histological measurements and grading follow Gustafson's efforts.

In 1978, Taylor[38] published a text on variation in tooth morphology relative to anthropologic and forensic aspects which emphasized the structural qualitative rather than quantitative differences of teeth and dentition. This text complements that of Rogers[36] and would be a useful reference in odontoanthropology studies. Taylor, in studying variations in dental patterns, suggested six parameters for evaluation:

1. Type of tooth structure — family characteristics,
2. Personal characteristics found throughout a dentition — crowns, occlusal ridges, cusps, and root robusticity, as well as branching patterns, furcation, and fusion,
3. Imposed characteristics based on the anatomical relationships of the crowns and roots,
4. Complexity factors such as tubercles, pits, additional ridges, grooves and fissures,
5. Acquired characteristics resulting from differences during tooth formation such as hypoplasia, pathology, trauma, function, personal habits, and restorations, and finally
6. Ethnic considerations.

Rogers and Taylor, both anthropologists, rely heavily on general dental structural characteristics and their relationship to the environment and cultural modifications.

Sex Determinants

Sex determination based on dentition is difficult for most forensic investigators. Sex differences in dentition are based largely on tooth size and shape. Male teeth are usually larger, whereas female canines are more pointed and a narrower buccolingual width. There also appear to be greater differences in size between maxillary central and lateral incisors in females as compared to males. Side-stepping metric differences, Seno and Ishizu[39] reported in 1973 on the use of the Y chromosome in dental pulp to determine sex differences. Success in sexing unknown remains based on this technique have resulted in several published accounts. In 1984, Mudd[40] reported on the use of the Y chromosome in hair specimens. Sundick in 1985 reported on sex determination by Y chromosome detection in unidentified remains at the annual meeting of the American Academy of Forensic Sciences in Las Vegas. Each of these studies involved the detection of the Y chromosome using quinacrine and fluorescent microscopy. This microscopic approach to sexing would appear more reliable to the forensic odontologist than metrics, at least on difficult, incomplete remains.

More recently, there have been a number of articles in the forensic literature[41-44] reporting the successful isolation of sex-specific banding patterns in DNA profiles of the X and Y chromosomes developed from fresh and degraded specimens. All reports indicate the need for high molecular weight genomic DNA.

Racial Determinants

Race determination in skeletal remains traditionally focuses on craniofacial characteristics such as the proportions of the orbital and nasal areas, nasal aperture characteristics, lower nasal border features, lower facial prognathism, palate form, cheekbone contours and incisor shoveling. St. Hoyme and Iscan[45] in 1989 reviewed the determinants of sex and race relative to accuracy and assumptions in *Reconstructions of Life From the Skeleton*. For each of the osteological clues, they pointed out the need to consider:

1. Its basic etiology: whether it is primarily biochemical, hormonal, or activity-related in order to predict its variation pattern,
2. Its range of variation by sex in various racial/ethnic groups,
3. Its manifestation by age: the age at which it appears and its pattern of change from childhood to old age,
4. How it is influenced by health, nutrition, occupation, or other circumstances of an individual's life,
5. Whether there are secular changes in its expression, and
6. Whether the characteristics are real, but temporary.

From a dental perspective, both the mandible and dentition reflect racial characteristics. Projecting chins are found in Europeans and some Asiatics. Rounded, almost receding, chins are found in Australian aborigines and in some South Pacific Islanders. Most African and Afro-American chins are intermediate. General jaw shape corresponds with general skull shape. Prognathous palates are associated with long, narrow mandibles with low rami; whereas large bizygomatic widths with wide mandibles have deep rami and significant gonial flare. The greatest eversion is found in Eskimos and Amerindians. Rocker jaws seem associated with Hawaiian crania. These general characteristics reflect relative ethnic dental markers.

According to these authors, the most useful racial clue in dentition is "shovel-shaped" incisors found in most Asiatic Mongoloids and Amerindians and in less than 10% of whites and blacks. Tooth size and shape including shovel tooth incisors, Carabelli's cusp or tubercle, enamel pearls, and dental pulp shape (taurodontism vs. cynodontism) have been listed as racial determinants.

Carabelli's tubercle or cusp is an anomalous cuspule on the mesiolingual surface of maxillary incisors appearing in 50% of American whites, 34% of Afro-Americans, and 5 to 20% of Amerindians. Taurodontism or "bull toothness", especially in maxillary molars, enamel pearls on premolars, and the frequent congenital lack of upper third molars, are commonly noted features in Mongoloids.

The form of the palate and the shape of the dental arches are subject to considerable variation. Stewart in 1946 described these forms as ovoid, "U"-shaped, and horseshoe-shaped. Martin and Saller in 1956 described these forms as semicircular, half ellipse, paraboloid, and broken angular line. The proportions of the palate and the associated dental arches are indicated by the palatal index, the ratio of the width to the length of the palate (width/length × 100). The resulting decimal fraction approaches 100.0 as the palate becomes wider and shorter. The anthropometric divisions of this index are below 80, 80 to 85, and above 85. An index of less than 80 indicates an elongated narrow palate typical of aboriginal Australians, Kaffirs and Zulus. Most Europeans and Amerindians have middle to high indices whereas numerous Orientals and some Pacific islanders have high palatal indices, indicating a short, rounded palate.

In general, there are large-toothed and small-toothed races. Aboriginal Australians, the Melanesians, and the American Indians including the Eskimos tend to be large-toothed, with wide crowns. The Lapps and Bushmen are small people with small teeth. American blacks tend to have large crowns.

Skull measurements have been used by many examiners as a basis for racial determination. In South America, the Bonwill triangle, an equilateral mandibular triangle connecting the apex of the mesial contact areas of the two central mandibular central incisors with the two mandibular condyles, has been used on the assumption that the studied population groups are not mixed and retain consistent hereditary characteristics.[48] According to Stewart,[46] metric means of cranial race determination usually follow the discriminant analyses of Howells and Giles-Elliot.

Dental decay and occlusal wear, often attributed to advancing technology and increased carbohydrate consumption, are not confirmed when a number of groups are studied such as prehistoric Amerindians, or Southeastern Asians, and ancient Hawaiians. However, cultural usages are often helpful such as black stains from betel nut consumption in Indonesia and other southeastern Asian regions or teeth with excessive slanted wear resulting from pulling fibrous, siliceous fern fronds in native peoples from South Pacific areas. Removal, modification, or decoration of anterior teeth can be useful indicators of sex or race. These cultural characteristics often reflect geographic ethnic patterns.

These craniofacial and dental issues take on some relevance when efforts are made to reconstruct likely visages based on skeletal craniofacial characteristics. Caldwell[49] described four current methods of facial reconstruction: (1) modeling in clay directly on the skull (three-dimensional), (2) construction of artists' drawings (two dimensional), (3) restoration of disrupted or damaged tissues, and (4) photographic or portrait superimpositions.

Webster et al.[50] reported on the identification of human remains using photographic reconstructions in two methods, comparative and superimpositions. This report used photographs, portraits, and dental studies to confirm the identifications. It is noteworthy not only for its success but also because it utilized several complementary methods of identification.

The process of facial restoration and the importance of physiognomic details is well known, largely based on the work of Krogman,[51] and has been used since by a number of forensic investigators, especially anthropologists and police departments, with reasonable success.[52-55]

Caldwell[49] also compared the facial reconstruction studies of Rathbun et al.,[56] Lenorovitz and Sussman,[57] and Zavala.[58] Rathbun et al. emphasized the eyes, lips, nasal form, and hair style as the most significant facial features in recognition. Lenorovitz and Sussman listed skin, hair, skin color, ears, face shape, eyebrows, eyes, nose, lips, eye color, chin age, and cheeks in order of importance to visual recognition. Zavala expanded that list twice-fold. These characteristics are also the same features which composite computer or overlay techniques such as the Identikit utilize in facial reconstructions. These efforts have also led to further computerized techniques such as computer age progression studies which have proven to be a valuable identification technique in missing persons investigations. Fierro[59] discussed this technique in a comprehensive review of human identification problems in unknown decedents and the variety of techniques used to resolve these problems. Computer age progression has been actively used by the FBI and by the National Center for Missing and Exploited Children. In contrast, computerized regression studies, that is, taking a visage and scientifically relating it to earlier ages of the individual are not currently available.

Forensic Odontological Databases

Applications in Mass Disasters

Forensic odontology plays an important role in medicolegal death investigations in mass disasters, especially transportation mishaps such as aircraft accidents where fragmentation and thermal injuries are common. A consistent effort has been made to computerize much of the data to improve comparative efforts. The Department of Defense uses two important databases in its forensic odontological identification efforts: (1) a pantomorphograph registry currently housed in Monterey, California which is periodically updated by copies of pantomorphographs in each servicemember's dental record, and (2) widespread use of a temporary computerized identification sorting tool known as CAPMI (Computerized Assisted Postmortem Identification System) developed by the U.S. Army Dental Research Institute. Lorton et al.[60-62] have reported on this system and its applications based on 35 combinations of restored tooth surfaces and missing teeth. A subsequent study using CAPMI on some 7030 soldiers of dental characteristics useful for identification by Friedman et al.[62] concluded that restoration identification and comparison showed a high degree of specificity. CAPMI has since been expanded to include a considerable number of anthropological measures as well. The civilian version of this program has reportedly met with mixed results. Several other dental computer sorting systems have been developed and are in beta testing. Current interest in the digitalization of radiographs for teleradiology and telemedicine purposes and its potential application to dental radiographs such as pantomorphographs, especially in established databanks, should improve such dental databases and provide an important tool in decedent identification efforts. This digitalized image retrieved from a databank could be compared with actual pantomorphographs and apical films in the victim's dental record as a validation means of premortem identification and then compared with postmortem dental records developed during the investigation. Forensic dental identifications remain the primary means of victim identification within the Department of Defense despite extensive use of fingerprints and growing utilization of DOD's DNA Identification Registry at the Armed Forces Institute of Pathology (Armed Forces DNA Identification Laboratory) which should have DNA samples (bloodstains and buccal smears) on all servicemembers by the year 2000. Current plans call for retention of these records for 40 years. This DNA material is not routinely typed, but rather stored in the registry under stringent environmental controls for possible use in the event of the servicemember's death in operational missions. The supporting AFDIL laboratory has applied DNA analysis in the identification efforts of several military aircraft mishaps and ordnance explosions. It also has played a supporting role in the identification of MIA remains repatriated from post-conflicts where other means of identification were not applicable.

There has been considerable debate on the applications of such databanks relative to an individual's constitutional rights of privacy and freedom from self-incrimination. This concern has been especially applied to proposed or existent DNA databanks. Nonetheless, these and similar databanks provide valuable information sources for identification efforts and should be encouraged providing adequate safeguards are in place and a strenuous quality control effort is made to preserve the integrity of the templates. It is these databanks that provide the population genetic studies so critical to the interpretation of DNA typing results relative to a specific identification. Currently, private DNA operations (Cellmark in Germantown, MD, Lifecodes in Stamford, CT, and Forensic Science Associates in Richmond, CA) as well as crime laboratories in the public sector, such as the FBI Laboratories, maintain population databanks for this purpose. These databanks are divided into four general populations: White, Black, Hispanic, and Asian. It is noteworthy that in each identification case, a presumptive identification is required in order to initiate a comparative identification process. The National Research Council's report on DNA Technology in Forensic Science in 1992 is a useful resource on the technologies and issues.[63]

Bite Mark Examinations

General Considerations

Although covered extensively in Chapter 7, we have elected to comment on several general features of bite mark examinations relative to scientific evidence and the potential use of ancillary technologies to resolve certain identification issues. A review of the published literature on bite marks underscores the significance in specimen examination and evaluation with any obtained templates or known impressions relative to: (1) the relationship of the jaws, (2) the form and size of arches, (3) missing teeth, (4) spacing between teeth, (5) presence of supernumerary teeth, (6) observed rotations of teeth, (7) the width of teeth, and (8) presence of special features such as fractures and ridges. Many published analyses, especially in the European literature, reference the work of Furness.[64]

Many of the discussions focus on the identification of bite marks, their documentation photographically, and the level of individualization possible based on the documented and preserved evidence against templates of dentition of individuals under investigation in the case. Benson et al.[66] in 1988 reviewed bite mark impressions relative to current techniques and materials. Wetli et al., all forensic pathologists,[67] described techniques used in the Dade County Medical Examiner's Office and reported the use of fingerprint powder or fingerprint ink on bite mark impressions to enhance impression visibility. Soft tissue radiography has also been used to enhance bite mark impressions.

Legal challenges to bite mark evidence seems to fall into two major categories of admissibility: (1) reliability of analysis, and (2) violations of constitutional rights (Fourth and Fifth Amendments) regarding search and seizure and self-incrimination protections. Hales[68] reviewed these issues in an often referenced report on the admissibility of bite mark evidence in 1978.

One aspect of bite mark investigations often neglected is the role of ancillary chemical and serological studies which either support the identification of the observed injury as a bite mark or the specificity of the bite mark relative to the biter's sex, race, or individuality. One such series of study focused on the presence of saliva and its serological characteristics. Another parameter, often mentioned, is the potential use of cytological examinations of exfoliated buccal epithelial cells, especially for sex determination and/or DNA analysis.

Saliva offers several routes of inquiry. Its identification in bite marks is directed towards the identification of inorganic anions such as thiocyanate or nitrites and polymorphic enzymes such as alkaline phosphatase and amylase. Further individualization, if pursued, is directed towards classical serological parameters including the detection of blood groups, serum polymorphic enzymes, and polymorphic studies unique to saliva based on electrophoretic variation of isoenzymes of hexose-6-phosphate dehydrogenase (Sgd), amylase, acid protein (Pa), basic protein (Pb), double band protein (Db), and proline rich protein (Pr).

Many of the reported studies refer to the seminal study by E.A. Azen in 1978 on the genetic polymorphisms present in human saliva. Both fluorescent ultraviolet examination and immunological studies have been reported.

Chemical Markers

The detection of the thiocyanate ion (3.1 to 27.5 mg SCN/100 ml) in saliva relies on the calorimetric reaction of thiocyanate with dilute ferric chloride to the slightly acidified specimen producing a pink to red product which is sensitive to 3 µg SCN. Thiocyanate in saliva persists for some time and has been reported present, although reduced, 28 months after deposition according to Nelson and Kirk.[69] A negative test for thiocyanate does not exclude the presence of saliva in a stain. When present in fresh samples, the average is 9.3 mg/100 mL and is about 2.5 times higher in smokers than nonsmokers.

Nitrite exists in saliva in concentrations of 4.6 to 10 µg NO_2/ml and is detected using the Griess test which using sulfanilic acid forms a diazonium compound which reacts with naphthylamine to form a pink to red p-benzenesulfone-acid-azo-naphthylamine compound. The test is sensitive but less specific for saliva and is limited to use in recent depositions. A reagent consisting of 0.5% alpha-naphthylamine in 5 N acetic acid and 0.8% sulfanilic acid in 5N acetic acid was used in the salivary stain studies.

A very sensitive and relatively specific general test for saliva is the demonstration of significant amounts of amylase in a suspect stain. A number of technologies have been described but those most used in forensic investigations utilize starch dye substrates using Renazol Blue R, Cibachrom blue F3G, or Procion Brillant Red M2BS. Studies on stamps and envelopes for saliva have used triphenyltetrazolium chloride to detect reducing sugars as a red, insoluble formazan. Positive reactions are also noted with ascorbic acid which has also been reported in saliva in 2.4 to 4.6 µg/ml concentrations.

Serological Markers

General serological parameters used for identification purposes rely on the presence and detection of blood groups in biological specimens other than blood detectable in 80% of the population based on secretor status. In addition to the ABH, Lewis, and Sda antigens, a number of serum polymorphic isoenzymes are present in saliva: alkaline phosphatase, amylase, esterases, G-6-PD, and parotid peroxidase (SAPX). Saliva also contains an interesting polymorphic protein system based on parotid glycoproteins; most if not all are acidic and proline rich. Both Gm and Km proteins are present and have been used for racial determinations. Harrington et al. in 1988 described their efforts to detect hemagglutinins in dried saliva stains for comparison with blood typing.[70] Although limited to stains up to several days old, their assay consisting of concentration and extraction with toluene, the addition of polyvinyl pyrrolidone, dextran albumin, and anti-immunoglobulin A (IgA) to the mixture, pretreatment of the mixture with bromelin, a proteolytic enzyme, low concentrations of RBC detector cells, and a low temperature (0°C) environment yielded useful data worth forensic consideration.

Typical serological studies of saliva are usually limited to detection of amylase, ABH, and Lewis antigens and several polymorphic markers. DNA profiling offers other possibilities, including greater individualization, if enough DNA can be extracted from any exfoliated cells.

Salivary Drug Detection

The use of saliva in drug detection has been explored, especially in monitoring therapeutic drug concentrations and detection of impaired drivers in a relatively noninvasive fashion. Peel et al. in 1984 reported on an RCMP (Royal Canadian Mounted Police) study which found measurable quantities of drugs in saliva extracted with methanol and analyzed by EMIT (enzyme multiple immunoassay technique) and gas chromatography/mass spectrophotometry.[71] Their work referenced that of Horning et al.,[72] Danhof and Breimer,[73] and Idowu and Caddy.[74] This methodology, both specific and sensitive appears to be a useful adjunct to serological testing in bite marks for identification purposes. A number of drugs such as phenobarbital, amphetamine and morphine have been detected in saliva and saliva stains by radioimmunoassay (RIA) by a number of investigators. Smith[75] described similar studies in blood stains for drug content.

Animal Bite Marks

Most medicolegal cases involving animal bite marks are relatively straightforward and are grossly identifiable as such by their general features and the character of the wounds inflicted. Rarely is the identification of the perpetrator unknown. Nonetheless, technology has provided several routes of inquiry when there may be a question of the perpetrator's identity.

Fletcher et al.[76] in 1984 described an ELISA (enzyme-linked immunoassay) technique using monoclonal antibody based on the presence of salivary IgA for species identification in stains up to 16 months old. Cross reactivity was limited and readily identifiable. Crossover electrophoresis and double gel diffusion techniques were used for comparison in cases with poor monoclonal antibody results. This technique would appear to have value in bite mark examinations from nonhumans where the biting animal is not known.

Sensabaugh and Blake,[77] in a review of DNA analysis using polymerase chain reaction (PCR) applications, commented on its use in species determinations. Evolutionary relationships among species are most directly determined by comparisons at the DNA sequence level. For routine species determination, simple yes/no amplification assays for species-specific sequences can be utilized. Alternatively, amplification coupled with dot blot hybridization with species-specific probes can be used. Both approaches are targeted to a species or set of species. A general unknown would require gene sequence analysis which would provide a direct measure of species relationships. If an unknown cannot be directly identified by sequencing, it can be placed into a genus, family, or order by comparing its sequence to corresponding sequences from other species groups. The sequence region for which most comparative sequence data exist is the cytochrome b gene on mitochondrial DNA. The gene has conservative sequence regions that allow the design of "universal" primers that will amplify the gene in most vertebrate species, according to Kocher et al.[78] Cytochrome b gene sequences are now known for most of the major vertebrate groups and additional sequence data appearing regularly in the literature.

Sex Determination in Bite Marks

The possibility of obtaining exfoliated buccal epithelial cells in saliva on bite marks has increased the possibility of sex determination of the perpetrator. The duration of this line of inquiry is apparently possible for several weeks postdeposition, depending on the materials containing the impressions and environmental factors. Two parameters have been proposed, both based on successful efforts to sex bloodstains: (1) the presence and detection of sex chromatin (Barr bodies in females, and F bodies in males); and (2) sex hormone level determinations based on detectable quantities and ratios of testosterone and 17B-estradiol by radioimmunoassay (RIA). The former parameter has been demonstrated successfully in saliva stains; this author is unaware of any successful attempt to identify sex in saliva by means of hormonal ratios.

Interpretation of such investigatory efforts must be dependent on an understanding of the possible variations that might be encountered. Discrepancies noted in tests for sex chromatin include (1) chromatin negative females, e.g., Turner's Syndrome and testicular feminization, (2) chromatin positive males, e.g., Klinefelter's Syndrome, and (3) genetic mosaics. In each case, a sufficient number of nucleated cells must be obtained, fixed, and stained. Alcohol fixation and H&E stains have been used successfully for detection of Barr bodies or "drumsticks" in materials containing at least 100 nucleated cells. An aceto-orcein staining process was described by Sanderson and Stewart in 1961.[79]

Determination of sex by DNA analysis according to Sensabaugh and Blake[77] is possible by using PCR based on the characteristics of the mammalian sex chromosomes, X and Y. Normal females have two X chromosomes and males have an X and Y chromosome. The development of a mammalian embryo as male is determined by genes on the Y chromosome and the phenotypic sex of individuals with an abnormal complement of sex chromosomes depends only on the presence or absence of the Y chromosome. According to the authors, a number of X and Y chromosome-specific sequences have been identified and serve as potential markers for sex determination. Several PCR-based approaches have been used. The simplest is the amplification of a Y specific sequence; the presence of a PCR product indicates the sample contains male cells. With this assay, the absence of a product cannot be interpreted unless there is an amplification control. An assay using the DYZ1 repeat sequence for the Y marker and either an Alu repeat or DQA sequences as amplification controls is an example of such testing.

Witt and Erikson[81] described an assay using both X and Y specific centromeric alphoid repeat sequences as the chromosome markers. Amplification of these two sequences employ different primer sets but can be co-amplified. Male DNA shows both X and Y PCR products, whereas female DNA shows only the X product. Gaensslen et al.[82] reported this application in 1992 on forensic specimens.

A third method, described by Aasen and Medrano[83] amplifies both the X and Y specific sequences using a single primer set. The human ZFY and ZFX genes possess regions of conserved sequence permitting the design of primers capable of amplifying both. The two sequences are then distinguished by a sequence-specific restriction assay using HaeIII. The ZFX gene is marked by a characteristic 400-base-pair fragment and the ZFY gene by a 317-base-pair fragment. Because both sequences are amplified from the same set of primers, the assay has a built-in control for the amplification reaction from both sexes. The gene sequences are also species-specific according to Aasen and Medrano.

DNA Analysis in Biological Specimens

DNA analysis has provided a significant advance in identification efforts and is routinely used in criminal investigations and mass disasters. The relative absence of general population DNA identification databanks against which putative specimens can be compared complicates identification efforts of unknown remains, especially when there is no presumptive identification of the decedent. If a presumptive identification is available, however, then it is often possible by using either nuclear or mitochondrial DNA profiling analysis to confirm the identification of the unknown and to reassociate remains when other methodologies are not applicable. In mass disasters, a common approach is to identify fragmentary remains by traditional means such as dental comparisons, fingerprints, or radiographic criteria (superimpositions), type recovered DNA from these fragments, and use that profile to reassociate other fragmentary remains producing the same DNA profile pattern. Current DNA profiling or fingerprinting techniques are either restriction fragment length polymorphisms (RFLPs) on variable number tandem repeats (VNTRs) or polymerase chain reaction (PCR) analysis. RFLPs analyze highly variable regions of human DNA, individualized by length polymorphisms, traditionally referred to as "junk DNA" by molecular biologists. The PCR technique or allele-specific analysis focuses in on and amplifies a specific DNA region. Differences among individuals at that site can be distinguished through the use of specialized probes that trigger a color change or through gel electrophoresis followed by a silver stain. Forensic PCR methods cannot discriminate among individuals as well as RFLP analysis does, but PCR requires only small amounts of DNA (approximately 1% that required for RFLP analysis) and can be used with some degraded DNA.

Approximately 70 to 80% of the DNA in the total human genome consists of unique sequences including spacer DNA, signal sequences, and protein coding DNA. The remaining 20 to 30% of the genome consists of repetitive, primarily noncoding sequences of uncertain function. It is on these sequences that DNA profiling depends. Repetitive DNA can be divided into two classes: (1) tandemly repetitive sequences, and (2) interspersed repeats. Tandem repetitive DNA accounts for approximately 1/3 of the repetitive DNA (10% of the genome) and is divided into two categories: (1) satellite DNA, ranging from 5 to 250 base pairs repeated many times, and (2) short tandem repeats, much shorter than satellite DNA (9 to 64 base pair "core" sequences) which exhibit a high degree of variability in overall length; these regions are also termed "minisatellites" or VNTRs (variable number tandem repeats) located at unique chromosomal loci. Minisatellites are relatively long tandem repeats whereas shorter repeats fall into the short tandem repeats (STRs) described above consisting of "core sequences". The different DNA profiling techniques focus on one or more of these repetitive sequence areas.

The largest amount of repetitive DNA (approximately 15 to 20% of the genome) are interspersed elements of specific sequences distributed widely throughout the genome. These sequences are about 300 base pairs in length and account for 5% of the genome. These elements are divided into two classes: (1) short interspersed elements called SINES composed of sequences of less than 500 base pairs, and (2) long interspersed elements called LINES which have sequences greater than 500 base pairs (1 to 2% of the genome)

DNA Contamination Issues

Invariably, such DNA analysis using RFLP or PCR techniques raise concerns of contamination and subsequently reliability in interpretation of so-called matches. A number of studies have addressed these issues, especially in regard to the use of RFLP (restriction fragment length polymorphisms) methodology.

Adams et al.[85] in 1991 reported on investigations conducted by the FBI relative to this issue based on profile results obtained from bloodstains and other biological stains subjected to a mixture of other biological stains, environmental insults (sunlight and temperature), different substrates (cotton, nylon, blue denim, glass, aluminum, and wood), and contaminants including gasoline, bleach, sodium hydroxide, soil, motor oil, detergent, phosphate salt, glacial acetic acid, and microorganisms. They found that in those samples which did produce profiles, those profiles were consistent with those of untreated control samples.

In 1993, Webb et al.[86] revisited this issue using microbial challenges of variable number tandem repeats (VNTR) probes for DNA profiling. Numerous polymorphic markers cloned from variable number tandem repeat sequences have been described and used for individual identification purposes. These clones usually consist of several kilobases of VNTR sequence suitable for isototopic labeling. Recently, however, synthetic oligonucleotides complementary to VNTRs have been used as DNA probes. Reporter molecules including biotin, digoxigenin, and alkaline phosphatase are covalently linked to the oligonucleotides facilitating nonisotopic detection methods. This study used probes challenged with DNA isolated from a variety of bacterial, yeast, and fungal sources. No DNA sequences of nonhuman origin were visualized on either autoradiographs or lumigraphs.

In 1994, Laber, et al.[87] conducted validation studies on the forensic analysis of restriction fragment length polymorphisms (RFLPs) with agarose gels without ethidium bromide staining and the possible effects of contaminants, sunlight, and the electrophoresis of varying quantities of DNA on RFLP patterns produced from DNA isolated from blood and semen stains. Computer-assisted image analysis was used to detect variations in RFLP band sizes in relation to control samples. The results demonstrated that high molecular weight DNA can be obtained when blood and semen stains are subjected to environmental and contaminating factors. Their studies further documented the reliability and validity of DNA typing in forensic applications.

DNA Dental Applications

Schwartz et al.[88] reported an interesting study of DNA obtained from teeth subjected to a variety of environmental conditions. The studies were on dental pulp using restriction enzyme digestion with PstI and restriction fragment length polymorphisms on loci DZS44, DXYS14, D18S27, and DXZ1. The authors obtained good results but observed band shifting of 2 to 4 kilobases with increased temperatures. This technical artifact can make pattern or band interpretation difficult in potential matches.

Smith et al.[89] in 1993 reported on a systematic approach to sampling dental DNA for identification purposes. The study was based on crushed and sectioned tooth specimens which were subjected to DNA typing with both sequence- and length-based analyses comparing teeth from the same individual and with other individuals. The authors concluded that crushing specimens maximizes the yield of dental DNA but with greater degradation, and that substantial yields could be obtained from more conservative sectioning efforts. The method of sampling did not affect the ability to do DNA typing. High molecular weight DNA was obtained from all specimens. DNA typing studies were also successfully performed on powdered dentin and dental roots, providing high molecular weight DNA. The dental roots yielded more DNA but it was also more degraded. The mitochondrial DNA control area was amplified for all molar pulp extracts. The result was a DNA band of approximately 1100 base pairs which co-migrated with the known control band.

When DNA is highly degraded, or in limited quantities, mitochondrial DNA (mtDNA) can be used for human identification and evidentiary materials. Mitochondrial DNA constitutes a fraction of 1% of the total DNA in a cell. However, there are hundreds to thousands of copies of mtDNA for every copy of nuclear DNA. The maternal inheritance pattern increases the availability of matching sequences of individuals with siblings and even distant maternal cousins who should carry the identical mtDNA sequence. Further use of this technology will be dependent on the establishment of DNA databases and population statistical studies to support interpretation of results.

The mitochondrial genome is 16,569 base pairs (bp) in length and circular, consisting of coding regions and a noncoding hypervariable control region. The control region spans more than 1100 base pairs and includes the origins for replication and transcription as well as the displacement loop. Holland et al.[90] in 1993 reported the successful use of mitochondrial DNA sequence analysis on human skeletal remains from MIAs in the Vietnam conflict when attempts at using nuclear genomic DNA (HLA-DQ alpha and VNTR locus D1S80) were unsuccessful using the polymerase chain reaction (PCR).

DNA Profiling or Fingerprinting

DNA profiling or fingerprinting is based on the fact that although most of the DNA molecule is common to all humans, parts differ from person to person. With the exception of identical siblings, the DNA of every individual is unique. DNA identification tests use sophisticated techniques of molecular biology developed over the last 25 years to compare samples taken from a suspect with those found in blood, semen, hair roots, or cells from saliva or skin discovered at a crime scene. In paternity cases, DNA from the alleged father is compared with that of the mother and child. The use of DNA profiling has mushroomed in the U.S. since its introduction in the mid-1980s. Paternity cases dominate, amounting to an estimated 100,000 profiles a year as opposed to approximately 5000 forensic cases, according to Mark Stolorow, director of operations for Cellmark Diagnostics in Germantown, MD. Cellmark is the largest commercial DNA profiling operation in the U.S. and has analyzed samples from the O.J. Simpson case. Lifecodes Corporation in Stamford, CT and Forensic Science Associates in Richmond, CA also perform DNA profiling. The FBI operates a large forensic DNA facility in the public sector in Washington, D.C. and offers training in the technique to forensic scientists from state, local, and foreign crime laboratories. Approximately 50 state and local forensic laboratories in the U.S. are carrying out some form of DNA profiling, according to Paul Ferrara, director of the Division of Forensic Science in Virginia, the first state to set up its own DNA typing operation. Ferrara is also chairman of the American Society of Crime Laboratory Directors' accreditation board.

The most useful DNA identification tests currently available analyze highly variable regions of human DNA called restriction fragment length polymorphisms (RFLPs). In this technique, genomic DNA is isolated from the cells' nuclei and cut into fragments by a restriction enzyme that cleaves the DNA at specific locations, recognizing only certain combinations of the ATCG codes on the DNA molecule. The sizes of the resulting fragments differ from individual to individual because of polymorphisms, highly variable DNA regions that contain a variable number of repeating units of certain small DNA sequences. The resulting fragments are separated by slab gel electrophoresis into different sized bands. The DNA is then extracted from the gel when it is blotted onto a nylon membrane using the Southern blotting technique where a series of radioactive probes are used to visualize fragments from certain regions where individual variations are common. The probes used are segments of known DNA impregnated with radioactive phosphorus-32 which bind to the precise DNA fragments tested, transferring their radioactivity selectively to those fragments. The membrane is then placed on X-ray film exposing the film to the radiation in the phosphorus and visualizing the DNA fragments. The process is lengthy, with each of the four or five loci exposed sequentially it usually takes 10 weeks. Once the film is developed it is inspected by the investigator and at least one other expert and often scanned into a computer for precise measurement and comparison of the resulting bands with known samples of DNA. Ambiguity in interpretation of these bands results from band shifts, degradation, missing bands, extra bands and combined bands, all due to technical problems. The dilemma faced by the analyst is how to distinguish differences induced by technical problems and artifacts from true genetic differences between samples.[92-94]

A second type of DNA profiling is polymerase chain reaction (PCR) which is a molecular copying process for developing gene sequences. A typical PCR test looks at six different inherited traits, each controlled by a specific gene, each with two alleles; one maternal allele and one paternal allele. If the alleles are the same, the individual is homozygous for that trait. If the alleles are different, the individual is heterozygous for that trait. For 6 different genes, there are just 21 possible combinations of alleles: 6 homozygous and 15 heterozygous. PCR looks for matches for these 21 combinations, some of which are extremely rare. The results are recorded as colored dots on a nylon strip. The PCR technique focuses on and amplifies a specific DNA region. The differences among individuals at that site are distinguished through the use of specialized probes which trigger a color change or through gel elec- trophoresis followed by a silver stain. Forensic PCR methods are less specific than RFLP analysis with probabilities of 1:100 to 1:2000 as compared with 1:10,000 to 1:1,000,000 reported for RFLP. However, PCR requires extremely small quantities of DNA and can be used on degraded specimens. A sizable evidence sample, however, does not guarantee a good yield of analyzable material. Heat, moisture, sunlight, surface contaminants, and other factors can speed DNA degradation. Contamination of evidence with DNA from animals or bacteria is usually not a problem because the probes used in DNA profiling are specific to humans or at least primates. Bacteria does have an effect on the stability of human DNA, especially soil bacteria which are rich in nucleases.[92,93]

Criminal cases generate more controversy than paternity suits. Both require a documented chain of evidence, however the forensic material may be limited as compared to samples from paternity cases. It often takes more work to isolate DNA from forensic specimens and more probes and controls. This is reflected in the costs for such work. Lifecodes, according to Michael Baird, vice president of laboratory operations, charges $200 per sample for paternity cases compared with $535 per sample for forensic cases. The most disputatious issue of forensic DNA identification efforts involves population genetics. Scientists disagree on how to calculate the probability that a sus- pect's DNA profile could match the evidence by chance. At issue is a method called the multiplication or product rule which assumes that the tested loci follow the Hardy-Weinberg equilibrium principle of independence. The chance that a suspect's DNA coincidentally matches the evidence depends on how frequently the particular pattern of genetic variants (alleles) present in the DNA profile occurs in the general population. Critics challenge the definition of "general population" arguing that in an heterogeneous popula- tion the frequency of a particular pattern could vary among ethnic groups.[84,92,95,96]

This issue arises because DNA profiling analyzes only a small sample of an individual's full complement of DNA, some 3 billion base pairs in the human genome. Both profiling methods reduce the possibility of random matches by evaluating more than one specific locus on DNA. In an RFLP analysis employing four or five single locus probes, each probe is designed to recognize a particular locus on a specific chromosome. Forensic labora- tories compile databases of the alleles that are found with each employed probe. These individual probes yield frequencies which in the multiplication rule provide a probability of matching patterns by the multiplication of the frequency of each of the used probes. The multiplication rule derives from population genetics models that assume that the DNA variations revealed by each probe are inherited independently of each other. This assumption is challenged by critics. Daniel Hartl, professor of biology at Harvard University, contends that unions within ethnic groups results in genetically differentiated subgroups that must be considered. Individuals who match at one locus might be more likely to match at another.[97]

The FBI and other forensic laboratories concede that the distribution of alleles is not completely random. Their databases are already separated into large population pools such as Whites, Blacks, and Hispanics. These laboratories report the calculated probabilities of a random match for each of these data groups and the frequencies can vary widely. Hartl argues that these large pools are not discriminatory enough because there is as much genetic variation among subgroups within races as there is between races. A National Research Council (NRC) panel in 1992 recommended against continued use of the multiplication rule concluding that genetic differences within ethnic groups should be taken into account in calculating the probability of a chance match between an innocent suspect and crime scene evidence. They recommended a more conservative approach called the ceiling principle in which forensic scientists would use the highest observed frequency of a given allele or 5%, whichever is larger, to calculate the likelihood of a random match. The report called for research to set these ceiling frequencies by using empirical data suggesting that determining the actual frequencies of particular DNA variations in 15 to 20 population subgroups of some 100 individuals per subgroup. While those data were being collected, an arbitrary frequency of 10% should be used. Many forensic laboratories now report both sets of calculations. Neil Risch and colleagues at Yale University support continued use of the multiplication rule. These statistical geneticists studied the FBI's databases and found only one instance in 7.6 million comparisons where one sample matched another by chance at three loci. Using four or five loci would make the likelihood of a random match infinitesimal.[92,100]

The issue of population genetics was addressed recently by Lander and Budowle[98] and the NRC recommendations relative to calculation of allele frequency probabilities by the multiplication rule vs. the ceiling principle. They noted that the subpopulation argument became a cause celebre, pitting luminaries such as Lewontin and Hartl[97,98] against Chakraborty and Kidd.[99] Six objections have been raised to the ceiling principle:

1. The ceiling principle is premised on the flawed analysis of Lewontin and Hartl that there is significant population substructure,
2. The ceiling principle is scientifically flawed because it is not used in population genetics; moreover, the plan to sample 10 to 15 representative populations is statistically unsound,

3. The ceiling principle makes unwarranted assumptions about the possible substructure of a population,
4. The ceiling principle is so conservative that it hampers the courtroom application of DNA fingerprinting,
5. The ceiling principle is not actually guaranteed to be conservative, and
6. The NRC report is causing DNA fingerprinting cases to be thrown out of court.

According to Lander and Budowie, each of the objections has been addressed and appears unfounded.[95-99]

During the first years that DNA profiling was applied to forensic cases, most criticism revolved around the lack of standards. In a 1990 report "Genetic Witness: Forensic Uses of DNA Tests" by the Office of Technology Assessment, the issue of setting standards for forensic applications of DNA testing was proclaimed fundamental to its admissibility in court. The NRC panel committee called for a mandatory accreditation program for DNA testing laboratories and for certification of laboratory personnel. An FBI-organized consortium of crime lab representatives, members of academia, and private companies called the Technical Working Group on DNA Analysis Methods (TWGDAM) first issued guidelines in 1989 which have since been updated. The guidelines specify analytical protocols for both RFLP and PCR profiling as well as general standards focusing on quality assurance, training and education of personnel, and proficiency testing. These guidelines have become the industry's *de facto* gold standard. Adherence to these guidelines is one criterion for accreditation by the American Society of Crime Laboratory Directors' Laboratory Accreditation Board. Roughly one third of public sector crime labs that perform DNA profiling have earned accreditation under the program. Cellmark was the first private laboratory to qualify. The DNA profiling standard introduced in 1992 by the National Institute of Standards and Technology (NIST) is a new tool for forensic laboratories to check their performance. The 20-component standard reference material for RFLP analysis is the most complex ever issued by NIST. The standard includes both male and female human DNA in three forms: approximately 3 million whole cells, whole DNA that has been extracted from such cells, and DNA that has been extracted and cut with the restriction enzyme in standard use in the U.S. NIST is expected to release a similar standard reference material for DNA profiling using PCR techniques, according to Dennis Reeder, group leader of NIST's DNA Technologies Group.[29]

The new crime bill adds further impetus to the movement toward quality assurance standards for forensic DNA labs. The DNA Identification Act requires the FBI director to set up an advisory board to recommend standards for quality assurance, including proficiency testing of forensic laboratories and analysts, within six months. Most expect that these standards will closely follow current TWGDAM guidelines, which should be used in the interim. Standardization is also being driven by the creation of the national DNA databank that the FBI has been working with local and state crime laboratories to develop. This system is called CODIS (combined DNA index system) and will enable investigators to compare DNA profiles derived from evidence from rapes or murders with DNA profiles from convicted offenders from throughout the country. They also will be able to compare evidence from unsolved crimes in other jurisdictions and check profiles of missing persons. The national database means that each laboratory must be able to reproducibly generate DNA profiles. Current studies involving some 22 laboratories show "remarkable consistency" among some 6000 measurements.[29]

According to the FBI, some 31 states have laws requiring criminals convicted of certain crimes to provide samples for DNA profiling. Most states limit the scope to convicted sex offenders, but a few, such as Virginia, include all individuals convicted of violent crimes. The U.S. Court of Appeals for the 4th Circuit has upheld its constitutionality and the U.S. Supreme Court refused to hear the case brought by a group of convicted felons.[92]

The threat of privacy posed by the expanding use of DNA databanks is an increasingly prominent issue according to some legal scholars. Although the DNA regions targeted by current profiling methods do not code for disease or any identifiable physical traits, some observers are disturbed by the government's access to such information. Congress has addressed this concern in its crime bill which limits access of CODIS to law enforcement and judicial purposes. The act sets fines of up to $100,000 for misuse of the databank.[92]

The creation of DNA databanks has fiscal impact on a state's resources. Many states are having difficulty keeping up with the number of convicts to be profiled. A year to a year and a half backlog is common. These large backlogs have highlighted the need for faster profiling procedures. Sensabaugh and Mathies are testing a high-throughput DNA profiling by using capillary electrophoresis in California.[92] The Armed Forces DNA Identification Laboratory (AFDIL) is also exploring the use of capillary electrophoresis. Williams et al.[103] published a recent article on the analysis of DNA restriction fragments and polymerase chain reaction products by capillary electrophoresis. Lifecodes and other companies have developed chemiluminescent probe systems that can replace the radioactive probes used in RFLP. Currently used in paternity testing, this methodology has forensic interest, according to the FBI.[92,99,100]

The application of this DNA technology to forensic odontology cases relies on the principles presented and the general condition that this analysis will be done by other than forensic odontologists. DNA has been isolated and characterized from dental pulp. This success provides a basis for reassociation of body parts that might not be otherwise possible because of decomposition. There is particular interest in mitochondrial DNA analysis because of its availability, especially in skeletal materials and its successful characterization by polymerase chain reaction.

Issues of Scientific Testing — General Principles

Scientific evidence has special relevance in medicolegal investigations and its admissibility in court is based on experiments and scientific tests where it can be demonstrated that it is reliable and will aid in understanding the facts in dispute. Admissibility is a question of weighing the probative value of such evidence against probative dangers such as misleading the jury, undue consumption of time, etc.

In general, the requirements for admissibility of scientific evidence includes (1) experiments conducted under substantially similar conditions, and (2) expert testimony as to the reliability of the testing procedures in which the procedure was conducted by qualified experts in the field who can appear in court to testify as to the conduct of the test and the reliability of the testing procedures. Judicial notice can be used in lieu of expert testimony when the reliability of the test is generally accepted but it does not substitute for proof that the test was properly administered. Finally, the probative value must outweigh probative dangers.

Identification issues presented to the court often involve probabilities in which it is attempted to show that the applied technologies were properly done and were specific, sensitive, and precise, and either exclude the individual or identify the individual with reasonable certainty.

Much discussion has been centered around what constitutes "scientific evidence" and when it can or will be accepted by the courts. The rules of admissibility vary from jurisdiction to jurisdiction but appear to follow the general principles. Frequently mentioned is the Frye Rule which is perhaps still the "gold standard" in some state courts. The Frye Rule focuses on scientific evidence which has achieved general acceptability within the scientific community and is specific, sensitive, and accurate. Modifications of this general acceptability principle also address relevance. Today many states and all federal courts follow the guidelines outlined in the Federal Rules of Evidence which were first drafted by the American Law Institute in 1942 and revised several times. These rules basically provide that unless there is some special circumstance "all relevant evidence is admissible."

Federal Rule 702 governs the admissibility of scientific evidence.

"If scientific, technical, or other specialized knowledge will assist the trier
of fact to understand the evidence or to determine as fact an issue, a witness
qualified as an expert by knowledge, skill, experience, training, or education,
may testify thereto in the form of an opinion or otherwise."

This position was reaffirmed by the United States Supreme Court in
Daubert v. Merrell Dow Pharmaceuticals, Inc. This case and its impact was
the focus of a recent article by Annas.[104] The adoption of Rule 702 eliminated
Frye's reliance on general acceptance as the exclusive requirement for admissibility. To qualify for "scientific", the Court concluded that the testimony
must be grounded in the "methods and procedures of science" and be more
than a subjective belief or unsupported speculation. The Federal Rules of
Evidence require that the "expert's opinion will have a reliable basis in the
knowledge and experience of his discipline."

Justice Blackmun (U.S. Supreme Court) in this decision and in a minority
position, proposed four "pertinent considerations" for federal trial judges to
take into account whether scientific evidence is reliable: (1) Is the hypothesis
set forward by the scientific expert falsifiable or testable? (2) Has the theory
or technique been subjected to peer review and publication? (3) What is the
potential rate of error in the method used? and (4) Has the method or theory
gained general acceptance, which "can be an important fact in ruling particular evidence admissible?". Although not uniformly accepted as reasonable
guidelines, these four questions reflect the general expectations of "scientific
evidence".

Because of the significance of admissibility of such scientific evidence,
the authors have elected to expand on these principles from the perspective
of a trial attorney and their relevance especially to DNA profiling and databases.

References

1. Helfman, P.M. and J.C. Bada, Aspartic Acid Racemization in Tooth Enamel
   from Living Humans, *Proc. Natl. Acad. Sci. U.S.A.,* 72(8) (1975).

2. Helfman, P.,M. and J.C. Bada, Aspartic Acid Racemization in Dentin as a
   Measure of Ageing, *Nature,* 262:279-281 (1976).

3. Ogino, T., H. Ogino, and B. Nagy, Application of Aspartic Acid Racemization
   to Forensic Odontology, *Forensic Sci. Int.,* 29:259-267 (1985).

4. Ritz, S., H.W. Schutz, and B. Schwarzer, The Extent of Aspartic Acid Racemization in Dentin: A Possible Method for a more Accurate Determination of
   Age at Death, *Z. Rechtsmed.,* 103:457-462 (1990).

5. Ohtani, S. and K. Yamamoto, Age Estimation Using the Racemization of Amino
   Acid in Human Dentin, *J. Forensic Sci.,* 36(3):792-800 (1991).

6. Gustafson, G., Age Determination on Teeth, *J. Am. Dent. Assoc.*, 41:45-52 (1950).

7. Gustafson, G., *Forensic Odontology*, Elsevier, New York, 1966.

8. Maples, W.R., Improved Technique using Dental Histology for Estimation of Adult Age, *J. Forensic Sci.*, 23(4):764-770 (1978).

9. Maples, W.R. and P.M. Rice, Some Difficulties in the Gustafson Dental Age Estimations, *J. Forensic Sci.*, 24(1): 343-356 (1979).

10. Skinner, M. and G.S. Anderson, Individualization and Enamel Histology: A Case Report in Forensic Anthropology, *J. Forensic Sci.*, 36(3):939-948 (1991).

11. Cook, D.C. Adult Age Determination from the Dentition, in *Human Identification: Case Studies in Forensic Anthropology*, Eds. T.D. Rathbun and J.E. Buikstra, Charles C. Thomas, Springfield, IL, 1984, chap. 22.

12. Johanson, G., Age Determination in Human Teeth, *Odontol. Revy*, 22 (Suppl.):1-126 (1971).

13. DeChaume, M., L. DeRobert, and J. Payen, De la Valeur de la Determination de laage par l'examen des dentes coupes minces, *Ann. Med. Leg. Criminol. Police Sci.*, 40:165-167 (1960).

14. Nalbandian, J. and R.F. Sognnaes, Structural Changes in Human Teeth, in Aging — Some Social and Biological Aspects, Ed. N.W. Shock, Publ. 65, American Association of Applied Science, 1960.

15. Burns, K.R. and W.R. Maples. Estimation of Age from Individual Adult Teeth, *J. Forensic Sci.*, 21:343-356 (1976).

16. Vlcek, E. and L. Mrklas, Modifications of the Gustafson Method of Determination of Age according to Teeth in Pre-historical and Historical Osteological Material, *Scr. Med.*, 48:203-208 (1975).

17. Fanning, E., The Relationship of Dental Caries and Root Resorption of Deciduous Molars, *Arch. Oral Biol.*, 7:595-601 (1962).

18. Lipsinic, F.E., E. Paunovich, G.D. Houston, and S.F. Robison. Correlation of Age and Incremental Lines in the Cementum of Human Teeth, *J. Forensic Sci.*, 31(3):982-989 (1986).

19. Kerley, E.R., Age Determination of Bone Fragments, *J. Forensic Sci.*, 14:59 (1969).

20. Kerley, E.R., Microscopic Determination of Age in Human Bone, *Am. J. Phys. Anthropol.*, 23:149-163 (1965).

21. Kerley, E.R. and D. Ubelaker, Revisions in the Microscopic Method of Estimating Age at Death in Human Cortical Bone, *Am. J. Phys. Anthropol.*, 49:545-546 (1978).

22. Singh, I.J. and D.L. Gunberg. Estimation of Age at Death in Human Males from Qualitative Histology of Bone Fragments, *Am. J. Phys. Anthropol.*, 33:373-381 (1970).

23. Carr, R.F., R.E. Barsley, and W.D. Davenport. Postmortem Examination of Incinerated Teeth with the Scanning Electron Microscope, *J. Forensic Sci.*, 31(1):307-311 (1986).

24. Fairgrieve, S.I., SEM Analysis of Incinerated Teeth as an Aid to Positive Identification, *J. Forensic Sci.*, 39(2): 557-565 (1994).

25. Smith, B.C., A Preliminary Report: Proximal Facet Analysis and the Recovery of Trace Restorative Materials from Unrestored Teeth, *J. Forensic Sci.*, 35(4):873-880 (1990).

26. Fulton, B.A., C.E. Meloan, and M. Finnegan, Reassembling Scattered and Mixed Human Bones by Trace Element Ratios, *J. Forensic Sci.*, 31(4):1455-1462 (1986).

27. Lambert, J.B., S.V. Simpson, J.E. Buikstra, and D.K. Charles, Analysis of Soils Associated with Woodland Burials, *Archaeological Chemistry III*, American Chemical Society, Washington, D.C., pp. 97-113, 1984.

28. Lambert, J.B., S.V. Simpson, C.B. Szpunar, and J.E. Buikstra, Ancient Human Diets from Inorganic Analysis of Bone, *Acc. Chem. Res.*, 17:298-305 (1984).

29. Kido, A., Y. Kimura, and M. Oya, Transferrin Subtyping in Dental Pulps, *J. Forensic Sci.*, 38(5):1063-1067 (1993).

30. Lopez-Abadia, I. and J.M. Ruiz de la Cuesta, A Simplified Method for Phenotyping Alpha-2-HS-Glycoprotein, *J. Forensic Sci.*, 38(5):1183-1186 (1993).

31. Lee, H.C., K.M. Berka, N.L. Folk, E.M. Pagliaro, J. Carroll-Reho, T.L. Brubaker, and R.E. Gaensslen, Genetic Markers in Bone, *J. Forensic Sci.*, 36(2):320-330 (1991).

32. Ibid., *J. Forensic Sci.*, 36(3):639-655 (1991).

33. Lasker, C.W. and M.C. Lee, Racial Traits in Human Teeth, *J. Forensic Sci.*, 2:401 (1957).

34. Atchison, J. Some Racial Differences in Human Skulls and Jaws, *Br. Dent. J.*, 116:25 (1964).

35. Harris, E.F. and J.H. McKee, Tooth Mineralization Standards for Blacks and Whites from the Middle Southern United States, *J. Forensic Sci.*, 35(4):859-872 (1990).

36. Rogers, S.L., *The Testimony of Teeth: Anthropologic and Forensic Aspects of Human Dentition*, Charles C Thomas, Springfield, IL, 1988.

37. Burns, K.R. and W.R. Maples. Estimation of Age from Individual Adult Teeth, *J. Forensic Sci.*, 21:343-356 (1976).

38. Taylor, R.T., *Variation in Morphology of Teeth: Anthropologic and Forensic Aspects*, Charles C Thomas, Springfield, IL, 1978.

39. Seno, M. and H. Ishizu, Sex Identification of a Human Tooth, *Int. J. Forensic Dent.*, pp. 8-11, 1973.

40. Mudd, J.L., The Determination of Sex from Forcibly Removed Hairs, *J. Forensic Sci.*, 29(4):1072-1080 (1984).

41. Naito, E., K. Dewa, H. Yamanouchi, and R. Kominami, Sex Typing of Forensic DNA Samples using Male and Female Specific Probes, *J. Forensic Sci.*, 39(4):1009-1012 (1994)

42. Vebovaza, L.V. and P.L. Ivanov, Sexing DNA on DNA Fingerprint Gel: An Internal Control for DNA Fingerprint Evidence, *J. Forensic Sci.*, 36(4):991-998 (1991).

43. Koboyash, R., H. Nakouchi, Y. Nakahori, Y. Nakagome, and S. Matsuzawa, Sex Identification in Fresh Blood and Dried Bloodstains by a Non-isotopic DNA Analyzing Technique, *J. Forensic Sci.*, 33(3):613 (1988).

44. Fukushima, H., H. Hasekura, and K. Nagai, Identification of Male Bloodstains by Dot Hybridization of Human Y Chromosome-Specific DNA Probe, *J. Forensic Sci.*, 33(3):621 (1988).

45. St. Hoyme, L.E. and M.Y. Iscan, Determination of Sex and Race: Accuracy and Assumptions, in *Reconstruction of Life From the Skeleton*, Eds. M.Y. Iscan and K.A.R. Kennedy, Alan R. Liss, New York, pp 53-93, 1989.

46. Stewart, T.D., *Essentials of Forensic Anthropology*, Charles C Thomas, Springfield, IL, 1979.

47. Martin, R. and K. Saller, *Lehrbuch der Anthropologie in Systematischen Darstellung*, Gustav Fisher Verlag, Stuttgart, Germany, 1961.

48. Keiser-Nielson, S., Geographic Factors in Forensic Odontology, *Int. Dent. J.*, 15:343-347 (1965).

49. Caldwell, P.C., New Questions (and some answers) on the Facial Reproduction Techniques, in *Forensic Osteology: Advances in the Identification of Human Remains*, Ed. K.J. Reichs, Charles C Thomas, Springfield, IL, pp. 229-255, 1986.

50. Webster, W.I., W.K. Murray, W. Brinkhous, and P. Hudson, Identification of Human Remains Using Photographic Reconstructions, in *Forensic Osteology: Advances in the Identification of Human Remains*, Ed. K.J. Reichs, Charles C Thomas, Springfield, IL, pp. 256-289, 1986.

51. Krogman, W.M., *The Human Skeleton in Forensic Medicine*, Charles C Thomas, Springfield, IL, 1962.

52. Bastiaan, R.J., G.D. Dalitz, and C. Woodward, Video Super-Imposition of Skulls and Photographic Portraits, *J. Forensic Sci.*, 31(4):1373-1379 (1986).

53. Hellmer, P., Identification of the Cadaver Remains of Josef Mengele, *J. Forensic Sci.*, 32(6):1622-1644 (1987).

54. Nickerson, B.A., P.A. Fitzhorn, S.K. Koch, and M. Charney, A Methodology for Near Optimal Computational Superimposition of Two-Dimensional Digital Facial Photographs and Three-Dimensional Cranial Surface Markers, *J. Forensic Sci.*, 36(2):480-500 (1991).

55. Ubelaker, D.H., E. Bubriak, and G. O'Donnell, Computer Assisted Photographic Superimposition, *J. Forensic Sci.*, 37(3):750-762 (1992).

56. Rathbun, T.D., Personal Identification: Facial Reproduction, in *Human Identification: Case Studies in Forensic Anthropology*, Eds. T.D. Rathbun and J.E. Buikstra, Charles C. Thomas, Springfield, IL, pp. 347-357, 1984.

57. Lenorovitz, D.R. and E.D. Sussman, The Discrimination Similarities and Differences in Facial Appearance: A Pilot Study, in *Personal Appearance Identification*, Eds. R.T. Zavala and T. Paley, Charles C Thomas, Springfield, IL, pp. 292-296, 1972.

58. Zavala, R.T., Determination of Facial Features Used in Identification, in *Personal Appearance Identification*, Eds. R.T. Zavala and T.Paley, Charles C Thomas, Springfield, IL, 1972.

59. Fierro, M.F., Identification of Human Remains, in *Spitz and Fisher's Medicolegal Investigation of Death*, 3rd ed., Ed. W.U. Spitz, Charles C Thomas, Springfield, IL, pp. 71-117, 1993.

60. Lorton, L. and W.H. Langley, Design and Use of a Computerized Assisted Postmortem Identification System, *J. Forensic Sci.*, 31(3):972-981 (1986).

61. Lorton, L., M. Rethman, and R. Friedman, Computer Assisted Postmortem Identification (CAPMI) System: A Computer Based Identification Program, *J. Forensic Sci.*, 33(4):977-984 (1988).

62. Friedman, R.B., K.A. Cornwell, and L. Lorton, Dental Characteristics of a Large Military Population Useful for Identification, *J. Forensic Sci.*, 34(6):1357-1364 (1989).

63. National Research Council, DNA Technology in Forensic Science, National Academy Press, Washington, D.C., 1992.

64. Furness, J., Teeth Marks and their Significance in Cases of Homicide, *J. Forensic Sci. Soc.*, 9:169 (1969).

65. Furness, J., A New Method for the Identification of Teeth Marks in Cases of Assault and Homicide, *Br. Dent. J.*, 124:261-267 (1968).

66. Benson, B.W., J.A. Cottone, J.J. Bomberg, and N.D. Sperber. Bite mark Impressions: Review of Techniques and Materials, *J. Forensic Sci.*, 33(5):1238-1243 (1988).

67. Wetli, C.V., R.E. Mittleman, and V.J. Rao, *Practical Forensic Pathology*, Igaku-Shoin, New York, pp. 93-103, 1988.

68. Hales, A., Admissibility of Bite mark Evidence, *South. Calif. Law Rev.*, Vol. 51(309):323-327 (1978).

69. Nelson, D.F. and P.L. Kirk. The Identification of Saliva, *J. Forensic Med.*, 10:14-21 (1963).

70. Harrington, D.J., R. Martin, and L. Kobilinsky, Detection of Hemagglutins in Dried Saliva Stains and their Potential Use in Blood Typing, *J. Forensic Sci.*, 33(3):628-637 (1988).

71. Peel, H.W., B.J. Perrigo, and N.Z. Mikhael, Detection of Drugs in Saliva of Impaired Drivers, *J. Forensic Sci.*, 29(1):185-189 (1984).

72. Horning, M.C., L. Brown, J. Nowlin, K. Lertratangkoon, P. Kellaway, and T.E. Zion. Use of Saliva in Therapeutic Drug Monitoring, *Clin. Chem.*, 23(2):157-164 (1977).

73. Danhof, M. and D.D. Breimer. Therapeutic Drug Monitoring, *Clin. Pharmacokinet.*, Vol. 3:39-57 (1978).

74. Idowu, O.R. and B.A. Caddy, Review of the Use of Saliva in the Forensic Detection of Drugs and other Chemicals, *J. Forensic Sci. Soc.*, 22:123-135 (1982).

75. Smith, F.P., The Detection of Drugs in Bloodstains, in *Advances in Forensic Science*, eds. H.C. Lee and R.E. Gaennslen, Biomedical Pubs., Foster City, CA, pp. 235-250, 1985.

76. Fletcher, S.M., P. Dolton, and P.W. Harris-Smith, Species Identification of Blood and Saliva Stains by Enzyme-Linked Immunoassay (ELISA) Using Monoclonal Antibody, *J. Forensic Sci.*, 29(1):67-74 (1984).

77. Sensabaugh, G. and E.T. Blake, DNA Analysis in Biological Evidence: Applications of the Polymerase Chain Reaction, in *Forensic Science Handbook*, Vol. III, Ed. R. Saferstein, Prentice-Hall, Englewood Cliffs, NJ, pp. 433-435, 1993.

78. Kocher, T.D., W.K. Thomas, A. Meyer, S.V. Edwards, S. Paabo, F.X. Villablanca, and A.C. Wilson, Dynamics of Mitochondrial DNA Evolution in Animals: Amplification and Sequencing with Conserved Primers, *Proc. Natl. Acad. Sci. U.S.A.*, 86:6196-6200 (1989).

79. Sanderson, A.R. and J.S.S. Stewart, Nuclear Sexing with Aceto-Orcein, *Br. Med. J.*, 2:1065-1067 (1961).

80. Sensabaugh, G. and E.T. Blake, DNA Analysis in Biological Evidence: Applications of the Polymerase Chain Reaction, in *Forensic Science Handbook*, Vol. III, Ed. R. Saferstein, Prentice-Hall, Englewood Cliffs, NJ, pp. 433-435, 1993.

81. Witt, M. and R.P. Erikson, A Rapid Method for Detection of Y Chromosomal DNA from Dried Blood Specimens Using the Polymerase Chain Reaction, *Hum. Genet.*, 82:271-274 (1989).

82. Gaensslen, R.E., K.M. Berka, D.A. Grosso, G. Ruano, E.M. Pagliaro, D. Messina, and H.C. Lee, A PCR Method for Sex and Species Determination with Novel Controls for DNA Template Length, *J. Forensic Sci.*, 37:6-20 (1992).

83. Aasen, E. and J.F. Medrano, Amplification of the ZFY and ZFX Genes for Sex Identification in Humans, Cattle, Sheep, and Goats, *BioTechnology*, 8:1279-1281 (1990).

84. Kobilinsky, L., Deoxyribonucleic Acid Structure and Function — A Review, in *Forensic Science Handbook*, Vol. III, Ed. R. Saferstein, Prentice-Hall, Englewood Cliffs, NJ, pp. 287-357, 1993.

85. Adams, D.E., L.A. Presley, A.L. Baumstark, K.W. Hensley, A.L. Hill, K.S. Anoe, P.A. Campbell, C.M. McLaughlin, B. Budowie, A.M. Giusti, B. Smerick, and F.S. Baechtel, Deoxyribonucleic Acid (DNA) Analysis by Restriction Fragment Length Polymorphisms of Blood and other Body Fluid Stains Subjected to Contamination and Environmental Insults, *J. Forensic Sci.*, 36(5):1284-1298, (1991).

86. Webb, M.B.T., N.J. Williams, and M.D. Sutton, Microbial DNA Challenge Studies of Variable Number Tandem Repeats (VNTR) Probes Used for DNA Profiling Analysis, *J. Forensic Sci.,* 1172-1175 (1993).

87. Laber, T.L., S.A. Giese, J.T. Iverson, and J.A. Liberty, Validation Studies on the Forensic Analysis of Restriction Fragment Length Polymorphisms on LE Agarose Gels without Ethidium Bromide: Effects of Contaminants, Sunlight, and the Electrophoresis of Varying Quantities of DNA, *J. Forensic Sci.,* 39(3):707-730 (1994).

88. Schwartz, E.A., L. Mieszerski, L. McNally, and L. Kobilinsky. Characterization of DNA obtained from Teeth Subjected to Various Environmental Conditions, *J. Forensic Sci.,* 36(4): 979-990 (1991).

89. Smith, B.C., D.L. Fisher, V.W. Weedn, G.R. Warnock, and M.M. Holland. A Systematic Approach to the Sampling of Dental DNA, *J. Forensic Sci.,* 38(5):1194-1209 (1993).

90. Holland, M.M., D.L. Fisher, L.G. Mitchell, W.C. Rodriques, R. Merril, and V.W. Weedn, Mitochondrial DNA Sequence Analysis of Human Skeletal Remains: Identification of Remains from the Vietnam War, *J. Forensic Sci.,* 38(3): 542-553 (1993).

91. Farley, M.A. and J.J. Harrington, Forensic DNA Technology. Lewis Publishers, Chelsea, MI, 1991.

92. Zurer, P., DNA Profiling fast becoming Accepted Tool for Identification, *Chemical and Engineering News,* pp.8-15 (1994).

93. Schefter, J., DNA Fingerprints on Trial, *Popular Science,* pp. 60-65 (1994).

94. Thompson, W. and S. Ford, The Meaning of a Match: Sources of Ambiguity in the Interpretation of DNA Prints, in *Forensic DNA Technology,* Eds. M.A. Farley and J.J. Harrington, Lewis Publishers, Chelsea, MI, pp. 93-152, 1991.

95. Berry, D.A., DNA, Statistics, and the Simpson Case, *Chance,* 7(4):9-12 (1994).

96. Berry, D.A., Statistical Issues in DNA Identification, in *DNA on Trial: Genetic Identification and Criminal Justice,* Ed. P.R. Billings, Cold Spring Harbor Laboratory Press, Cold Spring Harbor, NY, 91-108, 1992.

97. Lewontin, R.D. and D.L. Hartl, Population Genetics in Forensic DNA Typing, *Science,* 254:1745 (1991).

98. Lander, E.S. and B. Budowle. DNA Fingerprinting Dispute Laid to Rest, *Nature,* 371(6500):735-738 (1994).

99. Chakraborty, R. and K.K. Kidd, The utility of DNA Typing in Forensic Work, *Science,* 254:1735 (1991).

100. Budowle, B., K.L. Monson, and J.R. Wooley, Reliability of Statistical Estimates in Forensic DNA Typing, in *DNA on Trial: Genetic Identification and Criminal Justice,* Ed. P.R. Billings, Cold Spring Harbor Laboratory Press, Cold Spring Harbor, NY, pp. 79-90, 1992.

101. Bereano, P.L., The Impact of DNA-based Identification Systems on Civil Liberties, in *DNA on Trial: Genetic Identification and Criminal Justice,* Ed. P.R. Billings, Cold Spring Harbor Laboratory Press, Cold Spring Harbor, NY, pp. 119-128, 1992.

102. Wilker, N.L., S. Stawski, R. Lewontin, and P.R. Billings, DNA Data Banking and the Public Interest, in *DNA on Trial: Genetic Identification and Criminal Justice,* Ed. P.R. Billings, Cold Spring Harbor Laboratory Press, Cold Spring Harbor, NY, pp. 141-149, 1992.

103. Williams, P.E., M. Marino, S.A. Del Rio, L.A. Turni, and J.M. Devaney, Analysis of DNA Restriction Fragments and Polymerase Chain Reaction Products by Capillary Electrophoresis, *J. Chromatogr.,* A680:525-540 (1994).

104. Annas, G.J., Scientific evidence in the courtroom, *N. Engl. J. Med.,* 30(14): 1018-1021 (1994).

105. Boyde, A., "Estimation of Age at Death of Young Skeletal Remains from Incremental Lines in the Dental Enamel" presented at the 3rd International Meeting in Forensic Immunology, Medicine, Pathology and Toxicology Plenary Session IIA, London, England, April 1963.

106. Boyde, A., "Amelogenesis and the Structure of Enamel" Scientific Foundations of Dentistry, B. Cohen and J.R.H. Kramer, Eds., Heinemann, London, 1976 pp. 335-352.

107. Boyde, A. "Enamel" *Teeth,* B.K.B. Berkowitz, A. Boyle R.M. Fraule, H.J. Hohling, B.J. Moxham, J. Nalba and C.H. Tonge, Eds., Springer-Verlag, Berlin, 1989 pp. 309-473.

108. Azen, E.A., 1978. Genetic protein polymorphisms in human saliva: an interpretative review *Biochem. Genet.* 16: 79-99.

109. Azen, E.A., 1972. Genetic polymorphism of basic proteins from parotid saliva. *Science* 176: 673-674.

110. Azen, E.A., 1973. Properties of salivary basic proteins showing polymorphism *Biochem. Genet.* 9: 69-86.

111. Azen, E.A., 1977. Salivary peroxidase (SAPX): genetic modification and relationship to the proline-rich (Pr) and acidic (Pa) proteins. *Biochem Genet.* 15: 9-29.

112. Azen, E.A., cn C.L. Denniston, 1974. Genetic polymorphysm of human salivary proline-rich proteins: farther genetic analysis. *Biochem. Genet.* 12: 109-120.

113. Azen, E.A., C.K. Hurley, and C.L. Denniston, 1979 Genetic polymorphism of the major parotid salivary glycoprotein (Gi) with linkage to the genes for Pr, Db and Pa *Biochem. Genet.* 17: 257-279.

114. Azen, E.A. and F.G. Oppenheim, 1973. Genetic polymorphism of proline rich human salivary proteius *Science* 180: 1067-1069.

DNA Identification* 2

VICTOR WALTER WEEDN

Introduction

Forensic identification is based on finding differences — polymorphisms — between different individuals. These differences can take many forms, such as differences in facial appearance, differences in ear lobe conformation, differences in retinal arterial structure, differences in hair color, differences in height, etc. — some variations are unique and some are not. Indeed, individual variation is a tenet of biology. Fingerprint friction ridge patterns and dentition are useful for identification precisely because they are different in each individual. Furthermore, the DNA molecule is unique, except in identical twins.

Polymorphisms can either be acquired or inherited. A surgical scar is an obvious example of an acquired identifier. The friction ridge patterns of fingerprints have an obvious genetic component, but are predominantly established from local perturbations during fetal development, hence identical twins have different dermatoglyphics. Most acquired features used for identification may change with time, for example dental features can change over time. The polymorphisms within the DNA molecule are the basis for all inherited polymorphisms and they do not change over the lifetime of an individual.

Although dental identification is an excellent and convenient means of positive identification, there are limitations to its use. Dental identification requires the availability of a good quality, reasonably up-to-date dental radiograph. The dentist or orthodontist who has the radiograph in his file must be found. Due to the success of water fluoridation programs, there are now fewer dental restorations in younger people. Restorations have provided the basis for most dental identifications. Massive head trauma or decapitation

---

* The views expressed are those of the authors and do not necessarily reflect those of the U.S. Army or the Department of Defense.

may render dental identification impossible. Consequently, not all remains can be identified through dental comparison techniques.

Dental identification takes advantage of the polymorphic nature of the hardest structures in the body — precisely those structures which are most likely to remain available for identification purposes. Although dental structures are more likely to survive traumatic and decompositional changes than other traditional means of identification such as fingerprints, scars, facial appearance, etc., DNA has a still greater likelihood of survival. Any tissue or bone fragment can be used for DNA testing, with the possible exception of those which have undergone severe incineration or prolonged water (particularly saltwater) immersion. Perhaps most significantly, body fragments, unless of a hand with fingerprints, a portion of a jaw with teeth, or an articulable limb, will not ordinarily be identified except by laboratory tissue identification techniques.

A common obstacle to fingerprint and dental identification is the lack of antemortem data for comparison. The common availability of families as sources of reference material for comparison purposes is a particularly important aspect of DNA identification.

Furthermore, dental and fingerprint identification are relatively slow and tedious in a large mass disaster. Future DNA testing technologies will permit high-volume, low-cost testing. In significant mass disasters, the speed of batch laboratory testing may prove critical.

For many years, tissue identifications could only be accomplished by traditional serologic markers, particularly ABO blood group typing. DNA testing is far superior to those other tissue-typing techniques for a variety of reasons. DNA is the basis for all blood group types, red cell antigens, and protein isoenzymes. Due to the degeneracy of the genetic code, there will always be more polymorphisms in DNA than in the resultant phenotypes. The discriminatory power of DNA is far greater than any set of traditional markers, including HLA typing. Traditional markers typically yield values of one in thousands, whereas DNA tests often yield values of one in millions. DNA testing can be performed on any tissue or fluid. DNA tests, particularly PCR-based DNA tests, are more sensitive than traditional serologic markers. DNA tests can be performed on specimens which are far older than is the case with traditional markers and DNA is less susceptible to environmental insults.

The DNA Molecule

General

The basis for all inheritance is found within the DNA genome of cells. This information is coded within the chemical structure of the DNA molecule or, more accurately, the set of DNA molecules known as the genome. Nucleotide bases are arranged in specific sequences within the chemical structural scaffolding. Only four bases (adenine, cytosine, guanine, and thymine) make up the genetic alphabet that produces the words, sentences, paragraphs, and chapters which are eventually read into proteins that comprise biological organisms. These bases are present in pairs in a complementary fashion to form base pairs, such that every A is paired with a T, every C with a G, and vice versa. The consequence of this base pairing is that half of the molecule can be stripped away from the other half and the base sequence of one strand can be used to determine the sequence of the opposite strand, or to create a specific DNA hybridization probe.

Stability of DNA

DNA is a robust molecule which can tolerate a remarkable range of temperature, pH, salt, and other factors that destroy classical serologic markers. Validation testing in forensic science laboratories has shown that DNA mixed with detergents, oil, gasoline, and other adulterants did not alter its typing characteristics. Indeed, it is this ruggedness which allows DNA longevity and has permitted DNA typing of Egyptian mummies and 30-million-year-old insects preserved in amber. Bone or tissues that have been in soil environments for extended lengths of time often yield no DNA typing results by traditional means, especially when the soil is moist. However, even relatively ancient skeletal remains may yield an informative mitochondrial DNA sequence.

DNA Polymorphisms

DNA polymorphisms can be length-based or sequence-based. Length-based polymorphisms are a characteristic of repetitive DNA that generally does not code for any protein (so-called "junk" DNA). DNA fragments vary in size between individuals due to the presence of variable numbers of tandem repeats (VNTRs); i.e., a core of 7 bases may be repeated 3 times in one individual or 12 times in the next individual. Traditional restriction fragment length polymorphism (RFLP) analysis, as is commonly associated with the DNA testing in crime labs, involves cut fragments (restriction fragments) which include internal VNTR regions (loci) and thus vary in fragment length. VNTR fragments can also be amplified instead of cut, hence, amplified fragment length polymorphisms (AmpFLPs).

DNA identity information is found not only in fragment length variation, but also within the DNA sequence of similarly sized DNA fragments. Sequence polymorphisms consist of difference changes in one or more bases in a DNA sequence at a particular location in the genome. Sequence variations can manifest as regions of alternative alleles or base substitutions, additions, or deletions. Most sequence polymorphisms are mere point mutations. They may be found in coding or noncoding DNA. Sequence polymorphisms can be detected by DNA probes or by direct sequencing.

DNA Methods

RFLP Methods

The DNA typing method that was first described, and most commonly employed by crime labs initially, is known as restriction fragment length polymorphism (RFLP) analysis. The six steps in RFLP testing include:

1. Extraction of DNA from a biologic source
2. Cutting the DNA into relatively small fragments at specific sites with "restriction enzymes"
3. Separating the fragments by size using agarose gel electrophoresis;
4. Transferring and immobilizing the separated DNA fragments onto a nylon membrane
5. Denaturation of the DNA into single strands and hybridization to radioisotopically-labeled probes (small fragments of single-stranded DNA)
6. Autoradiography, in which an X-ray film is placed over the membrane for several days, resulting in exposure of the film at the point of the probe

RFLP testing is often called "Southern blotting" because the DNA transfer technique was first described by Professor Southern. Typically, RFLP testing will take several weeks to perform. For every probing, the membrane is stripped of the previous probe and rehybridized and autoradiography performed anew. However, alternatives to radioisotopic labels now exist, particularly chemiluminescent and fluorescent probe labels, which permit much faster testing.

Unfortunately, RFLP is not useful where the DNA is degraded, because random fragmentation thwarts detection of a specific large uncut fragment population. Since DNA rapidly breaks down after death, RFLP testing is of limited value in testing cadaveric tissue for identification of human remains, unless the remains are fresh.

PCR Methods

The polymerase chain reaction (PCR) is a method of copying or "amplifying" a particular segment of DNA. A few strands or even a single strand of DNA can be used to reproduce millions of copies of target DNA fragments. Kary Mullis was awarded the Nobel Prize in 1993 for the discovery of the PCR process, which has led to a revolution in the life sciences. PCR amplification is a sample preparation technique which enables further testing to detect various polymorphisms. Nonamplified DNA becomes undetectable against the amplified background target sequence. PCR testing is not only very sensitive, but it is quicker, less labor intensive, and less tedious than RFLP testing. Most significantly for remains identification, it is often successful even though the tissue specimen is degraded because only a few copies of relatively short segments need remain intact. However, PCR testing is susceptible to inhibition and the potential for cross contamination.

Dot/Blots

Sequence information can be obtained through the use of DNA probes. A DNA probe is a small piece of single-stranded DNA (oligonucleotide) which will bind to another single-stranded DNA with the complementary sequence. A sequence-specific oligonucleotide (SSO) probe, also known as an allele-specific oligonucleotide (ASO) probe, is a single-stranded DNA fragment sufficiently long to confer specificity, but short enough to bind only to the exact sequence complement. Commercial kits, i.e., DQ-alpha and Poly-Marker systems, are based on a dot/blot format for SSO typing and are currently in use by many crime labs. The resultant dot/blot strip has a series of spots that turn blue if the reaction is positive and in this way give a series of yes/no results. These dot/blot tests are quite rapid and work reasonably well despite sample degradation, but do not harbor the same discriminatory power as RFLP tests.

AmpFLPs and STRs

VNTR polymorphisms can be typed by both RFLP and by PCR methods. Since smaller loci are desired for amplification, generally the VNTR loci typed by PCR methods are different from those that are typed using RFLP methods. Regions with core repeat sequences greater than 7 bp have been called "minisatellite" or "long tandem repeat" (LTR) regions. Those with core repeat sequences of approximately 3 to 7 bp are called "microsatellite" or "short tandem repeat" (STR) regions. Dinucleotide repeats are not generally used in forensic science laboratories due to the artifactual production of so-called "shadow" and "stutter" bands.

The shorter STR fragments are generally preferable for a variety of technical reasons. A number of STR systems are available for use in identification, and commercial kits are available. These STR systems work well despite significant degradation and are quite amenable to automation. Sufficient numbers of STR systems can be performed to achieve discriminatory powers similar to current RFLP testing. The British and Canadian crime labs are moving towards using STR systems exclusively.

Mitochondrial DNA (MtDNA)

Not only is DNA present within chromosomes in the nuclei of cells, but DNA is also present in the mitochondria of cells. Mitochondria are known as the powerhouses of the cells as they are the primary machinery for accomplishing oxidative metabolism. Tens, hundreds, or even thousands of mitochondria are present within a single cell and each mitochondrion may contain several mitochondrial "DNA particles". Consequently, a cell contains only one copy of nuclear DNA, but literally thousands of copies of the 16,000-bp mitochondrial DNA (MtDNA) sequence; hence a mitochondrial DNA type can be obtained when the nuclear DNA type cannot.

Since no significant regions of repetitive DNA exist in MtDNA, only sequence polymorphisms are typed. The region of MtDNA which is analyzed for human identification is the noncoding region known as the displacement loop (D-loop) or control region. The degree of polymorphism in the D-loop is so great that direct sequencing may be the most efficient method of typing MtDNA, although a commercial dot/blot system is in development.

Another unique feature of MtDNA is its mode of inheritance — one half of nuclear DNA is from the mother and one half from the father. Mitochondria are inherited in a strictly mother-to-child manner; there is no paternal contribution. Because there is no recombination and because only a single (unpaired) copy is present in the cell, an exact sequence match is anticipated. Accordingly, MtDNA can be traced through a family via maternal lineages for many generations.

Mitochondrial DNA sequencing has great application to severely decomposed and skeletonized remains. However, the discriminatory power is limited; discriminatory powers are often of the order of one in a hundred. Very few laboratories are performing this kind of testing at this point in time.

Specimen Selection, Collection, and Preservation

DNA can be isolated and tested from virtually any postmortem tissue, although after death it will undergo progressive fragmentation. DNA is generally broken down (degraded) into fragments through autolytic and bacterial enzymes, specifically DNases. Nevertheless, the sequence information is still present within the DNA fragments and therefore the information is not completely lost despite the fairly extensive fragmentation which occurs from decomposition. However, not all DNA testing is appropriate or possible when the DNA is degraded. Traditional RFLP testing will require nondegraded high molecular weight DNA, whereas PCR-based analysis can be performed on degraded samples and mitochondrial DNA can be obtained from skeletal remains when nuclear DNA cannot.

In relatively fresh cadavers, unclotted blood (EDTA anticoagulated in a purple-top tube) is the preferable source of DNA. Although heme is an inhibitor of PCR, laboratories are accustomed to blood as a DNA specimen and although only white blood cells carry the DNA, ample DNA is present for testing. Due to the settling out of white blood cells, clotted blood may not be a good source of DNA. Blood is a good culture medium and bacterial growth may render blood samples useless. Virtually any tissue can be used successfully for DNA typing purposes. Brain tissue is said to be a particularly good source in intermediate post-mortem time periods. Hard tissues (bone and teeth) are the best source of DNA in cases of advanced decomposition.

The specimens should be kept cold or preferably frozen (although repeated freezing and thawing is not good). Desiccation, even simple air drying, may be an adequate method of storage of some DNA specimens, e.g., bloodstains and bone. Tissues in formalin are not optimal, but can often be used for PCR-based DNA testing. No tissues or biologic fluids should be discarded as inadequate without first attempting DNA testing.

Due to the degree of sensitivity of PCR-based technologies, great care should be taken to prevent contamination of one specimen by other sources of DNA. Specimens should be collected with gloves and pristine instruments. Fresh tissues should be collected by an incisional biopsy technique, where possible. Similarly, laboratory testing should be carried out with particular precautions against the possibility of contamination, including separating the pre-PCR sample preparation area from the post-PCR analysis area.

Teeth themselves can be excellent sources of DNA. In fact, the same reasons that permit the survival of teeth for dental identification similarly protect the DNA within teeth. Accordingly, teeth are a better source of DNA than skeletal bones, which are better than soft tissues in cases of very decomposed remains. DNA is present in the vascular pulp of the tooth, but it is also found throughout the tooth in varying levels, particularly in the odontoblastic processes, accessory canals, and cellular cementum. Most information necessary for traditional dental identification is present in the crown (enamel and dentin) of the tooth. Consequently, a tooth can be sectioned horizontally through the cervical root subjacent to the cementoenamel junction, preserving most restorations for traditional dental comparison purposes. Although somewhat greater amounts of DNA are obtained by crushing the entire tooth, this conservative method of sampling DNA from teeth has been found to be quite adequate.

The first step in extraction of DNA from bone or teeth is to break up the tissue to expose the DNA to the extraction medium. Early techniques involved the fracturing of bone by freezing it in liquid nitrogen, but subsequent protocols specify breaking the tissue with a mortar and pestle and then grinding the tissue into a coarse powder in a grinding mill. Protocols have differed in requiring or not requiring a decalcification step. We have found that decalcification is not only unnecessary, but approximately half of the DNA is lost through the dilution and imperfect recovery involved. The next step in most protocols is incubation in a proteinase-K solution to enzymatically digest proteins and release the DNA. After incubation in a buffer solution, standard DNA extraction procedures may then be performed.

Reference Samples/Databases

The lack of an antemortem dental X-ray or fingerprint record is the most common reason for the inability to obtain identification by traditional identification methods, whereas reference specimens for DNA testing are generally available from family members.

Specimens from the spouse and children will permit "reverse paternity" testing using nuclear DNA probes. Parental specimens, and possibly those from siblings, will permit identification, particularly in closed populations. Reconstruction from scattered relatives is often possible, but the statistical inference is substantially diminished. Mitochondrial DNA analysis must be performed on maternal kindred (mothers, siblings, children only in the case of a female), but unlike nuclear DNA identification, it can be performed even in distant relatives (maternal aunts and uncles, children of sisters).

It is not always possible or desirable to use families for reference specimens. Sometimes family members are no longer alive. Sometimes the family members are not known or their whereabouts cannot be determined. Some individuals are adopted into their families and therefore the family is not appropriate as reference specimens. Often it is awkward to approach families on the mere possibility of an identification. Except in the case of mitochondrial DNA sequence comparisons, pedigree analysis permits only inferential and less compelling conclusions than a sample from the individual himself. Furthermore, mutations render occasional identifications problematic.

Rather than secondary reference samples from family members, primary DNA specimens of the individual may be available from toothbrushes, biopsies or tissue slides archived in a hospital's pathology department, from stored blood donations, from licked envelopes and stamps, or in the case of mitochondrial DNA from locks of baby hair or clippings from an electric shaver. All states require the taking of bloodstains from infants for phenylketonuria (PKU) testing; some state health departments store these cards for significant periods of time.

Not only can DNA be obtained from teeth for primary identification, but it can also be obtained for reference DNA purposes. We have seen cases in which teeth have been identified, and the DNA from the tooth used as a reference DNA source to identify other tissue fragments.

The majority of states now have legislation creating DNA databases of convicted sex and violent offenders; other states will likely enact such legislation. These state DNA databanks will be linked by the FBI's National DNA Identification Index (also known as the Combined DNA Index System or CODIS) and will include a file for unidentified and missing persons. This computer system is separate and apart from the NCIC.

Due to the tremendous utility of DNA identification, the military established the DOD DNA Registry for the purpose of human remains identification. The DNA Registry is comprised of the Armed Forces DNA Identification Laboratory and the DOD DNA Specimen Repository. By the year 2001 all active duty military will have buccal swabs and dried bloodstain DNA specimen cards on file. The DNA Registry has already proven itself to be of great benefit. With the establishment of the DNA Registry, the military's duplicate panograph program will be phased out.

DNA identification represents a significant new adjunct to traditional methods of identification.

References

1. DeGusta, D., Cook, C., and Sensabaugh, G., Dentin as a source of ancient DNA, *Ancient DNA Newsletter,* 2(1):13, 1994.

2. Fisher, D.L., Holland, M.M., Mitchell, L., Sledzik, P.S., Wilcox, A.W., Wadhams, M., and Weedn, V.W., Extraction, and amplification of DNA from decalcified and undecalcified United States Civil War Bone, *J. Forensic Sci.,* 38(1):60-68, 1993.

3. Gaensslen, R.E., Berka, K.M., Pagliaro, E.M., Ruano, G., Messina, D. and Lee, H.C., Studies on DNA polymorphisms in human bone and soft tissues, *Anal. Chim. Acta,* 288:3-16, 1994.

4. Hagelberg, E., Gray, I.C., and Jeffreys, A.J., Identification of the skeletal remains of a murder victim by DNA analysis, *Nature,* 352:427-429, 1991.

5. Holland, M.M., Fisher, D.L., Lee, D.A., Bryson, C.K., and Weedn, V.W., Short tandem repeat loci: Application to forensic and human remains identification, in: *DNA Fingerprinting: State of the Science,* Pena, S.D.J., Chakraborty, R., Epplen, J.T., and Jeffreys, A.J., Eds., Birkhauser Verlag, Basel, Switzerland, pp. 267-274, 1993.

6. Holland, M.M., Fisher, D.L., Mitchell, L.G., Rodriguez, W.C., Canik, J.J., Merril, C.R., and Weedn, V.W., Mitochondrial DNA sequence analysis of human skeletal remains: Identification of remains from the Vietnam War, *J. Forensic Sci.,* 38:542-553, 1993.

7. Kirby, L.T., Ed., *DNA Fingerprinting: An Introduction*, Stockton Press, New York, 1990.

8. Kobilinsky, L., Recovery and stability of DNA in samples of forensic science significance, *Forensic Sci. Rev.*, 4:67-87, 1992.

9. Lee, H.C., Gaensslen, R.E., Bigbee, P.D., and Kearney, J.J., Guidelines for collection and preservation of DNA evidence, *J. Forensic Ident.*, 41:344-356, 1991.

10. Lee, H.C., Pagliaro, E.M., Berka, K.M., Folk, N.L., Anderson, D.T., Ruano, G., Keith, T.P., Phipps, P., Herrin, G.L., Garner, D.D., and Gaensslen, R.E., Genetic markers in human bone. I. Deoxyribonucleic acid (DNA) analysis, *J. Forensic Sci.*, 36:320-330, 1991.

11. Shibata, D., Kurosu, M., and Noguchi, T.T., Fixed human tissues: A resource for the identification of individuals, *J. Forensic Sci.*, 36:1204-1212, 1991.

12. Smith, B.S., Holland, M.M., Sweet, D.L., and Dizinno, J.A., DNA and the Forensic Odontologist, in: *The Manual of Forensic Odontology*, C. Michael Bowers, Ed., American Society of Forensic Odontology, Chicago, IL, 1995.

13. Smith, B.S., Weedn, V.W., Warnock, G.R., and Holland, M.M., Histologic considerations in the sampling of dental source DNA, *J. Forensic Sci.*, 38(4):1194-1209, 1993.

14. Weedn, V.W. and Roby, R.K., Forensic DNA testing, *Arch. Pathol. Lab. Med.*, 117:486-491, 1993.

Issues Regarding Scientific Testing

3

GLENN N. WAGNER
LARRY D. WILLIAMS

Introduction

In 1992, the National Research Council (NRC), in giving its stamp of approval on the use of forensic DNA typing to obtain identification information, observed "… DNA technology is at least as reliable as other forensic methods and is therefore more likely to result in definitive identification and exclusion."[1]

In its 1990 report,[2] the Office of Technology Assessment specifically noted:

> The Office of Technology Assessment (OTA) finds that forensic use of DNA tests are both reliable and valid when properly performed and analyzed by skilled personnel. Molecular genetics techniques can accurately disclose DNA patterns that reflect DNA differences among humans. Questions about the validity of DNA typing — either the knowledge base supporting technologies that detect genetic differences or the underlying principles of applying the techniques per se — are red herrings that do the courts and the public a disservice.[3]

However, the NRC also cautioned that the introduction of a powerful new technology is likely to set up unwarranted or unrealistic expectations.[4] Chief among these expectations is the perception that trial judges and lay juries will give more credence to the improbability that two people will have the same allele or gene component at the same location on a chromosome.[5] Moreover, there is the "inappropriate" expectation that, given the magnitude of this technology, juries will, perhaps, overlook errors in quality assurance and laboratory mistakes. Indeed, this new scientific evidence may "assume a posture of mystic infallibility".[6]

This section addresses this powerful technology from the standpoint of some of the constitutional issues relating to obtaining DNA blood specimens from criminal suspects and, to a lesser extent, tissue specimens from cadavers. The plethora of issues surrounding its reliability and relevancy at criminal trials will also be examined. Finally, an assessment of the impact of establishing and using DNA databanks will be covered.

0-8493-8103-7/97/$0.00+$.50
© 1997 by CRC Press LLC

Body Intrusions

There are many scientific techniques[7] or procedures that are employed to test physical artifacts such as semen, skin, hair follicles, blood, or bone and organs found at a crime scene or mass disaster to establish the identity of the contributor. DNA analysis is but one of these procedures which compares samples of known and unknown origins in order to determine the possibility of a common origin of the samples.

The focus on body intrusions will be to assess the constitutional impact on a suspect's rights when he is involuntarily required to provide a sample of his blood for DNA analysis. While the courts appear uniform in their handling of these cases, two constitutional arguments are usually advanced: that it is unreasonable to extract blood for DNA analysis without a warrant and, failing there, the seizure of blood represents a violation of one's right against self-incrimination.

In criminal proceedings, as a general proposition, it is fairly well established that a suspect has a constitutional right to be free from unreasonable searches and seizures,[8] as well as the right not to provide self-incriminating evidence.[9] The Fourth Amendment right protects suspects against intrusions into their body (search) and the extraction (seizure) of body fluids unless there is a search warrant. The Fifth Amendment protects "communications" and "testimony".[10]

Schmerber v. California[11] is the leading Supreme Court case on intrusions into the body for the collection of evidence. *Inter alia,* the case stands for the proposition that, in the absence of an "emergency" (to preclude destruction of evidence such as alcohol or other contraband), extracting blood must be done after securing a warrant[12] based on "probable cause".[13] The Court supported its reasoning for a warrant by observing: "The importance of the informed, detached and deliberate determinations of the issue whether or not to invade another's body in search of evidence of guilt is indisputable and great."[14] The Court, in carefully balancing the privacy rights of a defendant on the one hand and the rights of a state to secure evidence where there is the possibility of its rapid destruction, allowed the seizure without benefit of a warrant. It follows then that a seizure of blood for DNA analysis (the components of the blood will not be destroyed) will not be supportable absent a search warrant.[15]

It was also argued in *Schmerber* that the involuntary taking of his blood for analysis of its alcoholic content represented a form of communication or testimony and, hence, violated his right not to provide self-incriminating "evidence" in the form of blood. In rejecting Schmerber's characterization of the taking of his blood as amounting to a communication or testimony, the Court said:

It is clear that the protection of the privilege reaches an accused's communication, whatever form they might take. On the other hand, both federal and states courts have usually held that it offers no protection against compulsion to submit to fingerprinting, photographing, or measurements, to write or speak for identification, to appear in court, to stand, to assume a stance, to walk, or to make a particular gesture. The distinction which has emerged, often expressed in different ways, is that the privilege is a bar against compelling "communications" or "testimony," but that compulsion which makes a suspect or accused the source of "real or physical" evidence does not violate it.[16]

One final caveat must always be observed when such intrusive procedures are employed, namely, that the extraction be done in a reasonable fashion using medical personnel with appropriate qualifications.[17]

Of course, consent from the person whose blood for DNA analysis is sought may obviate the above constitutional issues. Two underpinnings support consent searches. The first is that when one consents, he or she "waives" his or her Fourth Amendment rights. The second theory is that consent is a valid exception to the warrant requirement of the Fourth Amendment. Naturally, consent to the search must be an act of free will, unfettered by police pressure and restraint.[18]

Testing Human Remains

Obtaining and testing DNA specimens from human remains or cadavers will largely depend upon the circumstances surrounding the death. If, for example, the death investigation falls within the statutory authority of the coroner or medical examiner, obtaining a specimen to complete the investigation requires no consent of the next of kin.[19] Mass disasters such as the conflagration in Texas involving David Koresh and his followers, or the myriad airplane crashes where identification of fragmented remains is crucial, are other examples where the statutory authority of the local coroner is yet again invoked. This legislatively imposed authority is generally not the subject of case law or a problem area.

Novel Scientific Evidence and the Courts — An Introduction

With regard to the admissibility of scientific evidence in trials, Judge Cox[20] found it instructive to group evidence into three levels. At the top rung, the reliability or acceptance of the scientific principles are so overwhelmingly accepted by the courts that a proponent need not establish the principle each time. Fingerprint identification[21] and bite marks[22] are examples. At the bottom rung, "lies a junk pile of contraptions, practices, techniques, etc., that have been so universally discredited"[23] that a judge will reject them as a matter of course. Examples include astrology and voodoo. At the middle rung is where novel scientific evidence is placed because the evidence can neither be accepted nor rejected out of hand. To this third category, we assign polygraph evidence[24] and DNA identification evidence. Moreover, "a proponent must lay a proper foundation [using experts in the area], focusing on the underlying principles and techniques of the procedures involved."[25]

Two other methods have also been employed to recognize the validity of a particular scientific technique. Namely, through the use of legislative action[26] and through the use of a trial technique called stipulation.[27]

Professors Gianelli and Imwinkelried[28] offer an analytical framework for the admissibility of scientific evidence. They observe that "[t]he reliability of evidence derived from a scientific theory depends on: (1) the validity of the technique applying that theory and (2) the proper application of the technique on a particular occasion."[29] They refer to this approach, which will be discussed later, as relevancy. Irrespective of the approach courts take, any new technique is established primarily using expert testimony.

The Frye Test

An analytical approach using the "general acceptance" test to establish the reliability of scientific evidence was first espoused in *Frye v. United States*.[30]

With notable exception in the federal courts,[31] Frye currently reigns as the "gold standard" in a large number of state court jurisdictions.[32]

The Frye rule of "general acceptance" was first enunciated over 70 years ago in a District of Columbia criminal trial where the defendant sought to introduce results of a systolic blood pressure deception test. This test, a precursor to the modern-day polygraph machine, was proffered to establish that the defendant was telling the truth.

In excluding the proffered evidence, the court said:

> Just when a scientific principle or discovery crosses the line between the experimental and demonstrable stages is difficult to define. Somewhere in this twilight zone the evidential force of the principle must be recognized, and while the courts will go a long way in admitting expert testimony deduced from a well-recognized scientific principle or discovery, the thing from which the deduction is made must be sufficiently established to have gained general acceptance in the particular field to which it belongs.[33]

Clearly, those jurisdictions following the Frye test seek to ensure that the evidence is reliable. The D.C. Circuit has observed: "The requirement of general acceptance in the scientific community assures that those most qualified to access the general validity of a scientific method will have a determinative voice."[34] Reliability is critically important because scientific evidence takes on "an aura of infallibility,"[35] with judges and juries whose comprehension, given the complexities of modern science, quite often is lacking.

Utilizing the Frye test, several key questions arise. First, is it the *principle* or the *technique* that must first be generally accepted.[36] The term "principle" relates to possible theories or scientific rules scientists usually rely on in developing the technique. The term "technique" generally means the actual procedure, to include instrumentation used. In the Frye case, the court, in focusing on the principle, stated that there was no generally accepted connection between variations in blood pressure and deception.[37]

The second question revolves around the meaning of "acceptance." Some courts have expressed the view that the acceptance must be "substantial",[38] or a demonstration that a "clear majority" was needed.[39]

In DNA analysis, the case of *People v. Wesley*[40] provides some insight into the relevant fields of acceptance. In *Wesley*, bloodstained apparel was seized from the defendant. As is the customary procedure, law enforcement officials wanted blood and hair specimens as reference specimens when DNA testing was done of the clothing and specimens taken from the body of the victim. Applying the Frye test to forensic DNA analysis, the court determined that the broad fields of acceptance were genetics, population statistics, and molecular biology.

Criticisms of Frye

Despite its popularity, the Frye test has not been without its critics. Maletskos and Spielman observed: "A literal reading of *Frye v. United States* would require that the courts always await the passing of a 'cultural lag' during which period the new method will have had sufficient time to diffuse through scientific discipline and create the requisite body of scientific opinion needed for acceptability."[41]

Another Frye criticism suggests that the validity issue is reposed in the scientific community and not in the courts where it belongs.[42] Professors Gianelli and Inwinkelried sum up some of the criticism with their observation that irrespective of the test applied, the objective should be "preventing the admission of unreliable scientific evidence."[43]

Relevancy Test of the Federal Rules

The second approach to the evaluation of the reliability of scientific evidence is the relevancy test. Using this approach, novel scientific evidence is treated no differently that other expert testimony. Although of recent origin, it certainly seems the more enlightened approach.

The "relevancy" test is largely an outgrowth of criticism lodged against Frye and the 1975 enactment of the Federal Rules of Evidence (FRE). The thrust of the test lies in FRE 401, 402, and 403.

FRE 402 indicates: "All relevant evidence is admissible, except as otherwise provided by the Constitution of the United States, by Act of Congress, by these rules, or by other rules prescribed by the Supreme Court pursuant to statutory authority. Evidence which is not relevant is not admissible."

FRE 401 defines "relevant evidence" as "evidence having any tendency to make the existence of any fact that is of consequence to the determination of the action more probable or less probable than it would be without the evidence."

FRE 403 even warns the judge who must rule on its admissibility to exclude even relevant evidence

> ...if its probative value is substantially outweighed by the danger of unfair prejudice, confusion of the issues, or misleading the members [juries], or by consideration of undue delay, waste of time, or needless presentation of cumulative evidence.

FRE 702 controls the use of expert testimony. It provides that,

> [I]f scientific, technical, or other specialized knowledge will assist the trier of fact [judge or jury] to understand the evidence or to determine a fact in issue, a witness qualified as an expert by knowledge, skill, experience, training, or education, may testify hereto in the form of an opinion or otherwise.

Prior to the Supreme Court's pronouncement in *Daubert*,[44] one of the leading cases interpreting this new approach was *United States v. Downing*.[45] *Downing* was a mail fraud case where the issue was whether the defendant was in fact a person using the alias "Reverend Claymore". After 12 witnesses said that he was Claymore, the defense proffered the testimony of an expert witness on the unreliability of eyewitness testimony. The Court rejected the testimony and relied on FRE 702. The court opined that the proffered testimony was not "helpful". The court then proceeded to outline what has been referred to as the Downing criteria:

1. The soundness and reliability of the process or technique used in generating the evidence
2. The possibility that admitting the evidence would overwhelm, confuse, or mislead the jury
3. The proffered connection between the scientific research or test result to the presented, and the particular disputed factual issues in the case[46]

The seminal case and the only Supreme Court case to address this new approach is *Daubert*.[47] Prior to the Court's ruling, there had been considerable division in the federal circuits. The issue was whether the Federal Rules of Evidence superseded Frye in providing the standard for admitting expert scientific testimony in a federal trial. The Supreme Court answered in the affirmative and rejected the Frye "general acceptance" test.[48] In reviewing FRE 702, the Court listed several factors a trial judge should consider in evaluating a proffer of expert scientific testimony. Those nonexclusive factors include:

1. Whether the theory or technique in question can be tested
2. Whether it has been subjected to peer review and publication
3. Its known or potential error rate and existence and maintenance of standards controlling its operation
4. Whether it has attracted widespread acceptance within a relevant scientific community

The Court noted that the inquiry is a flexible one requiring focus on principles and methodology and not on the conclusions they generate.[49] In focusing in on the "helpfulness" standard of FRE 702 (the evidence must assist the trier of fact to understand the evidence or to determine a fact in issue), the Court's use of the following example is instructive:

> The study of the phases of the moon, for example, may provide valid scientific "knowledge" about whether a certain night was dark, and if darkness is a fact in issue, the knowledge will assist the trier of fact. However, (absent creditable grounds supporting such a link), evidence that the moon was full on a certain night will not assist the trier of fact in determining whether an individual was unusually likely to have behaved irrationally on that night.[50]

The Court found nothing in the text of FRE 702 which "establishes 'general acceptance' as an absolute prerequisite to admissibility."[51] The Court continued by proclaiming that since the Rules have liberal application, the rigid "general acceptance" approach of Frye is at odds with this new approach.

Problems Applying DNA Test Results

Irrespective of the analytical approach — general acceptance or relevancy — courts, legal commentators, and the treatise writers generally agree DNA profiling, as a novel scientific procedure, has received broad support and has been admitted into evidence.[52]

Professor Imwinkelried, in a comment,[53] provides an in-depth discussion into the debate surrounding admissibility of DNA evidence. He concludes that courts have been receptive to the technology and most have found DNA typing a trustworthy technique. If there are shortcomings in which technicians conduct DNA tests, such shortcomings do not affect the *admissibility* of the test results, only the *weight* a judge or jury should accord it. Hence, a judge or jury might give little or no weight at all to the expert's testimony.

The success of the application of DNA profiling in the identification of defendants, by its very nature, depends largely on a case-by-case analysis. This approach is in keeping with Judge Cox's classification that some novel scientific evidence can neither be accepted nor rejected outright.[54]

However, the most frequent challenges that opponents to DNA profiling raise are (1) adequacy of genetic interpretations; (2) quality assurance of testing procedures; and (3) the inference of unfairness to defendants.

Adequacy of Genetic Interpretations

After a proponent has successfully proffered evidence establishing the DNA technique and that sound laboratory procedures were followed, there must be a scientifically reliable method of determining the probabilities or frequency of a matching profile. The purpose of frequency estimates is to give meaning to the match by showing the likelihood that an unrelated person in the reference population would be a chance match.[55] As the NRC noted, it is meaningless "[t]o say that two patterns match, without providing any scientifically valid estimate (or, at least, an upper bound) of the frequency with which such matches might occur by chance."[56]

To develop their frequency estimates, forensic laboratories establish databases of analyzed blood specimens (usually several hundred) of different ethnic groups from different parts of the U.S. By using its RFLP[57] radioactive probes on the samples, the laboratory creates band patterns or images on the autoradiograph. Each band represents one particular match allele. The bands are then grouped by the size of DNA fragments and then placed into "bins" for purposes of comparing the percentage of the public that has that band.

> The percentage of bands falling into a particular bin is established as the percentage of the population possessing that particular allele. The percentages for each allele, reflected in each "probe" [citation omitted] in the "series" [citation omitted] performed for a particular DNA analysis, are multiplied together. That result is then multiplied by 2, reflecting the composition of an individual's DNA from the combination of each parent's DNA. The result of this final multiplication is the statistical probability of that particular DNA being repeated in the general population.[58]

The NRC emphasizes that when calculating population frequency estimates, the scientifically accepted Hardy-Weinberg equilibrium[59] and linkage disequilibrium[60] principles must be applied and that no significant deviations should exist. Proper application of these principles will also reduce criticism about the population database being too small to provide an accurate statistic probability or population substructure.

Recent state court cases[61] are instructive of the importance of statistical probability. *State v. Bible*[62] opined that although DNA sample matching met the Frye test, there was no general acceptance in the relevant scientific community of the procedures used to calculate statistical probability of a random match. The court excluded expert opinion that the chances were "one in fourteen billion or, more conservatively, one in sixty millions that the blood on [the] defendant's shirt was not the victim's." Similarly, in *Illinois v. Watson*,[63] the court stated that the FBI's method for estimating the probability that the "match" between the evidence seized at the crime scene and defendant's DNA could occur at random is not "generally accepted" as reliable among populations geneticists. Hence, the FBI statistics and the expert's testimony were excluded.

In *People v. Barney*,[64] the California court excluded the DNA profile product rule method of determining statistical probability of a match because the methodology was found not generally accepted in the scientific community.

Quality Assurance of Testing Procedures

In years past, most of the problems DNA forensic laboratories experienced in quality assurance/quality control centered around lack of controls, inadequate population statistical data, or a failure to share or reveal those procedures. The decisions in *Castro*[65] and *Schwartz*[66] which excluded the proffered evidence reflect those earlier deficiencies.

The FBI, due to its proactive approach, is the recognized leader in the development of "guidelines" for DNA forensic laboratories. In 1989, it assembled the Technical Working Group on DNA Analysis Methods (TWGDAM) to discuss methods, protocols, and results for DNA RFLP analysis.[67] The guideline this working group developed is the "gold standard".

Moreover, other organizations such as the National Committee on Forensic DNA Typing (NCFDT) and the National Institute of Standards and Technology (NIST) are working to develop standards and controls.

While forensic laboratories have made great strides in shoring up their procedures, each time a proponent of DNA profiling seeks its admission there must be a demonstration of strict adherence to all laboratory procedures.

Inference of Unfairness to Defendants

Aside from the previously mentioned discussions concerning the theories of admissibility of DNA profiling technology, arguably, calculating the population profile frequency and expressing it in terms of probability (1 in 135,000,000)[68] carries with it grave dangers of undue prejudice and misleading a jury. While it cannot be gainsaid that the seminal purpose for using scientific evidence is to assist a judge or jury in resolving a particular fact, many courts have recognized the danger of undue prejudice to a defendant's due process rights when controversial probability statistics are used. This conclusion in no way lessens the powerful probative value assigned to the argument that once a "match" has occurred, statistical rules allow the use of such probability estimations. However, some courts have opted to exclude such expert DNA testimony relying on "due process" and "fairness" to support their reasoning. In *State v. Schwartz*,[69] the Court, in excluding DNA evidence, merely expressed grave reservations that juries in criminal trials would give undue deference to these statistical probabilities. Subsequent to this decision, the state legislature passed a law providing for the admission of statistical probability evidence relating to DNA test results.[70]

Establishment and Use of DNA Databanks

Introduction

Despite enormous potential benefits, particularly in the identity of criminal defendants and the elimination of unidentified soldiers in future wars, the establishment and use of DNA databanks has not been without its critics. The principal threat is to individual privacy.[71] In a 1988 speech to the California Criminalistics Institute Seminar on DNA Identification, Attorney General Van de Kamp had this to say:

> "It is one thing to have fingerprints and criminal histories easily accessible to thousands of peace officers. It is quite another to have information on-line that can mark you as a carrier of AIDS or prove that you are not genetically related to either of your parents. Which of us would like to know that we are genetically predisposed to Alzheimer's disease or other illnesses? And which of us would be willing to have such information easily available to others?"[72]

Similarly, the Office of Technology Assessment recognizes the potential for abusing information that is difficult "to access, to verify, or to correct."[73] One commentator[74] also recognizes that "the technology for information collection, storage, and retrieval has outpaced the technology for safeguarding databanks of personal information."[75] Others[76] point out that "perhaps the strongest single pressure motivating interagency information transfers is that the cost effectiveness of any data collection activity depends in part on the number of users who can share its fruits."[77]

In summary, following are some of the privacy concerns generated by DNA databanks:

1. Will insurers, health and life, have access to results to deny, increase, or limit coverage based on genetic predisposition to various diseases?
2. Who will have accessibility and why?
3. Will employers improperly use results to make hiring decisions, promotion decisions, or specific job placement decisions?
4. Will educational institutions use testing as part of the admissions process?

Law Enforcement Use

It is not surprising that state and federal law enforcement officials, showing a new resolve borne of desperation, have turned to the establishment of databanks in their war against crime. The theory is that if this powerful technology may assist in either inculpating or exculpating a particular suspect, perhaps it could be used to *find* them as well. Hence, when trace biologic evidence such as hair follicles, blood, semen, or other DNA-rendering specimens are found at a crime scene, law enforcement officials may now compare the results of their DNA typing to other profiles already stored. The use of DNA analysis from these databanks, however, will not be a panacea for the detection of criminals. One significant role of this forensic evidence will be to corroborate other evidence of criminal misconduct. Davies[78] provides an excellent review of the London Metropolitan Police Forensic Science Laboratory's DNA Index. This Index functions to (1) identify serial crimes; (2) link a suspect to a previous unsolved case; and (3) nominate a suspect for a current case. The Index records DNA profiles from personal samples, fluid stains from offenders in unsolved cases, and bloodstains from other crimes.

The use of DNA databanks, notwithstanding privacy considerations, should be no different than the Automated Fingerprint Identification System (AFIS) databank currently employed by the FBI.[79] Once the evidence from the specimen has been profiled, the "pattern of bands" or prints will be digitized for easy retrieval and comparison.

While there are similarities between AFIS and a DNA databank, including the requirement that both use trained technicians to read and interpret the data, the DNA databank would prove a more powerful quantitative statement when two samples are found to "match". Hence, while one's fingerprint might be helpful in establishing one's presence at the scene of a crime, evidence of his unique DNA would be offered to help establish that he could be the source of the evidence, and therefore, is guilty of the crime.

State and Federal Databanks

Several states[80] have enacted DNA statutes mandating that convicted felons and sex offenders provide a blood sample for DNA analysis and storage. The Virginia statute[81] is fairly representative. Generally, the blood specimens are collected upon entry into the prison system or as a condition of release on probation if no confinement is adjudged. In addition to analysis and storage, the Virginia statute allows for the release of databank information to federal, state, and local law enforcement officials in furtherance of an official investigation.[82] Unauthorized use is also prohibited.[83]

The rationale supporting these databank statutes is a state's special interest in detecting future suspects. Studies have established that felons and sex offenders have a high rate of recidivism.[84]

The FBI, in cooperation with states' crime laboratories, has established its own databank called Combined DNA Index System (CODIS). This national databank will contain DNA profiling information from the various states' crime laboratories on convicted felons and sex offenders and serve as a repository and clearing house. The databank will be especially helpful in comparing profiles in unsolved crimes in other jurisdictions and the identity of missing persons.

Military Databank

The primary means of remains identification within the military are fingerprint and dental comparisons.[85] According to Dr. Weedn, the FBI is missing a percentage of service members' fingerprint records which were rejected for a variety of technical reasons. Moreover, fingerprint identification may be of little assistance on fragmented, decomposed, or incinerated remains.[86] Even dental identifications are lacking where there are no restorations in service members' records or where the remains are so fragmented, no teeth can be found for analysis.[87]

The timely and accurate identification of service members' remains and the expeditious return of remains to next-of-kin is critically important. Hence, in 1991, and largely as a result of the Persian Gulf conflict, the Department of Defense (DOD) created the Armed Forces DNA Identification Laboratory and authorized the use of DNA analysis to aid in the identification of remains.[88] According to Dr. Weedn, without reference specimens of service members' DNA, the DNA laboratory's primary role at that time was one of reassociation of body fragments using antibody profiling.[89] Of course, traditional methods of identification such as fingerprint comparison, serological analysis, and medical and dental radiograph comparisons were and still are employed.

In 1993, as a result of the limitations of tissue identification, the Assistant Secretary of Defense for Health Affairs established the DOD DNA Repository of Specimen Samples at the Armed Forces Institute of Pathology, Walter Reed Army Medical Center, Washington, D.C.[90]

The DOD DNA Registry was created "to facilitate remains identification."[91] In addition to the DOD security measures, the Privacy Act of 1974[92] limits access to the data bank. Reference specimens,[93] when completed, will be collected from all active and reserve components service members. Specimens from relatives of service members who are missing in action (MIAs) may also be collected for later testing should MIA remains be repatriated.[94] Given the capabilities of this new database and identification laboratory, the DOD may never have to bury the remains of another unknown soldier. This is a stark contrast from previous wars where a significant number of service members were never identified.

References and Notes

1. *DNA Technology in Forensic Science,* by the National Research Council (U.S.), National Academy of Science, (U.S.) National Academy of Sciences, 1992, p. 140. [Hereinafter as NRC Report].

2. U.S. Congress, Office of Technology Assessment, OTA-BA-348 (Washington, D.C.: U.S. GPO, *Genetic Witness: Forensic Uses of DNA Tests,* (July, 1990).

3. *Id.* at 7–8.

4. NRC Report supra note 1 at 7–9.

5. *Id.* 7–10. *See* also, Hoke, DNA Tests in Criminal Prosecutions: Too Much Evidence or Not Enough?, *J. Legal Med.,* 11:481–482 (1990).

6. *United States v. Addison,* 498 F.2d 741, 744 (D.C. Cir. 1971). *See also,* Epstein and Klein, *The Use and Abuse of Expert Testimony in Product Liability Actions,* 17 Seton Hall L. Rev. 656 (1987).

7. For instance, ABO blood group markers and antibody profiling.

8. Amendment IV, U.S. Constitution states: "The right of the people to be secure in their persons ..., against unreasonable searches and seizures, shall not be violated, and no Warrants shall issue, but upon probable cause, ..."

9. Amendment V, U.S. Constitution states: "No person shall be ... compelled in any criminal case to be a witness against himself, ..."

10. *Schmerber v. California,* 384 U.S. 757 (1966); *State of California v. Simpson* represents an excellent modern day example of the application of DNA technology and Fourth Amendment issues. Simpson, a professional football Hall of Famer, movie star, and sportscaster, is charged with the June 1994 brutal murders of his former wife and her friend. Critical to the prosecution's case is the admissibility of crucial evidence seized from Simpson's Los Angeles home

without benefit of a search warrant and the identity of the likely perpetrator based upon traces of the blood left at the crime scene. Traces of blood found at the crime scene and blood taken from Simpson's body match based upon PCR and RFLP DNA typing techniques. Jury selection in the case is not expected to be completed until December, 1994; *Coolidge v. New Hampshire,* 403 U.S. 443 (1971). *See also,* W. LaFave, Search and Seizure (1978).

11. *Schmerber,* 384 U.S. at 770.

12. Securing a warrant usually requires the filing of sworn affidavits by law enforcement officials to a neutral and detached magistrate seeking to search a particular person or place. *Id.* at 770.

13. "Probable cause" is a "practical common-sense decision [that], given all the circumstances, ... there is a fair probability that contraband or evidence of a crime will be found." *United States v. Gates,* 462 U.S. 213, 238 (1984).

14. *Schmerber,* 384 U.S. at 770.

15. *Graves v. Beto,* 301 F. Supp. 264 (E.D. Tex. 1969), aff'd 424 F.2d 524 (5th Cir.), cert. denied, 400 U.S. 960.

16. *Schmerber,* 384 U.S. at 763–64.

17. *Schmerber,* 384 U.S. at 771–72; *See* also *Note, Search and Seizure: Compelled Surgical Intrusions,* 27 Baylor L. Rev. 305 (1975).

18. *Schneckloth v. Bustamonte,* 412 U.S. 218 (1973), *Brent v. White,* 398 F.2d 503 (5th Cir.) (1968) (Consent to blood extraction).

19. *Section 11-2304* of the District of Columbia code is fairly representative. Categories of death investigations include violent deaths; sudden deaths caused by readily recognizable disease; deaths under suspicious circumstances; deaths of persons whose bodies are to be cremated; deaths related to disease resulting from employment; and deaths related to disease which might constitute a threat to public health.

20. *U.S. v. Gibson,* 24 M.J. 246 (CMA 1987).

21. *Piquet v. United States,* 81 F.2d 75, 85 (7th Cir.) *cert. denied,* 298 U.S. 664 (1936).

22. *People v. Middleton,* 54 N.Y. 2d 42, 45, 429 N.E. 2d 100, 101, 444 N.Y.S. 2d 581, 582 (1981).

23. *U.S. v. Gibson* at 249.

24. *Id.* at 249.

25. *Id.* at 249.

26. Ark. Stat. Ann. §75-1031.1 is an example where blood tests are used to determine paternity.

27. In *State v. Dean,* 103 Wis. 2d 228, 307 N.W. 2d 628 (1981), the prosecution and the defense stipulated that the results of a polygraph examination are admissible. Such a stipulation obviates the necessity to establish the validity of the basic theory of polygraphs.

28. P. Gianelli and E. Imwinkelried, *Scientific Evidence,* (1993).

29. Id. at Section 1-1.

30. *Frye v. United States*, 293 F. 1013 (D.C. Cir. 1923).

31. *See Daubert v. Merrill Dow Pharmaceuticals, Inc.* 113 S.Ct. 2786 (1993).

32. *People v. Kelly*, 17 Cal. 3d 24 (1976); Comment, *DNA Identification Tests and The Courts*, 63 Wash. L. Rev. 903 (1988); Schmitt and Crocker, DNA Typing: Novel Scientific Evidence in the Military Courts, *Air Force Law Review*, 1990, p. 231. [Hereinafter cited as Schmitt and Crocker].

33. Frye, 293 F. at 1014.

34. *United States v. Addison*, 498 F.2d 741, 743 (D.C. Cir. 1974).

35. Schmitt and Crocker, *supra* note 32 at 229.

36. *Id.* at 230 footnote 15.

37. Frye, 293 F. 1014.

38. *United States v. Gould*, 741 F. 2d 45, 49 (4th Cir. 1984).

39. *People v. Guerra*, 37 Cal. 3d 385, 690 P.2d 635, 656, (1984).

40. *People v. Wesley*, 533 N.Y.S. 2d 643 (Albany Co. Ct. 1988).

41. Maletskos and Spielman, Introduction of New Technology Methods in Court, in Law Enforcement, *Science and Technology*, 957, 958 (S. A. Yefsky, Ed., 1967).

42. *United States v. Williams*, 583 F.2d 1194, 1198 (2d Cir. 1978), cert. denied, 439 U.S. 1117. (1979).

43. Gianelli and Imwinkelried, *supra* note 28, at Section 1-5(E).

44. *Daubert*, 113 S.Ct. 2786.

45. *United States v. Downing*, 753 F. 2d 1224 (3d Cir. 1985).

46. 753 F.2d at 1237.

47. Since *Daubert* did not involve constitutional law issues, state courts may continue to follow the dictates of *Frye*.

48. *Daubert*, 113 S.Ct. 2793.

49. *Id.* at 2797.

50. *Id.* at 2796.

51. *Id.* at 2799.

52. Jonakait, DNA and the Courts: Cases and First Impressions, *Expert Evidence Reporter* (Shep./McG.-Hill) 1:121 (Jan. 1990).

53. *Imwinkelried*, The Debate in the DNA Over The Foundation For The Admission of Scientific Evidence: The Importance of Human Error As a Cause of Forensic Misanalysis, *Criminal Law Symbolism*, 69 Wash. U.L.Q. 19 (1991).

54. *Gibson*, 24 M.J. 249.

55. Neufeld and Scheck, Factors Affecting the Fallibility of DNA Profiling: Is There Less Than Meets The Eye?, *Expert Evidence Reporter* (Shep./McG.-Hill) 1:93–94 (Dec. 1989).

56. NRC Report *supra* note 1 at Ch. 3.

57. "RFLP" or restriction fragment length polymorphism is currently the most popular DNA typing technique that uses single-locus or multi-locus probes to detect variation in a DNA sequence based on differences in the length of fragments created when DNA is cut with an enzyme. *NRC Report* supra note 1 at Ch. 8.

58. Hoke, DNA Tests In Criminal Prosecutions, *J. Legal Med.,* 11:481, 497 (1990).

59. *People v. Wesley,* 140 Misc. 2d 306, 327–28, 533 N.Y.S. 2d 643, 657 (Albany County Ct., 1988).

    The "Hardy-Weinberg" equilibrium principle states that, in a large, random, intrabreeding population, not subject to excessive selection, migration, or mutation, the gene and genotype frequencies will remain constant over time.

    The "Product rule" (2Pq) is used in conjunction with the "Hardy-Weinberg" principle under which chance frequencies are multiplied against each other to give the probability of concurrent incidence.

60. "Linkage disequilibrium" is a phenomenon in which a specific allele at one locus is nonrandomly associated with an allele at another locus. *NRC Report,* Ch. 8.

61. *State v. Bible,* 175 Ariz. 549, 859 P.2d 1152 (1993); *Illinois v. Watson,* 1994 WL 30084 (Ill. App. 1994); and *People v. Barney,* 8 Cal. App. 4th 798, 10 Cal. Rptr. 2d 731 (1992).

62. 175 Ariz. 549.

63. *Illinois v. Watson,* 1994 WL 30084.

64. *People v. Barney,* 8 Cal. App. 4th 798.

65. *People v. Castro,* 144 Misc. 2d 956, 545 N.Y.S. 2d 985 (Sup. Ct., Bronx County, 1989).

66. *People v. Wallace,* 14 Cal. App. 4th 651 (1993); *State v. Schwartz,* 447 N.W. 2d 422 (Minn. 1989).

67. *NRC Reports supra* note 1 at Ch. 14. The text of the TWGDAM guidelines may be found at Appendix B of Schmitt and Crocker's *supra* note 32.

68. *Spencer v. Commonwealth,* 238 Va. 275, 384 S.E. 2d 775 (Va., 1989).

69. *Schwartz,* 447 N.W. 2d 422; *Wallace,* 14 Cal. App. 4th 651.

70. Subsequent to this legislative action, in *State v. Nielsen,* 467 N.W. 2d 615 (Minn. 1991) the Minnesota Supreme Court affirmed a conviction by ruling that the admission of DNA evidence was a harmless error.

71. De Gorgey, The Advent of DNA Databanks: Implications for Information Privacy, *Am. J. Law Med.,* XVI, No. 3, 381, 396 (1990).

72. Transcript on file with the *American Journal of Law and Medicine.*

73. U.S. Congress, Office of Technology Assessment, Criminal Justice, New Technologies and The Constitution: Special Report 9 (May 1988).

74. Shattuck, *In the Shadow of 1984: National Identification Systems, Computer Matching, and Privacy in the United States,* 35 Hastings L.J. 991 (1984).

75. *Id.* at 991.

76. A. Miller, The Assault on Privacy (1974).

77. *Id.* at 142.

78. A. Davies, The Use of DNA Profiling and Behavioural Science in the Investigation of Sexual Offenses, *Med. Sci. Law,* (1991) Vol. 3d:95–101.

79. "AFIS" uses a computer to scan and digitalize fingerprints and then "translates the spatial geometry of the unique ridge patterns into a binary code for the computer's searching algorithm." De Gorgey, *See supra* footnote 70 at page 383.

80. According to the FBI Investigative Law Unit which, *inter alia,* tracks court decisions and DNA statutes, there are currently 31 states with mandatory requirements for DNA specimens.

81. Va. Code Ann. §19.2-310.2 (1990). *See* also note *DNA Fingerprinting: The Virginia Approach,* 35 Wm & Mary L. Rev. 767 (1994).

82. Va. Code Ann. §19.2-310.5 (1990).

83. Va. Code Ann. §19.2-310.6 (1990).

84. *Violent Crime in Virginia,* Virginia Department of Criminal Justice Services, May 1989; Recidivism of Prisoners Released in 1983, Special Report, Bureau of Justice Statistics, April 1989.

85. Conversations in November 1994, with Dr. Weedn, Armed Forces Chief Deputy Medical Examiner and the Chief, Armed Forces DNA Identification Laboratory, (AFDIL), Department of Defense and DNA Registry, Armed Forces Institute of Pathology, Washington, D.C. [Hereinafter cited as Weedn].

86. *Id.*

87. *Id.*

88. Deputy Secretary of Defense Memorandum #47803, dated 16 December 1991, The Pentagon, Washington, D.C., 20301-1200.

89. Antibody profiling, a non-DNA technique, involved the identification of individual proteins called antibodies that circulate in the blood. Each person should have a unique set of antibodies that can/could be tested and individualized.

90. Memorandum from The Assistant Secretary of Defense for Health Affairs, dated 5 Jan. 1993, Subject: Establishment of a Repository of Specimen Samples to Aid in Remains Identification Using Genetic Deoxyribonucleic Acid (DNA) Analysis.

91. *Id.*

92. 5 U.S.C. §552a governs releasibility of repository information. The Act prohibits federal agencies from revealing personal information collected for one purpose and then used for another without the requisite consent of the individual.

93. Reference specimens consist of blood droplets on special paper, a thumb print, a buccal swab, and personal information such as name, signature, social security number, and bar code labels for specimen identification. Since the first collections started in 1993, over 800,000 specimens have been collected and stored. DNA typing is only done for quality assurance purposes. Otherwise, typing will be dictated by circumstances. Conversations with Dr. Weedn.

94. Weedn *supra* note 85.

Forensic Anthropology

4

WILLIAM R. MAPLES

Introduction

Forensic odontologists often work with specialists in other fields of forensic science. Besides the forensic pathologist, the forensic anthropologist is perhaps the next most common collaborating colleague.

The application of physical or biological anthropology in the legal identification process was described in lectures at Harvard before the end of the last century (Stewart, 1979) and was used in the courtroom by a Harvard Ph.D., George Dorsey, in Chicago homicide trials in 1897 and 1898 (Stewart, 1976). While this forensic application of physical anthropology dates to the time of the beginnings of physical anthropology in this country, forensic anthropology was not widely practiced on a regular basis until after World War II. The last 20 years have seen rapid growth of the field, both in cases and practitioners, but even today, full-time forensic anthropologists are rare. Most forensic anthropologists are employed as faculty in universities or museums. Approximately 45 are diplomates of the American Board of Forensic Anthropology. The average individual forensic work load is probably a dozen or less cases per year.

While forensic odontologists and anthropologists are both primarily interested in the hard tissues of the body, the forensic anthropologist usually devotes more attention to the osseous material rather than dental evidence. That is not to say that physical anthropologists do not study the evolution and variation of human dentition, nor does it imply that the dentist is unschooled in the anatomy of the skull.

Role of the Forensic Anthropologist

Forensic anthropologists may be asked for very specific information such as an estimation of age at death, or they may be asked to give all information that can be determined from the skeletal remains. The anthropologist can be useful in cases when the remains of the deceased cannot be fully evaluated during a normal post-mortem examination by the pathologist. These remains may include those where the soft tissues have partially or completely decomposed, or where the remains have been burned or mutilated by intent or accident. In cases where the body is intact, the specialist in human osteology may be helpful in determining weapon characteristics from damage to the skeletal system. Lastly, the anthropologist may be able to establish identification by a number of means, including the comparison of antemortem and postmortem radiographs.

The anthropologist must remove remaining soft tissue from the skeletal evidence before any analysis can be done. In a mass disaster this is not always possible because of the time factor, and in those instances the techniques must be modified or limited to those that can be used with remaining soft tissue. Usually, more radiography is necessary when soft tissue cannot be removed.

Removal of soft tissue, sometimes after initial radiography of the remains, is usually accomplished by boiling, preferably under an odor hood. Forensic anthropology laboratories that are properly equipped have odor hoods over stainless steel sinks, an X-ray machine, radiograph dry processing and duplicating equipment, osteometric instruments, video superimposition equipment, and ample macrophotographic capabilities. Adequate space for layout and storage of skeletal remains must be available. Perhaps 40 years ago, anthropologists were brought only dry skeletal remains, but today more remains come to the anthropologist with soft tissue and other malodorous materials. Today, it is increasingly difficult for the anthropologist to handle the cases in a faculty office or small laboratory in an academic building shared by faculty members who fail to share the forensic anthropologist's interest in the recently dead.

The boiling of remains also reduces the biohazard exposure for the staff of the anthropology laboratory, as well as those handling the remains afterwards, such as the forensic dentist, prosecutors, and other attorneys.

Techniques

The various techniques used by the forensic anthropologist are discussed in detail in a number of books (Stewart, 1979; Rathbun and Buikstra, 1984; Krogman and Iscan, 1986; Reichs, 1986). This chapter will be confined to techniques that are particularly useful to the forensic dentist or those that may produce conflicting conclusions between the dentist and the anthropologist. Remember, no single thing is always the best indicator of age, sex, or race. The experienced forensic scientist considers a range of the available features and techniques before reaching a conclusion. Multiple indicators are the key — not single indicators or techniques. Some techniques are poor in most cases, some good in many cases, and some are good in most cases, but none are reliable in every case. Remember too, that the first step must be to confirm that the remains are human and how many individuals are present. Incorrect conclusions at this point quickly lead to embarrassment or worse.

Dental aging techniques based on formation of the crown, eruption, and root tip completion are commonly used by dentists, often with very satisfactory results, but occasionally age estimates derived from dental information may be in conflict with skeletal age determinations. Anthropologists have learned in case after case that multiple aging techniques usually give somewhat different ages for any particular set of remains. It is now common practice to derive age estimates using as many techniques as possible before using one's experience and judgment to arrive at the best estimate, which is usually stated in overlapping age estimates. So it is with dental aging. Very often, especially in remains of teenaged victims, the anthropological age estimate and the dental age estimate may not be in agreement, and occasionally there may be extreme differences. The most often-used dental age data comes from Schour and Massler (1940). However, this study was based on a sample that was very limited in number, race, and socioeconomic background (white upper-middle class). It is usually best to consider other aging information before a final age estimate is determined.

Several years ago, a skeleton was found in Pennsylvania that was obviously immature both skeletally and dentally. Dentists estimated the age at death to be 12 or 13 years, not over 14. An anthropologist, who only did the occasional forensic examination, said that the skeleton was in her middle or late teens. A teenager who had disappeared nine years earlier was suggested as a possible identification, but the forensic dentists maintained that the missing teenager was several years too old. The only ante-mortem radiographs available were dental radiographs made before the missing girl entered her teen years, hence before the extensive dental changes of very active years of growth.

After almost a year of disagreement, the remains were taken to an experienced forensic anthropologist for further analysis. The dentist who escorted the remains was careful to withhold all details of the missing girl. The anthropologist first radiographed the jaws and suggested the dental age at approximately 14 years. Then a detailed analysis was made of the state of epiphyseal union exhibited throughout the skeleton. Finally, the anthropologist said the deceased had reached her 16th birthday, but died before her 18th. Armed with that conclusion, the anthropologist asked the dentist for the age of the missing girl, which turned out to be 16 years and 11 months. Video superimposition of dental details in antemortem and postmortem dental radiographs and of facial details in a photograph of the girl superimposed on the skull were used to confirm this long-overdue identification. All available age indicators should always be considered, particularly in children.

When very poor oral health is present, such as in transient people, the dental age may appear to be greater than normal. Indeed, transients and migrant workers often show increased periarticular lipping in the joints and osteophytic lipping in the vertebrae. Increased caution is always indicated when very poor oral health is present.

Two of the best-known and most experienced forensic anthropologists of their time, Wilton Krogman and T. Dale Stewart (Krogman, 1962; Stewart, 1951) could determine the sex of skeletal remains correctly in about 80% of the cases using the skull only, but in about 90% correctly when the pelvis was used. Forensic dentists usually confine their analyses to the skulls, or even the jaws. The forensic anthropologist can usually bring greater precision to gender determination by using the entire skeletal remains.

The male skull is larger than the female skull, has better-marked muscle attachment areas (nuchal and temporal lines), larger and *blunter* mastoid processes, more superciliary development, much blunter superior orbital margins, heavier zygomatic arches, larger jaws, and more sloping foreheads. Males may show everted or neutral gonial angles, while females usually show inverted or neutral gonial angles. The anterior mandible (chin) may be squared or rounded in males, but is usually pointed or rounded in females.

Determination of sex in prepubescent remains is very difficult. Puberty begins the development of many secondary sexual characteristics. Skeletally, these are particularly distinctive in the male. For that reason, immature skeletal remains that show male features of the cranial or postcranial skeleton are probably male. One usually does not count the female and male features in the immature skeleton to find which predominate. If such a skeleton shows any male features, it is probably male.

There is less gender variation in the age of dental development than there is in skeletal development. Hunt and Gleiser (1955) proposed that a dental age estimate should first be determined in immature remains, and then compared with male and female age estimates from techniques such as Greulich and Pyle (1950) if the hand and wrist are intact, or the Pyle and Hoerr (1955) age estimates for the knee. The females should show better agreement of dental and skeletal ages using female standards, but very different ages using male standards. The reverse is true for males, since males lag behind females in skeletal maturation. This seems to be a very useful technique for the determination of gender of immature remains.

There are many indicators of gender in the postcranial or infracranial skeleton. Male joints are larger than those of females, so every long bone end is useful. For example, a maximum diameter of the head of the femur that is 46 mm or more suggests that the deceased was male, while 43 mm or less suggests female (44 mm and 45 mm are measurements shared by the tails of male and female distributions). Muscle attachment areas, such as the linea aspera on the femur, the supinator crest on the ulna, and the deltoid tuberosity on the humerus are examples of some useful features.

There are numerous discriminate function analyses available to determine sex, as well as race, from osteometric results using standardized measurements. These are not only useful for initial conclusions, but may also be used for added confirmation or for objective tests to demonstrate to others, such as medical examiners and coroners, the basis for the conclusions. A comprehensive collection of these formulas can be found in Bennett (1992).

Race is a population concept. Races are "populations which differ in the frequency of some genes" (Dobzhansky, 1950). Since individuals within that population vary considerably in their genes, it is very difficult to assign any individual to a particular race with any reliability. The racial identity that we carry with us throughout our lives is a sociological label, not a biological reality. When we are asked to identify the race of a skeleton, the question is really, "What racial label did society give him"? The forensic anthropologist, the forensic odontologist, or the forensic pathologist may be able to give an answer with reasonable certainty, based on skeletal and dental characteristics, but as racial admixture is increasingly common in the last few decades, and as immigrants flow into this country from distant areas of the world in large numbers, racial identification becomes more difficult instead of more reliable. Any attempts to be too specific on race are likely to obfuscate rather than elucidate. In most cases it is best to simply say, "black, white, mongoloid, or perhaps an admixture of two of the major categories." Racial classification is difficult enough without the constant danger of socially unacceptable terminology in this age of heightened sensitivities. The more one attempts to use socially correct terms, the deeper the mire. For instance, if the skeleton appears to be from a black person, the currently accepted term "African-American" may seem reasonable. What we cannot usually diagnose from skeletal remains is nationality. The deceased may have been an African-American, but could also have been a Nigerian, Kenyan, or even Haitian. Keep it as simple and free of additional social baggage as possible.

While the postcranial skeleton shows racial variation, the head — that anatomical structure of shared interest of the forensic anthropologist and the forensic odontologist — gives the most useful characteristics for racial diagnosis.

Obviously, there is considerable racial information in the teeth, but individual teeth are seldom diagnostic. Shovel-shaped maxillary incisors (trace, semi, or full), for example, are considered a Mongoloid trait and are found in 100% of Aleuts studied (Cadien, 1972), but they may be found in individuals from any racial group in the world. The fact that a forensic skeleton

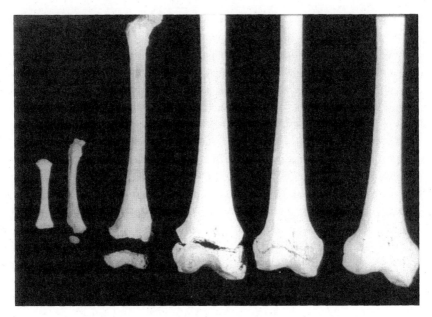

Figure 4.1 An example of skeletal aging, the development and eventual union of the distal epiphysis of the femur (from left to right) from before birth, neonatal, approximately 4 years, subteen, mid-teen years, and adult.

has shovel-shaped incisors may suggest the possibility of Asian origins, but does not exclude Eastern Europeans, Africans, or even Polynesians. Similarly, large mesiodistal incisor diameters suggest African or Oceanian ancestry, but the range of variation in all races precludes any absolute conclusion.

The shape of the upper dental row (v-shaped in whites, u-shaped in blacks, and horseshoe-shaped in mongoloids), the width and shape of the nasal aperture, the development of the nasal spine and the shape of the lower margin of the nasal aperture, orbital and supraorbital shapes, the relative length and height of the braincase, and the shape of the occipital bone are some of the cranial features that are useful in the identification of racial affinity. Alveolar prognathism, defined by anthropologists as the anterior projection of the jaws, is also a good trait for race determination.

Height can be estimated after age, gender, and race of the remains are determined. For the adult (other formulas must be used for immature remains), the Trotter and Gleser (1952) formulas are probably the best. Separate formulas are available for each of the six major long bones. In the case of the humerus, radius, ulna, femur, and fibula, the measurement used is the *maximum* length. The maximum length, not the bicondylar length, of the femur is used. The tibia is measured from the most superior point on the lateral condyle to the most inferior point on the medial malleolus, *parallel to the shaft of the bone*. It must not be measured in a straight line between

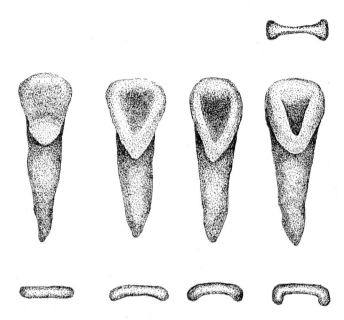

Figure 4.2 From left to right (upper view is lingual aspect, lower view is incisal aspect), normal "unshoveled" incisor, slightly shoveled, moderate shoveling, shoveled. Occasionally a very shoveled tooth will show the lingual shoveling and some labial shoveling as well. (Illustration courtesy of Gina Collins.)

the two points with the shaft slanted on the measuring board. The intercondylar eminence (lateral and medial intercondylar tubercles) is not included in the measurement. When left and right bones are both present, the two sides are averaged.

Always use the formula which has the lowest standard error of the estimate for the best estimate of stature. In all formula sets (white females, black males, etc.) except for Mexican males, the formula for the combined lengths of the tibia and femur gives the statistically most successful results. The fact that the legs, not the arms, are better correlated with stature is not surprising. Never average results from several formulas. That merely combines the best results and the worst results to give a mediocre estimate.

After the age, sex, race, and height are determined, possible identifications are usually proposed by investigators assigned to the case. This critical stage in the identification process is fraught with difficulties. Jewelry, credit cards, clothing, automobile ownership, old fractures, or skeletal disorders are not individually adequate to make civilian identifications (manifested crew on a military aircraft can under certain circumstances be treated differently). The identification must be proven biologically: by fingerprints, a good dental record showing multiple restorations or extractions, antemortem/postmortem radiograph comparisons, complex medical histories involving the skeleton or teeth, or sometimes, by superimposition. If an identification is accepted without a firm biological basis, information from the remains may not be admissible if the remains are no longer available for defense experts, e.g., after cremation.

The investigators must secure all useful records on the deceased. Obviously, dental records and radiographs must be sought, but medical radiographs, medical records, DNA reference samples from appropriate relatives, and photographs (especially "mug shots") must be secured. If any ridge detail remains in the soft tissue, fingerprints may still be useful. Fingerprint records or latent fingerprints from rooms or personal belongings of missing persons must be obtained. If hair is still present in the remains, reference samples may be obtained from combs, hairbrushes, or handbags of the missing person (hair alone cannot be used to confirm an identification). While most of the techniques are well known, further discussion of medical records, antemortem/postmortem radiograph comparisons, DNA, and superimposition may be useful.

Medical records alone are usually not adequate for identification. A pattern of rib, clavicular, and even mandibular fractures, for instance, are frequently seen in many accident victims. Occasionally, however, multiple injuries received in different accidents and/or surgical intervention leaving sutures or other evidence that may be conclusive, as those seen in one case: nasal fractures and a fracture of the left zygomatic arch with depression of the arch (fight), a fracture of the right ulna (fell down), a fibular fracture with a suture securing soft tissue to the proximal end of the tibia (struck by car), and a fracture of the styloid process of the left ulna with radiographic evidence of metal debris (gunshot wound) were deemed sufficient to make a conclusive identification even in the absence of antemortem radiographs. The same injuries were noted in the skeletal remains as those in the medical records which also listed the circumstances of the injuries.

Isolated healed fractures, interpretations of postural and other skeletal problems (scoliosis, "bad back", joint conditions, etc.) are often unreliable.

Antemortem radiographs may be compared with postmortem radiographs. Most frequently, these are dental radiographs that show restorations or distinctive dental anatomy, but virtually any antemortem radiographs may be used. The earliest radiographic comparison mentioned in the literature compared the remains of a man killed in 1925 in Kashmir with radiographs made in 1918 (Law, 1927). With the improvement of quality of radiographs, morphology of spinous and transverse processes, pedicle and laminar outlines, vertebral osteophytes (seen in relatively recent radiographs), healed fractures, clavicular shapes, shapes of anomalous structures (cervical and lumbar ribs, ununited vertebral arches, mandibular or palatine tori, extravertebral articulations [especially cervical], etc.), shapes of the twelfth ribs, cranial sutures, and trabecular details are all useful. The best trabecular details are found in dental radiographs, in hand or foot radiographs, and in clavicular or long bone radiographs. Trabecular details in ribs (complicated by lung image) and complex trabeculae in calcanea and long bones are not very satisfactory. In the latter, extremely slight differences in radiographic angle result in very different images.

Video superimposition may be used with great effect in comparison of radiographic details such as morphological variations and trabeculations.

Nuclear (genomic) DNA is difficult to obtain from decomposed remains, even using PCR (polymerase chain reaction), but mitochondrial DNA (mtDNA) persists for decades or longer. Although both male and female gametes have mtDNA, it is located in the tails of sperms which break off and are lost when the ovum is fertilized. As a result, only female mtDNA is passed on generation after generation without change from mothers to their offspring, both males and females. Teeth are an excellent source of mtDNA since it is protected in the pulp chambers, but bone cortex may also be used. Reference samples may be used for maternal relatives (the mother and her siblings, maternal grandmothers and their siblings, offspring, maternal cousins, etc.). The identification probability is not as high for mtDNA as it is using nuclear DNA, but mtDNA is important because of its durability and the relative abundance of reference donors.

Austin-Smith and Maples (1994) demonstrates that video superimposition is adequate for identification when multiple photographs from different angles (e.g., full face and profile) are available. Reliable identifications are possible using video superimposition from single photographs which show distinctive details such as teeth exposed by broad smiles (seldom seen in "mug shots").

Video superimpositions are best prepared by scientists experienced in using the video equipment in their laboratory, not by video production companies. Images digitalized by computers may be unduly manipulated by the incautious or unscrupulous. Fast video wipes and incomplete fades will also produce video images that may suggest a good identification when it is not.

Manipulating and holding the skull in the correct position relative to the skull image has been achieved by complex and expensive equipment (Iscan and Helmer, 1993), but the easiest and least expensive technique is to employ vertical camera stands to use vertical lab space rather than the more precious horizontal space, and place the occipital portion of the cranium with the mandible attached by using dental utility wax in a cork flask with the camera directed downwards toward the face.

At some point during the analysis of the remains, trauma analysis is necessary. While skeletal damage may be obvious, sometimes skeletal evidence of perimortem injury is very subtle, such as fractures of the alveolar margins, chipped teeth, longitudinal enamel fractures, or damage to the very thin cortex of articular bone, such as the mandibular condyles. The remains, where skin is no longer intact, should be radiographed prior to maceration to locate metal fragments from knife tips or debris from gunshot wounds. Damaged bone should be radiographed once again after maceration to demonstrate any metal debris or lead streaks from gunshot wounds. Usually, more lead remains on the bones before maceration as some lead evidence is usually lost during cleaning efforts. Lead debris may still be found on bones that have remained exposed to the surface environment for more than a decade.

If it becomes necessary to prove the metal debris located radiographically on bones is in fact lead, proton-induced X-ray emission (PIXE) analysis may be used. Physics and nuclear science departments at universities with an accelerator can do this nondestructive analysis.

Fragmented skulls, and sometimes other bones, must be reconstructed to visualize perforations from gunshot wounds. Fractures must be recorded by photographs and diagrams. Patterns of radiating fractures can demonstrate the type of weapon used, the site or sites of impact, the number of wounds, or the sequence of wounds. Bevelling on gunshot wounds will frequently show the direction of the projectile, although keyhole fractures may present potentially confusing bevelling.

The literature abounds with articles stating that firearm caliber cannot be accurately determined from the wounds. While this is true in the case of soft tissue injuries, perforations through bone, especially in the absence of displacement of fragments by fracturing, will usually show a minimum diameter not greatly exceeding the caliber (e.g., about 0.27 or 0.28 in. in the case of .25-caliber wounds, etc.). The diameter, plus the presence or absence of metal debris (abundant in .22-caliber wounds, present in larger unjacketed projectiles fired from revolvers, and usually absent in jacketed projectiles fired from semiautomatic pistols) will allow some conclusions concerning the type of weapon.

Skulls fractured in blunt trauma may show patterns characteristic of the weapon (Maples, 1986). Hammers, pry bars, jack handles, handgun butts and muzzles, beverage bottles, axe handles, and many other common tools and weapons often leave very distinctive patterns. A few guidelines are useful to remember.

The damage or perforation is the result of the maximum cross section of the weapon that has passed through the surface of the bone. For example, a slot screwdriver passing through a sternum at a perpendicular angle will first create a rectangular perforation the size and shape of the tip of the blade. Fragments may be hinged inward along the margins. As the tool continues inward, the long sides widen as these two flat, broad tool surfaces move out toward the diameter of the shaft. The two short sides move more slowly apart, and not at all if the screwdriver is merely a sharpened shaft, until the triangular shoulders of the blade pass through. At that point, the breadth of the perforation remains the same, but the shaft will produce semicircular or triangular (round shaft vs. square shaft) defects along the two long sides. At each point of penetration, the cross sections that break bone from the margins will leave their marks. Measurements may be obtained, but some caution is indicated as hinged bone may close somewhat. In this example, when the tool penetrates the posterior wall of the sternum the tool measurements from the anterior and posterior walls of the sternum should be approximately the same as those found on two points of the tool separated by the distance between the entrance and exit from the sternum.

Incised wounds (cuts and stabs) are commonly found on bones. Great care should be used to avoid adding nicks to the bone during any stage of the autopsy, preparation, or analysis. Scalpels should not be used to open the body near any skin perforated by decomposition or wounds. During macerations, no metal instruments should be used that could scrape, nick, or cut the bones.

Bones should be removed from fresh victims if it is necessary to determine weapon characteristics from the bones. Radiograph the plastron or other tissue containing portions of multiple ribs. The radiographs can be used to identify (and number) each costal cartilage and rib. The same radiographs can be used to determine approximate distances between damaged structures (e.g., two adjacent ribs damaged by the back of the blade and the cutting edge).

In examining bones for incised marks, every bone surface should be examined with magnification (×2 to ×3 is ideal). The anterior surfaces of the cervical vertebrae, inferior margins of the mandible, ribs, sternum, clavicles, and posterior portions of the thoracic and lumbar vertebrae should receive particularly careful attention. Run your fingers along the superior and inferior margins of ribs (nicks will catch on the skin). After incised marks are located, consider the anatomical relationships of that bone to surrounding tissue. A fine cut across the anterior surface of the body of a cervical vertebra may not appear significant, but considering the soft tissue structures that must be penetrated or severed for the blade to reach the bone surfaces, the mark takes on added significance.

When bones are found disarticulated, it is important to place damaged bones back into articulated positions with adjacent bone when trauma is considered. If a stab wound severed a transverse process of a thoracic vertebra, one would expect damage to the rib at that location if the injury occurred around the time of death with the bones in their proper anatomical positions. (The same consideration should be given to burned bones that were found scattered to determine if the body was burned or a grass fire had damaged the disarticulated bones of a decomposed body.)

Figure 4.3 Two skeletons in place after roofing material was removed and before the two skeletons were commingled (as approximately 10,000 fragments) into a single body bag.

Dismemberment or decapitation will inevitably leave evidence on skeletal remains. The type of saw used for dismemberment is important. The grooves made from the saw teeth may travel in straight parallel lines (band or other power saw), straight but overlapping lines (hand saws), curved lines (oscillating or rotating circular blade), or the very coarse cuts of a chainsaw. Chainsaws may leave chainsaw oil on the bones and hacksaw blades may leave distinctively colored paint on the cut bone surfaces. Large bones from the meat market may be cut by a selection of saws and kept in the laboratory as a reference collection.

The number of lawsuits and other inquiries involving remains (cremains) cremated in crematoria are rapidly increasing around this country. The forensic anthropologist and dentist should work together closely in these cases. While the allegations may vary and thus affect the way each case in conducted, certain procedures are usually indicated.

Before an expert begins analysis of cremains, or releases them to other experts for the first examination, the cremains should be weighed, radiographed in thin layers on as many radiographic cassettes as necessary, and photographed on the cassettes before or after radiography.

Before beginning analysis, the expert may separate the cremains by particle size using proper analytic sieves (not the round-bottom sieves available in hardware and houseware stores). Unless one is willing to devote great time and caution to clean the sieves before use (since particles may become lodged along the margins of the mesh), new sieves should be used in each case, but receivers and lids for sieves may be reused after washing. Sieve sizes of 4, 2, and 1 mm meshes are recommended.

After separation by particle size, a magnet should be used in each of the separated samples to remove ferrous metallic particles. Magnets incased in plastic coating, such as laboratory stirring bar retrievers, are preferable since the particles can be thoroughly removed. The separated samples should be weighed and radiographs again made, using metal grids (1 in. plastic-covered grids made from metal shelving are ideal). Radio-dense particles can be located after radiography by grid location. Important metallic objects should be cross-checked on both preanalysis and laboratory radiographs.

Metal identification tags with names and/or numbers are frequently in cremains. These should be carefully documented. Occasionally, radiographs may be useful when the tags have been severely corroded during cremation.

The particles not passing through the 1 mm mesh are now systematically manually searched using some magnifier such as a magnifying ring light. At this time any identifiable material such as distinctive bone fragments, cremation slag and other debris, and dental fragments are isolated. These may then be examined with a stereomicroscope.

Bodies are cremated with various internal accruements such as prosthetic joints, surgical staples, vascular clips, surgical wire and wire catheters, as well as orthopedic pins, nails, plates, and screws. Pacemakers are supposed to be removed before cremation, but this is not always done. Other material may be found in cremains, such as nails and staples from the container in which the body was cremated, dental materials from bridges, crowns, and dentures, wires from cardboard tags, snaps from hospital wristbands, hardware from

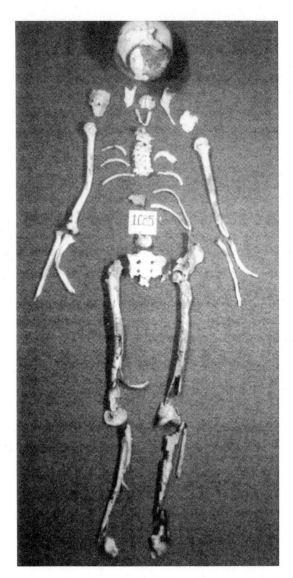

Figure 4.4   The final reconstructed bones from the female (Jennings).

eyeglasses, and miscellaneous clothing materials (snaps, clasps, and buttons). Jewelry is seldom found, although some crematory operators say that they remove jewelry before cremation and place it in the cremains when they are put into the final urn.

In most cases, the medical and dental hardware within the body at death is the most important evidence to confirm or reject the name association for the cremains. Dental posts, crowns, and bridgework may be useful for record comparison, but may also be individually identified by comparison with

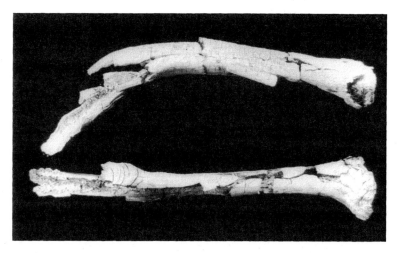

Figure 4.5 Reconstructed tibiae from the male showing extreme checking and warping seen in cremated flesh-covered bones.

antemortem radiographs. Porcelain fragments with metal pins indicate denture teeth, but when one or two are found in cremains with abundant dental roots, etc. the denture teeth may have come from incidental commingling from previous occupants of the cremation retort.

Large objects such as bridges, crowns, joint prostheses, and orthopedic plates are removed before processing (grinding) the cremains, but orthopedic screws from the plates may be present in cremains. Surgical wire, staples, and vascular clips do find their way into the urns, and are very useful. Besides determining whether these materials are ferrous or not by using a magnet, it may be necessary to have chemical microprobes used to determine the actual metals present in the objects. Unusual metals such as tantalum or titanium may be found in medical records as well as the cremains.

Everything of importance must be fully documented metrically and by weight, radiographs, and photographs. These materials cannot be retained or seldom reexamined, so all documentation must be thoughtfully done.

An expert working in a lawsuit where millions of dollars may be at issue, must use every bit of evidence and analysis that is available. The expert should examine medical records, radiographs, and other documents about the deceased before the examination of cremains. This is not the time to say that such information might "bias" the examination. This is not the time for ego games and working blind. Informed knowledge of what may be present can be extremely useful.

At the conclusion of the examination, the material may remain separated by particle size in zippered plastic bags and any important specimens (e.g., dental posts, etc.) may be placed into glass or plastic vials. Alternatively, all material and specimens may be returned to the original container. The choice of combining the material or leaving it separated is made after consideration of whether or not the expert wants to save the next expert time. Of course, sometimes an expert may think that a particularly devious colleague has separated meaningless material for misdirection. In our opinion, it is probably best to recombine after clearing the decision with the attorney who employed you.

The skeletal evidence is rich in information. The forensic anthropologist, working as part of a team of forensic pathologists, odontologists, and other forensic scientists, can greatly add to the results of the analysis. Indeed, the results of the scientists working as a team and discussing the case at all stages of the investigation greatly exceed what each expert can do individually.

References

1. Stewart, T.D. Essentials of Forensic Anthropology. Charles C Thomas, Springfield, IL, 1979.

2. Stewart, T.D. Evidence of handedness in the bony shoulder joint. *American Academy Forensic Science Book of Abstracts* (Annual Meeting, Washington, D.C.), p. 68, Feb. 1976.

3. Rathbun, T.A., Buikstra, J.E. *Human Identification: Case Studies in Forensic Anthropology.* Charles C Thomas, Springfield, IL, 1984.

4. Krogman, W.M., Iscan, M.Y. *The Human Skeleton in Forensic Medicine,* second edition, Charles C Thomas, Springfield, IL, 1986.

5. Reichs, K.J. Forensic Osteology: *Advances in the Identification of Human Remains.* Charles C Thomas, Springfield, IL, 1986.

6. Schour, I., Massler, M. [Chart entitled "Development of the Human Dentition"] 2nd ed. Chicago, American Dental Association, 1944.

7. Krogman, W.M. *The Human Skeleton in Forensic Medicine.* Charles C Thomas, Springfield, IL, 1962.

8. Stewart, T.D. What the bones tell. *FBI Law Enforcement Bulletin,* 20(2):2-5, 19, 1951.

9. Hunt, E.E., Jr., Gleiser, I. The Estimation of age and sex of preadolescent children from bones and teeth. *American Journal of Physical Anthropology,* 13:479-487, 1955.

10. Greulich, W.W., Pyle, S.I. *Radiographic Atlas of Skeletal Development of the Hand and Wrist.* Stanford University Press, Stanford, CA, 1959.

11. Pyle, S.I., Hoerr, N.L. *Radiographic Atlas of Skeletal Development of the Knee.* Charles C Thomas, Springfield, IL, 1955.

12. Bennett, K.A. *A Field Guide for Human Skeletal Identification,* second edition, Charles C Thomas, Springfield, IL, 1993.

13. Dobzhansky, T. Evolution in the tropics, *American Scientists* 38:209-221, 1950.

14. Trotter, M., Gleser, G.C. Estimation of stature from long bones of American whites and Negroes. *American Journal of Physical Anthropology,* 10:463-514, 1952.

15. Culbert, W.L., Law, F.M. Identification by comparison with roentgenograms of nasal accessory sinuses and mastoid process. *Journal of the American Medical Association* 88:1634-1636, 1927.

16. Austin-Smith, D., Maples, W.R. The Reliability of Skull/Photograph Superimposition in Individual Identification. *Journal of Forensic Sciences* 39(2):446-456, 1994.

17. Iscan, M.Y. Helmer, R.P. *Forensic Analysis of the Skull.* Wiley-Liss, New York, 1993.

18. Maples, W.R. Trauma Analysis by the Forensic Anthropologist. *Forensic Osteology: Advances in Forensic Anthropology.* K.J. Reichs, Ed., Charles C Thomas, Springfield, IL, 218-228, 1986.

Buried Crime Scene Evidence: The Application of Forensic Geotaphonomy in Forensic Archaeology

5

MICHAEL J. HOCHREIN

Introduction

The science of taphonomy maintains its origins in the 1940 proposal of Russian paleontologist I. A. Efremov to include it as a branch of paleontology (Considine, 1989). A compendium of papers on the topic (Behrensmeyer and Hill, 1980) formally announced establishment of the field. A generally accepted definition of taphonomy is that of the study of the processes by which animal and plant remains become fossilized. The *McGraw-Hill Encyclopedia of Science and Technology* (1992) expands upon the common association between taphonomy and paleosciences: "Taphonomy is a recent addition to paleobiology with most work having occurred since 1960. Taphonomic studies have influenced field recovery techniques by showing the importance of the body-part composition of fossil assemblages as indicative of specific preservational processes. Taphonomy has introduced new quantitative techniques into the analysis of fossil assemblages, including mathematical models of disarticulation and scattering of fossil assemblages with different preservational probabilities ... The central aim of taphonomic studies is to elucidate how biological information has been altered from the original living systems." Shipman (1981) defines taphonomy as, "The study of the transition of skeletal elements from parts of living animals to fossilized fragments; also, the processes or events affecting bone destruction or preservation during this transition."

Early twentieth century work, such as that of geologist and paleontologist Johannes Weigelt, is recognized for its contributions as early taphonomic research. Weigelt referred to processes leading to the embedding and preservation of organic remains as "biostratinomy" (Weigelt 1989). Biostratinomy is close in principle to current applications of taphonomy in forensic analyses.

0-8493-8103-7/97/$0.00+$.50
© 1997 by CRC Press LLC

In their forward to Weigelt's *Recent Vertebrate Carcasses and Their Paleobiological Implications,* Anna Behrensmeyer and Catherine Badgley mention that later usages of Weigelt's term, "restricted biostratinomy to transformations of organic remains from death through burial" and exclude later processes related to fossil formation (Weigelt 1989). Following Weigelt, "diagenisis" was recognized as a subdiscipline of taphonomy. Diagenisis is defined as the study of the postburial effects of the environment on remains (Lyman 1994).

In general, the application of taphonomic principles by physical anthropologists has retained the basis of the science as examining transitions from the biosphere to the lithosphere. Garland (1987) says of taphonomy:

> "… the investigation of death, decomposition and burial in modern environments is also a part of taphonomy since it allows the initial transformation phases of the taphonomic history of a bone to be studied. This period may be conveniently divided into three phases: from death to burial, from burial to excavation, and from excavation of the grave to the laboratory examination of the human skeletal remains."

Given the term's derivation from the Greek word "taphos", meaning tomb, "taphonomy" might literally be defined as the study of the tomb or grave itself. Yet, neither the paleontological or physical anthropological applications of taphonomy routinely emphasize the examination of geophysical characteristics of the grave. Instead, analyses typically concentrate on the condition of remains following their removal from the matrices in which they were interred. Lyman (1994) devotes an entire chapter to "Burial as a Taphonomic Process"; however, he defines burial as a natural process of sedimentation. Lyman adds, "What I have found truly amazing is that despite that while faunal remains typically come to us in buried form, there is very little written about the burial process itself" (Lyman 1994).

As it relates to buried body crime scenes, forensic anthropologists are normally presented with remains without the benefit of being present at their exhumation. In such situations, study of the grave feature is reduced to an ad hoc interpretation based upon the condition of the remains, recollections of the individuals who collected the remains, and soil or botanical evidence adhering to the remains. Primary evidence from the crime scene itself often cannot be examined *in situ*, or firsthand, by the forensic scientist.

In this chapter, the study of the grave or feature which contains buried evidence is referred to as "geotaphonomy". Geotaphonomy is herein defined as the study of the geophysical characteristics of, and changes in, subterranean features associated with the interment of buried evidence. Such an analysis requires the use of archaeological field techniques for the recovery and interpretation of phenomena introduced, or altered, during the construction of a grave or other burial feature.

Recognizing the Value of Geotaphonomy

Perhaps, the foremost premise every student of field archaeology learns is that the recovery of artifacts through excavation is a destructive process. Likewise, elementary crime scene training for law enforcement personnel contains repeated warnings that the collection of evidence during the processing of a crime scene inherently disrupts the original condition of that scene. Archaeology and criminalistics have evolved separately and, in the process, each discipline has stressed that their field applications constitute singular opportunities to collect information *in situ* (i.e., in the condition it was last left prior to discovery). In cases where crime scene processing and archaeology are combined in buried body cases, the importance of preserving or recording the original context of the scene becomes even more fundamental. However, despite the caution emphasized during training for crime scene processing, it remains common for buried evidence scenes to be processed with a disproportionate effort placed on collecting the body and associated evidence rather than examining the context from which the remains were derived. Such efforts, which tend to disregard geotaphonomic evidence, are not necessarily intentional. Rather, they involve a fundamental failure to recognize that the actual graves or features constitute an important source of evidence related to the crime. Of course, with crime scenes there is almost always an unfounded urgency to transfer remains to a laboratory setting.

The recent work of renowned forensic anthropologists, many diplomates on the American Board of Forensic Anthropology, have enlightened the law enforcement community about the abundance of information which may be obtained from the anthropological and odontological analyses of human remains by forensically trained scientists. The works of Bass and Birkby (1978), Boyd (1979), Brooks and Brooks (1984), France et al. (1992), Killam (1990), Mann and Ubelaker (1990), Maples (1994), Morse et al. (1976), Morse et al. (1984), Skinner and Lazenby (1983), Ubelaker (1989), and Ubelaker and Scammell (1992) have emphasized the principle that thorough analyses of buried remains are influenced by the care with which remains are exhumed.

The ability to employ professional archaeologists is often not recognized by, or thought to be outside the fiscal means of rural police departments in whose jurisdictions buried evidence cases predominate. The author's experience has been that news on the aforementioned techniques of proper exhumation either has not reached or has been generally ignored in the processing of many rural crime scenes. Commonly, the results are "best efforts" in extracting the evidence, rather than a detailed examination and documentation of the subterranean features in which they were contained. Once human remains are removed from the grave, and the excitement of the dig has waned, little effort is placed in the collection of geotaphonomic evidence. Universally, forensic anthropologists have experienced nightmarish cases in which human remains were handed them without photographs of their original positions, sketches, accurate recollections, or descriptions of their systematic recovery. The writer has had occasion to intercede in well-meaning attempts to search for remains as delicate as those of a neonate using the toothed bucket of a backhoe! Obviously, such practices obliterate opportunities to more completely understand how, when, and by whom, the body of a victim may have been buried.

Boddington (1987) infers the importance of viewing crime scenes from the vantage of geotaphonomy. In addressing observations at a tenth- or eleventh-century Anglo-Saxon cemetery, Boddington notes the value of recognizing and recording the context of remains:

> "Detailed scrutiny reveals a more subtle set of characteristics, variations in arm and leg position, differences in decay and, most odd of all, a chaotic disorganization of the bones of the thoracic and lumbar regions. The archaeologist here must address the question: are these mere random irregularities in depositional events or do they reflect, however indirectly, on the nature of the burial rite and society...? ...while some of the observed patterns are difficult to interpret, archaeologists have much to gain from a detailed examination of skeletons *in situ.*"

Such observations constitute just one example of how archaeologists have interpreted sites by combining anthropology, osteology, biology, and geology. It is also clear that the geophysical attributes of an interment endure the passage of time. In discussing the effects decomposing remains have on "burial environments", Janaway (1987) speaks of the necessity for accurately recording the location and positions of interred evidence:

> "Organic materials are sometimes preserved on a number of different metal artefacts, hence, in order to understand the spatial arrangement of organic materials in the grave, precise recording of grave goods is essential. This should include full three dimensional plotting of position and should in particular record which face of an object is uppermost."

Concerning the most recent type of archaeological site, the buried body crime scene, Morse et al. (1983) describes excavation techniques used to reveal evidence of tool marks and footprint evidence:

> "The upper four inches of the grave should be excavated in such a manner as to leave approximately one inch of soil shielding the suspected walls of the grave. This soil can be excavated after the upper four inches of soil have

been removed by picking or slicing it away from the grave walls paying careful attention to any soil changes, cracks, or cut roots which indicate the precise location of the grave wall. This is particularly important since it has been demonstrated that harder soil types such as clay, can retain clear impressions of the tools used to originally excavate the grave."

Such a technique should be routinely applied throughout the excavation of a grave or pit. As marks are encountered they should be photographed, provenienced, and cast with dental gypsum. In one case, tool marks were discovered three years after the original interment. The marks, identified as deep as 50 cm below ground surface, retained the glossy surface resulting from the shovel slicing through the silt-clay matrix. Theoretically, such evidence could be preserved indefinitely. Any implement used in digging a grave or pit must have a portion of the tool impressed into the soil at a point which acts as its fulcrum. The tool's surface slices through, or penetrates, soil layers; therefore, the feature cannot be constructed without leaving marks. Tool marks are not limited to shovels. The use of picks or mattocks also leave unique impressions (Figure 5.1 to 5.3), as do post-hole diggers or heavy equipment. Accounts of buried body cases document everything from tire irons to clam shells used by subjects who hastily dug graves to conceal the remains of their victims (Anonymous, 1981a, 1981b, 1984; Ross, 1994).

Another example of how the recovery of geotaphonomic evidence contributes to the identification, collection, and interpretation of buried body crime scenes is evident in an account of Dorothea Puente's burial of homicide victims around her Sacramento, California home during the 1980s. Wood (1994) details how an examination of crime scene photographs after the conclusion of the case resulted in a disturbing revelation:

"Body number six had been buried at about the midpoint in the backyard. Like most of the bodies, it was found in a shallow grave, only about twelve inches of dirt covering the blanket-wrapped, taped-up victim.

(The detective) told the coroner's conference that he and the anthropologist saw an unusual compaction of dirt on either side of the victim's wrapped legs, and a moundlike effect above the knees, as if the soil had been forced upward. A tunnel had been created between the victim's wrapped legs, caused by the packing of the dirt on either side...

(The detective's) opinion was consistent with the open mouths of some of the other victims. He believed, and the anthropologist agreed it was possible, that (the victim) had awakened from her drugged stupor and begun jerking her wrapped legs, trying to kick to the sides or above her. But she succeeded only in mounding the dirt, packing it up on either side. She was too weak or restrained to do more."

Figure 5.1 An impression of a shovel handle left hear the top edge of the feature. This is a relatively common toolmark left during construction of a grave but one which is often overlooked.

Such information may be vital for the prosecution of a case. Yet, examination of geophysical features which could document a victim's movement within a grave are generally overlooked during the recovery of remains.

Case Histories

What follows are two buried body case histories which demonstrate how evidence was retrieved through the appropriate application of geotaphonomic field techniques. Techniques described for both cases are standard practice in archaeology and should be adopted for buried evidence crime scenes. The first case demonstrates how delays in recognizing the importance of the grave itself can adversely affect potential evidence. The second case is an example of additional evidence which may exist in buried environments and which could reflect chronology in the construction and alteration of a grave.

Figure 5.2   Depicts another common toolmark, an impression left in the side of a feature when the axe blade of a mattock (see Figure 5.3) is forced into the excavated walls of a feature by the rocking action of the tool needed to loosen it and the dirt during the digging of a pit or grave.

Case I

The teenage son of a midwestern family was reported missing one January day. In March of the same year, the partially buried body of an individual, later identified as the victim, was discovered at the rear of an abandoned structure. The human remains, clothed and buried in a shallow grave, were first encountered by a local resident who had been walking her dog. The body appeared to have been disturbed by animals which uncovered the cranium and arm of the otherwise buried body.

In August, the crime scene was reexamined by the author, at the request of the investigators, to determine if there was any additional evidence which might be gleaned from the grave. Critical to this reexamination was a clear understanding of the techniques used in processing the scene five months earlier. The interview of detectives who were present at the crime scene revealed their excavations involved scraping dirt from above the body and pulling it out of the grave. The area of the grave where the victim's head lay was then "dug up" and the soil screened to determine the presence of any bullet fragments. The detectives were certain the portion of the grave from the victim's torso to his feet had not been excavated. With that information,

Figure 5.3   A mattock.

geotaphonomic excavations first attempted to locate the back-filled shallow grave which, by August, was overgrown by tall grass. Once located, the boundaries of the grave which interfaced unexcavated soil matrix were examined on the basis of shape (to include both the plan view and profile aspects). This procedure was performed to determine whether the instrument(s) used in digging the original grave had either a flat/straight or curvilinear cross section.

The field methods used in evaluating the geotaphonomic evidence from the crime scene began with a pedestrian reconnaissance of the grave-site area. Vegetation and rodent activity in the form of burrows obliterated most surface indicators of the grave's position. The presence of a shallow, oblong depression along with an examination of original crime scene photographs determined the approximate location of the grave. After carefully clearing away the vegetation a 1- × 2-m grid was emplaced over the apparent grave. The grid was subsequently expanded to 2 × 3 m. The area within the grid was then completely defoliated revealing surface contours.

A base line was established from which all excavation units within the grid reckoned. Each unit or square, comprising 1 m², was designated by a number referring to the unit's southwest corner in relation to the 0 meter, or base line.

Archaeological excavation began within the southeastern quadrant of square 3L0 (a 1 × 1-m unit with its southern, or left, side oriented parallel

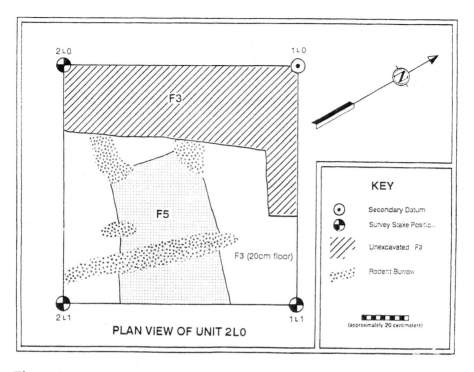

2L0 1L0

F3

F5

F3 (20cm floor)

KEY

⊙ Secondary Datum

◑ Survey Stake Positic..

//// Unexcavated F3

⠇⠇ Rodent Burrow

■□■■■□
(approximately 20 centimeters)

2L1 1L1

PLAN VIEW OF UNIT 2L0

Figure 5.4   This plan view diagram of the excavation unit, found to contain remnants of the grave described in the first case history, shows the intrusion of rodent burrows into the grave feature (F5). Although the feature demonstrated straight walls, animal intrusions into the grave after the removal of the body interfered with the determination of the type of digging implement used to dig the grave.

and 3 m left of the base line). The southern margin of the excavation was the roughly east-west 3-m line. From that edge, a trench was excavated toward the north, and perpendicular to the base line. Soil matrix (referred to as "F3" or feature number 3), was removed by thin scrapes with a boned trowel in arbitrary levels, each 5 cm in thickness.

At a depth between 28 and 40 cm below an arbitrary datum (an established survey point of a known height above ground surface from which all depths and distances are measured), a feature was identified. The feature, designated "F5", had a color and texture indicative of disturbed soil and was different in character from the surrounding matrix. The texture of F5 was more friable and less compact than F3, and its color was slightly darker than that exhibited by the undisturbed matrix. The feature was defined by clear boundaries to the north and south sides. Also observed were many rodent burrows or tunnels intruding into the matrix of F3 and F5 (Figure 5.4).

The feature designated F5 was consistent with the location of the shallow grave primarily processed during the homicide investigation in the spring.

The nature of the fill within F5 and the feature's shape were characteristic of an excavated depression subsequently in-filled by natural or human forces. This evidence indicated that F5 represented the remains of the northwestern end of the shallow grave. The entire grave feature was not excavated since investigators could not insure that the southern end of the grave had not been disturbed during their initial search for bullet fragments and other potentially buried evidence.

After Feature F5 was photographed and mapped, 2 cm of matrix was removed across the entire excavation unit. What remained was a faint but distinguishable F5 matrix with poorly defined borders within the F3 matrix. Severe rodent disturbance was also in evidence. Excavation ceased at this level, given that the lowest extent of F5 was encountered and the number of rodent burrows obliterated important areas of the feature. The sides, or walls, of the grave appeared very linear in plan view as if dug by a flat-sided instrument. However, the same could not be testified to given the presence of rodent disturbances (see Figure 5.4) and the possibility that those disturbances could arguably have altered the configuration of the grave. Had the original processing of the crime scene included a careful search for geotaphonomic evidence, it may have revealed the presence of tool marks before they were altered by burrowing creatures.

During the search of a subject's residence, a short-handled, flat shovel was found hanging in the garage. A variety of other evidence and testimony collected by the original investigators ultimately led to the conviction of that subject.

Case II

In another midwestern homicide case, a couple was reported missing one summer evening from their rural farm. One year later, a group of subjects confessed to the double homicide, and told investigators how they concealed the victims by burying them in a common grave. A preliminary examination of an area possibly containing the grave revealed only the remnants of a manure pile spread over an area approximately 3 m in diameter. The site of the possible grave was photographed, mapped, and subjected to an inventory of measurements referred to as an Intrusive Sensing Battery (ISB) Survey (Hochrein, manuscript in preparation). ISB, developed by the writer, is defined as the contemporaneous application of five soil tests conducted, with limited intrusion/destruction, to determine near-surface anomalies associated with buried features. The principle of the ISB survey is that the digging of a grave or pit interrupts the normal stratification, compaction, thermal absorption-retention, moisture absorption-retention, and chemical make-up of a previously undisturbed soil profile. The differences between backfill and the original soils may be detectable long after visual indications of the

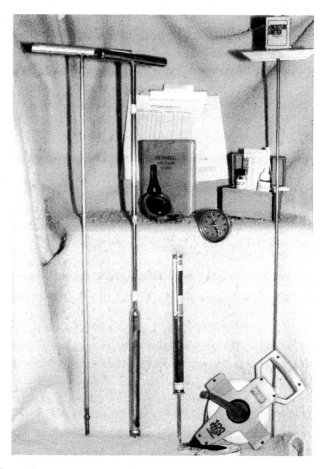

Figure 5.5 A basic Intrusive Sensing Battery (ISB) kit is represented in this photograph. It contains, from left to right, a modified tile probe; a soil core or tube sampler; a compass; a Munsell Soil Color Chart; logs for recording field data; a turf penetrometer; a soil thermometer; a soil pH testing kit; reel tape; and soil moisture meter. Although the kit represents low technology, the instruments are reliable, portable, and affordable.

disturbance have been obscured. Equipment used to detect compaction, moisture, temperature, chemical, and stratigraphic differences include a turf penetrometer/soil compaction tester, soil moisture meter, soil thermometer, soil pH meter/soil test kit, and soil core sampler (Figure 5.5). In place of taking individual penetrometer readings over the relatively large search area, four search team members formed a "shoulder to shoulder" north-south line at the east side of the manure deposit. At 30.5-cm intervals, tile probes were gently inserted into the soil by each team member. Probes which met less relative resistance were flagged. Penetration was deepest, and met with less resistance, in the most depressed portions within the disturbed area.

A slotted soil core sampler was used to extract soil samples. In addition to noticeable differences between the soil profiles from within and outside the disturbed areas, one sample had a strong odor of decomposition. With indications of a subsurface anomaly, the decision was made to excavate the area. Excavation units were oriented in what appeared to be a generally north-south pattern of less compacted matrix. During the excavation, soil moisture and temperature were recorded to determine the boundaries of the grave. Consistencies in moisture contents recorded adjacent to excavated margins of the grave, as well as a consistency in temperatures within 20 cm of the excavated edge, confirmed that the eastern boundary of the grave did not extend far beyond the excavations. This notion was supported by the probing, in which it was determined that greater penetration was concentrated just west of the 1-m north-south grid line. The grid system consisted of 1 m × 1 m squares positioned to the left (east) of a base line.

Following photography of both the search area and specific area of the grave, the outline of grid squares was established with string and metal pins known as surveyor's arrows (Figure 5.6). Contour measurements of all squares were acquired by plumbing to the ground surface from an arbitrary datum point. Data were recorded at 10-cm intervals across each square. Measurements were taken by recording the distance from the surface of the ground to a level string extending from the datum. Excavations entailed the removal of fill in arbitrary levels using sharpened flat-blade shovels and trowels. All unit fill was wet-screened through 0.25 and 0.0625 in. hardware cloth.

All fill was removed by carefully following the ground surface contour. At approximately 1 to 2 cm below the original ground surface (underlying a veneer of composted manure), the first indications of a feature were encountered. The outline of a pit (designated feature F4), of distinctly different color and texture was clearly visible among the undisturbed soil (F3). Matrix in the apparent grave had a greater capacity for moisture retention than immediately surrounding areas. Uniformity in color and the very cherty and irregular nature of F3 made it difficult to visually distinguish the eastern edge, or side, of F4. Eventually, ISB moisture and temperature measurements, along with test excavations, revealed that the eastern edge did not extend beyond the probable human remains. In sum, the grave appeared to have been dug only wide enough to accommodate the human remains.

The grave's fill was carefully removed with sharpened trowels and other delicate implements. At 36 cm below the ground surface, a fibrous, rope-like material was encountered. It lay directly over a blue, plastic-like material. By gently pressing on the excavated portion of the blue plastic-like material tactile confirmation was obtained that it covered a portion of skeletal material and a substantial amount of soft tissue. Further excavation revealed the remains were wrapped in a tarpaulin and bound with rope.

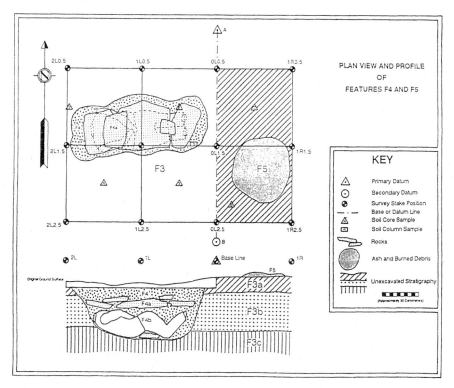

Figure 5.6 This theoretical example of a typical, albeit simplistic, buried body site map details the orientation of surface and subterranean features and evidence in plan view and profile. Careful measurements in three dimensions result in a drawing which accurately reflects: the orientation of a portion of the larger site grid system; the relationship of the body (F4b) below a layer of rock (F4a) used to conceal the remains within the grave (F4); the configuration and relationship of that evidence to the undisturbed soils (F3a,b,c) and possible associated evidence (F5); and the locations of multiple soil samples. In this example additional maps, supported by photographs, would be made of evidence found during the excavation of the ash pile (F5).

Excavations also revealed numerous cobble-sized and smaller fragments of a concrete-like material above the human remains at the same depth as a more continuous layer of the same material across the lower portion of the grave. The fill also contained a concentration of broken tree branches along the western edge of the grave. Their position within the fill coincided with that area of fragmented concrete.

Several key observations may be drawn from this detailed geotaphonomic examination of the grave. Above the approximate center of the grave, a thin veneer of concrete was truncated, which indicated that at some time following the burial, the grave had been reexcavated, thus causing disturbance to layering above the human remains. The grave's stratification was otherwise undisturbed. A large section of the concrete layer covered the foot end of the grave. That section was not fragmented and a portion of the tarped remains extended through the poured and hardened layer. This indicated that although the burial was disturbed after the original interment, the remains were not removed from the grave. At some time following the inhumation, but prior to processing of the crime scene, other minute fiber evidence had been introduced into the grave fill. The exact positions of fibers were only determined through the application of exacting archaeological field techniques. It was also revealed that either during the process of the original inhumation, or later disturbance to the burial, tree limbs and twigs became intermixed with the upper layers of fill. This was significant because of the potential for information which could be interpreted by experts such as forensic botanists and palynologists. In this case, the plant remains were obviously inconsistent with the grave fill matrix and only present in that area where the grave was disturbed. Collection of such botanical evidence and detailed documentation of its position within the grave could have shed light on its origin, as well as a time frame in which it may have been introduced into the grave (Hall, 1988; Willey and Heilman, 1987).

Discussion

Clearly, practical and potentially valuable applications of forensic anthropology and taphonomy exist in the contemporary analyses of human remains. We must reinforce the fact that proper archaeological field techniques not only aid laboratory examinations, but they also reveal additional key evidence for the physical anthropologist, odontologist, pathologist, and investigator. Such evidence could be cultural, as that left by those who buried evidence or subsequently intruded into the site. It might also be biological in the form of entomological, botanical, palynological, or scatological remains left during the natural evolution of the burial site. Alternatively, such evidence could include geophysical characteristics in the form of stratigraphic changes induced to the natural soil profiles.

For proper exhumation techniques to be most effective, buried evidence training for law enforcement personnel must include at least a cursory knowledge of archaeological field techniques. It would be advantageous for students receiving formal training in law enforcement and criminalistics to be encouraged to learn proper excavation and survey techniques which have principles applicable to all crime scene processing. Minimally, law enforcement personnel must become aware of archaeologically trained personnel located within respective jurisdictions. Furthermore, members of the archaeological community must be made aware of how they might assist law enforcement officials in criminal investigations. Discrete outreach programs, if not already established, should be developed to institute effective and reliable contacts within the archaeological community, particularly at local colleges and museums. Once these vital bridges have been established, both the anthropologist and the law enforcement officer need to recognize how their varied backgrounds contribute to common goals in processing the crime scene. Law enforcement must have the patience to allow the archaeologist several hours, perhaps even days, to conduct detailed excavations. The archaeologist must realize the processing of a crime scene is not an academic undertaking with unlimited resources and time to waste.

Certainly, a common ground can be reached whereby both sides may conduct investigations with mutual respect and cooperation, without sacrificing its condition. Unfortunately, no pat formula exists for conducting such investigations. The procedures applied will be unique for each crime scene. Communication between parties with the intent of cooperation and organization is vital. The types of documentation which will be prepared during the excavation and ultimately become part of the evidentiary record should be discussed. A clear understanding as to who will be part of the chain of custody is a primary concern of this preplanning stage. A working timetable should also be established to allow law enforcement to arrange shift changes and become accustomed to the length of time necessary for the archaeologist to conduct detailed excavations. The archaeologist and law enforcement agent will also find that having descriptive information about the victim(s), subject(s), and crime scene on hand further expedites the excavations. Such information should include aerial photographs and photographs of the area prior to the victim(s) burial, topographic maps, soil surveys, as well as descriptions of indigenous plant and animals (including insects).

Most important is a clear understanding that personal conduct at a crime scene is always expected to be discreet and appropriate toward the gravity of the circumstances. The detail and care with which the forensic archaeological excavation is performed will not only enhance the accumulation and quality of evidence, but will afford the dignity owed the decedent and his family.

Acknowledgment

Special thanks go to Dr. Anthony Boldurian of the University of Pittsburg Department of Anthropology and Special Agent Homer P. Hoffman, Jr., F.B.I. for their insight and support in the preparing of this chapter.

References

Anon., 1981a, Regional News, Texas, United Press International, January 30, 1981, Dateline: Galveston, TX.

Anon., 1981b, Regional News, New York, United Press International, February 18, 1981, Dateline: Johnstown, NY.

Anon., 1984, "Court Upholds Murder Convictions". Regional News, Texas, United Press International, February 29, 1984, Dateline: Austin, TX.

Bartlett, N., 1992, *MCGraw-Hill Encyclopedia of Science and Technology,* Vol. 18, 7th ed., McGraw-Hill, New York, pp. 130–132.

Bass, W. M. and W. H. Birkby, 1978, Exhumation: The Method Could Make the Difference. *FBI Law Enforcement Bull.,* 47(7):6–11.

Behrensmeyer, K. and A. P. Hill, Eds., 1980, *Fossils in the Making, Vertebrate Taphonomy and Paleoecology,* University of Chicago Press, Chicago, IL.

Boddington, A., 1987, Chaos, disturbance and decay in an Anglo-Saxon cemetery. In *Death, Decay and Reconstruction, Approaches to Archaeology and Forensic Science,* A. Boddington, A. N. Garland, and R. C. Janaway, Eds., Manchester University Press, Manchester, U.K., pg. 27.

Boyd, R. M., 1979, Buried Body Cases. *FBI Law Enforcement Bull.,* 48(2):1–7.

Brooks, S. T. and R. H. Brooks, 1984, Problems of Burial Exhumation, Historical and Forensic Aspects. In *Human Identification,* T. A. Rathbun and J. E. Biukstra, Eds., Charles C Thomas, Springfield, IL.

Considine, D. M., Ed., 1989, *Van Nostrand's Scientific Encyclopedia,* 7th ed., Van Nostrand Reinhold, New York, pg. 2762.

France, D. L., T. J. Griffin, J. G. Swanburg, J. W. Linemann, G. C. Davenport, V. Trammell, C. T. Armbrust, B. Kondratieff, A. Nelson, K. Castellano, and R. Hopkins, 1992, A Multidisciplinary Approach to the Detection of Clandestine Graves, *J. Forensic Sci.,* 37(6):1445–1458.

Hall, D. W., 1988, Contribution of the Forensic Botanist in Crime Scene Investigations, *The Prosecutor,* Summer: 35–38.

Hochrein, M. J., Intrusive Sensing Battery (ISB) Surveys in Buried Evidence Investigations. (Manuscript in preparation.)

Garland, A. N., 1987, A histological study of archaeological bone decomposition. In *Death, Decay and Reconstruction, Approaches to Archaeology and Forensic Science,* A. Boddington, A. N. Garland, and R. C. Janaway, Eds., Manchester University Press, Manchester, U.K., pg. 120.

Janaway, R. C., 1987, The preservation of organic materials in association with metal artefacts deposited in inhumation graves. In *Death, Decay and Reconstruction, Approaches to Archaeology and Forensic Science,* A. Boddington, A. N. Garland, and R. C. Janaway, Eds., Manchester University Press, Manchester, U.K., pg. 128.

Killam, E. W., 1990, *The Detection of Human Remains,* Charles C Thomas, Springfield, IL.

Lyman, R. L., 1994, *Vertebrate Taphonomy*, Cambridge University Press, Cambridge, MA, pp. 16, 506.

Mann, R. W. and D. H. Ubelaker, 1990, The Forensic Anthropologist, *FBI Law Enforcement Bull.*, July:20–23.

Maples, W. R., 1994, *Dead Men Do Tell Tales*, Doubleday, New York.

Morse, D., D. Crusoe, and H. G. Smith, 1976, Forensic Archaeology, *J. Forensic Sci.*, 21(2).

Morse, D., J. Duncan, and J. Stoutamire, Eds., 1983, *Handbook of Forensic Archaeology and Anthropology*, Florida State University Foundation, Tallahassee, FL, pg. 39.

Ross, R., 1994, "Two Pairs of Sneakers Found Near Bodies: Overpass Searched Slowly", *The Times-Picayune*, May 29, 1994, Metro, p. B1.

Shipman, P., 1981, *Life History of a Fossil, An Introduction to Taphonomy and Paleoecology*, Harvard University Press, Cambridge, MA, pg. 204.

Skinner, M. and R. A. Lazenby, 1983, *Found! Human Remains — A Field Manual for the Recovery of the Recent Human Skeleton*, Archaeology Press, Simon Fraser University, Burnaby, B. C.

Ubelaker, D. H., 1989, *Human Skeletal Remains — Excavation, Analysis, Interpretation*, 2nd ed., Taraxacum, Washington, D.C.

Ubelaker, D. and H. Scammell, 1992, *Bones — A Forensic Detective's Casebook*, HarperCollins, New York.

Weigelt, J., 1989, *Recent Vertebrate Carcasses and Their Paleobiological Implications*, University of Chicago Press, Chicago, IL, pg. viii.

Willey, P. and A. Heilman, 1987, Estimating Time Since Death Using Plant Roots and Stems, *J. Forensic Sci.*, 32(5):1264–1270.

Wood, W. P., 1994, *The Bone Garden, The Sacramento Boardinghouse Murders*, Pocket Book, New York, pg. 3-7.

Forensic Photography

6

FRANKLIN D. WRIGHT
GREGORY S. GOLDEN

Introduction

Accurate photography is crucial to forensic investigation as a means of documenting evidence. The need to photographically record injury patterns as they appear on skin is paramount to the odontologist and pathologist. Since vast amounts of time often elapse between the commission of a crime and the trial of the perpetrator, photographs frequently are the only permanent record of the injuries to the victims. Therefore, it is imperative that the forensic investigator be able to properly photograph injury patterns as a means of preserving such evidence.

This chapter requires the reader to have a good grasp of photographic terminology and the skills for operating basic camera equipment. It is beyond the scope of this chapter to attempt to teach basic photography. There are many publications that can provide the necessary background to improve the understanding of the photographic principles described in this chapter. Two readily available and easy to read books are *KODAK Guide to 35mm Photography: Techniques for Better Pictures*[1] by the Eastman Kodak Company and *The Photographer's Guide to Exposure*[2] by Jack Neubart.

In addition to the photographic principles, information about the physiology associated with injuries to skin and the techniques utilized by the forensic dental photographer to properly record the injuries by using photographs is discussed.

The process of photographically recording images on film, videotape, or other media occurs through the capture of electromagnetic radiation (light) of specific wavelengths. These wavelengths, measured in millionths of millimeters, are referred to as nanometers and abbreviated as (nm). Photographic images are recorded on photographic films which are sensitive to light wavelengths in the range of 250 to 900 nm (Table 6.1). Visible light, which comprises the range of electromagnetic radiation seen by the unaided human eye, is from 400 to 760 nm in range. Most modern camera equipment and film is specifically designed to record images seen in the visible range of light.

**Table 6.1   Spectrum of
Electromagnetic Radiation**

Wavelength (nm)	Defined Light
0.1	X-ray
250–375	Ultraviolet
400	Violet
470	Blue
530	Green
600	Yellow
700	Red
750+++	Infrared

Adapted from *Dermatology in General
Medicine*, 4th ed., McGraw-Hill, New
York. With permission.

In the visible spectrum, the image is recorded on the film as it is seen by the
eye through the lens when the lens is focused on the image. It is also possible
to record images specifically illuminated in the shorter ultraviolet range (210
to 400nm), and longer infrared range (750 to 900 nm) wavelengths. Because
ultraviolet and infrared light are outside the visible range of electromagnetic
radiation, they are commonly referred to as "nonvisible light". Photography
using nonvisible light requires special techniques to record the injury. It may
also require some minor focusing adjustments, called "focus shifts", to correct
for the optical properties of lenses which were designed for visible light
photography. These special photographic techniques and focus shifts will be
described in more detail in other sections of this chapter.

When light strikes skin, four basic events occur.[4] The first of these is
reflection, which occurs when some of the electromagnetic radiation hits the
skin and bounces back from it. It is this reflection of visible light that accounts
for the colors seen by the human eye.

Not all light energy on an object is reflected. Some of the light can be
absorbed. It is the absorption of light by an object that makes it appear black.
The action of the absorption of light associated with the injury being photographed is significant in nonvisible light photography, as will become evident later in the chapter.

A third reaction of light striking skin is the *transmission* and scattering
of the energy associated with the light through successive layers of cells until
the energy of the light has dissipated.

The final reaction that occurs when light energy strikes an object is a
molecular excitation called *fluorescence.* Excitation at the molecular level
causes the emission of a faint glow that lasts only as long as the excitation

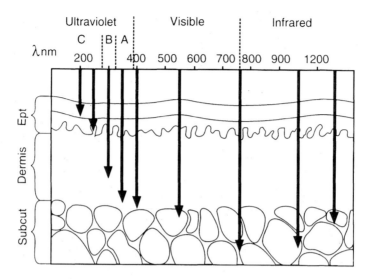

Figure 6.1 Diagrammatic representation of the variation in penetration of UV, visible, and near-infrared radiation into tissue (not drawn to scale). (Adapted from *Dermatology in General Medicine*, 4th ed., McGraw-Hill, NY. With permission.)

energy is applied to the object. Once the excitation energy is spent, the fluorescent glow ceases. Fluorescence is not readily seen because of the short duration of the emittance, lasting only about 100 ns (10^{-8} s),[5] and because the reflected light energy is so much greater that it overwhelms any fluorescent light detectable by the naked eye.

When light strikes human skin, all four of the previously mentioned events occur simultaneously. Depending on the wavelength of the source of the incident light and the configuration of the camera, it is possible to record, individually, any of the four reactions of skin to light energy (Figure 6.1).

Ultraviolet light only penetrates a few microns (thousandths of millimeters) into skin whereas infrared light can penetrate skin to a depth of up to 3 mm.[3] What is usually seen when visible light strikes the skin is reflected light energy. What isn't seen, however, is the light energy that is absorbed by the skin. By varying the wavelength of incident light used for illumination and setting up the appropriate configuration of the camera, lens, filters, and film, it is possible to photograph any of the four events which occur. This ability creates an opportunity for interesting pictures, especially when looking at bruises and other injuries to skin. Sharp surface details can be seen with ultraviolet light, while images well below the surface of the skin can be seen using infrared light. The techniques and photographic protocol for documenting injuries to human skin in visible and nonvisible light will be described.

Basic Physiology of Injured Skin: Inflammation and Repair

Having covered how skin reacts to light energy, it is equally important for the investigator to understand what physiological changes occur in living tissue when skin is injured. These changes from normal to an injured or healing state are what allow the discriminatory recording of the bruises when illuminated by light sources of various wavelengths.

When skin is injured, a progression of events occurs, beginning with a process called **inflammation,** and ending with **repair.** Inflammation is the response of living tissues to all forms of injury. It involves vascular, neurologic, humoral (blood related), and cellular responses at the site of injury.[6] Repair is the process by which lost or damaged cells are replaced by vital cells.[6] Although inflammation and repair are separate processes, they are closely interwoven in the response of tissues to injury. Inflammation dominates the early events and repair assumes major importance later.[6] During the inflammatory and reparative stages of wound healing, many organic components are found in the injured tissues that are not present in the same amounts in the surrounding healthy tissues. These include collagen, porphyrins from the blood, clotting factors, histamine, white blood cells, fibroblasts, and many others. The injured skin and the surrounding healthy tissue are very different in appearance. Injuries, such as bruises, are commonly seen and can be recorded photographically. Since the healing process is ongoing, it is often possible to photograph the healing process long after the injured tissue appears to have "healed" to the naked eye.

The organic components of the damaged tissue react to light energy differently than the undamaged adjacent tissues. Because of these differences, it is possible to photograph these tissues with different wavelengths of light and record images of the injured or healed tissue on film. Success in photographing healing bruises over time will depend on several variables, including the composition of the injured skin, the thickness of skin, the wavelength and intensity of light used to photograph the damaged area, the equipment used, and the type of film used. Depending upon the specific injury, it may be necessary to photograph injuries both in color and in black and white film, using visible light as well as nonvisible light. The injury may also vary in appearance in the photographs of each of these incident light sources.

The location and type of skin injured has profound effects on the ability to photograph the injuries. For example, thick skin of the palm of the hand is usually much easier to photograph immediately after an injury than after it has partially healed. The thick, keratinized covering of the palm of the hand often exceeds the ability of most light energy to penetrate it enough to record the subepithelial injuries. Such cases require fluorescent photography due to the highly fluorescent nature of thick skin. In contrast, thin skin found in areas such as the face or female breast tissue can frequently lend itself to recording injury patterns long after the visible damage from the injury has faded when viewed under room lighting with the naked eye. Again, this is directly related to the ability of the light energy to penetrate the skin to a sufficient depth to record the injury.

It is important to understand one final concept about the physiology of injured skin. In the living victim, at any given time after the initial response to injury occurs the composition of the injured skin is continuously changing as the injury heals. These changes will affect the response of the tissues to the selected wavelength of light energy over time, and may change the appearance of the injured tissue when photographed. This is especially true in a living victim, but it is also true in a deceased victim for the first few days after death. If the anticipated photographic evidence is not obtained with the first attempts, one should continue to re-photograph the injuries over time. If the victim is deceased, one should attempt to have the medical examiner or coroner delay any invasive autopsy procedures of the tissues associated with the injury until all attempts to photograph the injury have been exhausted.

Forensic Photography: Types and Techniques

When presented with an injury, the forensic dentist or investigator must decide what information the injury may contain, the extent of the injury, and how best to photographically record it. As previously mentioned, preserving the detail of the injury with photographs may involve a combination of color and black and white visible light photographs as well as the use of the nonvisible ultraviolet and infrared photographs. The photographer should develop a *standard technique* which includes orientation photographs showing where the injury occurred on the body. Additionally, this protocol should include close-up photographs for detail, and photographs placing the lighting source (flash and light guide) at different angles in relation to the injury.

Photographs should be taken with and without a scale. The use of a scale serves as a reference to record the relative size of the injuries in the photographs. While there are a number of acceptable scales, including coins, when unavailability of appropriate scales occurs, many forensic investigators use the ABFO #2 scale in their photographs. This right-angled scale was developed by a photogrammetrist (Mr. William Hyzer) and a forensic dentist (Dr. Thomas Krauss) for the purpose of minimizing photographic distortion and assuring accuracy in measurement. It has a black, white, and gray scale for color correctness, as well as three perfect circles and metric scales (Figure 6.2).

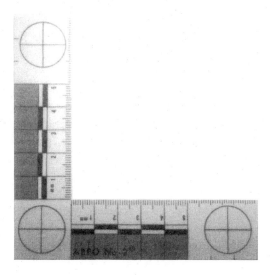

Figure 6.2   ABFO #2 scale.

The ABFO #2 scale is available from Lightning Powder Company, Inc., Salem, Oregon. The photographer should retain the original scale used in the photograph in the event enlargement to life-sized reproductions becomes necessary.

It is essential that the **standard technique** developed by the forensic photographer includes exposing many photographs for each case. One should not be hesitant about using several rolls of film for a photo shoot. Typically, most beginning forensic photographers do not take enough photographs in the first few cases in which they become involved.

Visible Light Photography

By far, the most common type of photography utilized today is photography using visible light, both in color and black and white. Manufacturers of photographic equipment and films develop and market equipment and supplies that are specifically designed to have an optimal performance in the 400- to 760-nm range of the electromagnetic spectrum. For the photographer wishing to take pictures in this range of light energy, there is relatively little practice required to ensure highly detailed and sharply focused photographs.

Many 35-mm SLR cameras available today are considered "automatic" point-and-shoot cameras. By definition, the object to be photographed is viewed through the lens and the camera *automatically* adjusts the focus and exposure variables before exposing the film. These types of cameras have been manufactured for optimal photography in the *visible light spectrum*. However, depending on the type of film used and the spectrum of electromagnetic radiation to which the film has sensitivity, it can become possible to "fog" (alter or distort) a visible light exposure with ultraviolet and infrared light.

With visible light photographic techniques, ultraviolet light may cause color shifts toward an undesirable bluish tint in the photographs, while infrared light may create more red tints than desired. To prevent ultraviolet and infrared wave energy from fogging visible light photographs, modern-day manufacturers produce coated lenses and filtered flash units, allowing only visible light to reach the film. This coating can work for or against the photographer, depending on what light range he or she is using. Older lenses and flash units may not have this filtration built in and may, therefore, be acceptable for ultraviolet or infrared photos. Conversely, the older optics could also require the use of filters for color correction in visible light.

Most 35-mm cameras have serious size limitations when it comes to recording life-size images. The limitation comes from the small area of film (24 mm × 35 mm rectangle) which records the image. Since there are very few objects which will fit into that small an area, considerable enlargement of the photographs may be necessary to see the injuries life-sized. Since evaluations and comparisons of the injuries to the teeth, weapons, or tools which created them are often done in direct relation to the life-sized object, it is necessary to have photographs that can be enlarged to life-size without loss of the detail necessary for the comparison.

Film manufacturers have designed photographic films that record light wavelengths from 250 to 700 nm. Special infrared films are available that can record photographs taken in light from 250 to 900 nm. Choosing the proper film is critical for successfully recording the detail of an injury. The film must be sensitive to the wavelength of light being used to photograph the injury or no image will appear when the film is developed. There are many quality photographic negative films manufactured, both in color and black and white. Table 6.2 suggests some readily available films, processing techniques, and their potential uses in forensic photography.

In addition to the photosensitivity range of the film, the correct film speed must also be determined. Films come with a rating, referred to as the ASA/ISO number, which serves as an indicator of the amount of light energy necessary to properly expose the film. The higher the ASA/ISO number, the faster the film; in other words, less light is needed to expose an image. Films with high-speed ratings (ASA 1600 or 3200) require very little light energy exposure, but caution must be exercised. The higher the ASA/ISO number, the lower the grain density on the film where the image is recorded, which translates into less versatility during enlarging. Large-grain fast films tend to produce prints which appear to lose focal sharpness and detail as they are enlarged toward their normal limits, i.e., life-sized or 1:1.

Table 6.2   Common Films Used in Forensic Dentistry

Film	Type	ASA/ISO Speed	Light Sensitivity (nm)	Processing
		Black and White prints		
Kodak Plus X Pan	(*Prefer for UV*)	125	250–700 nm	D-76 or HC110
Kodak Tri X Pan		400	250–700 nm	D-76 or HC110
Kodak TMAX		100 or 400	250–700 nm	D-76, TMAX or HC110
Kodak High-Speed Infrared	(*Prefer for IR*)	(For Infrared Prints: Camera set range:) 25–64	250–900 nm	D-76 or HC110
		Color Prints		
Kodak Royal Gold	(*Prefer for color prints*)	25 or 100	250–700 nm	C-41
Kodak Gold		100 or 400	250–700 nm	C-41
Fuji Color		100 or 400	250–700 nm	C-41
		Color Slides		
Kodak Ektachrome		100	250–700 nm	E-6
Fuji Chrome	(*Prefer for Color Slides*)	50 or 100	250–700 nm	E-6
Kodak Kodachrome		64	250–700 nm	K-14 (Must send to Kodak)

Just as there are good and bad attributes for high-speed films, slower-speed films can also have limitations. Using a film speed that is too slow for the amount of available light will result in an underexposed picture that may also lack clarity and detail. There are some situations where the photographer *does* need to underexpose for better detail, particularly during fluorescent photography. This will be discussed in a later section. The basic recommendation is to use the slowest film speed which will have the most grain density for the lighting present. Problems caused by having the wrong film or improper lighting may be minimized by bracketing the exposures over a wide range of camera settings. (*Bracketing means to expose individual photographs in a range of f-stops and shutter speeds.*)

At the time this book is being published, a relatively new method for capturing photographic images is evolving. It is referred to as "digital photography" and utilizes a special computer hard disk in the camera that stores the image s as digital information. These images can be later written to CD-ROM for storage. The advantage of digital photography is that the image can then be immediately viewed on a computer monitor or printed on a color printer. The image could also be transferred to traditional photographic films. This technology works superbly for color and black and white visible light photographs, but requires special computer chips for nonvisible light photographs. Currently, this specialized camera and equipment is very expensive. As the technology and the evolving market mature, the cost of the equipment should decline.

To understand the capabilities of any individual camera, it will be necessary to expose several rolls of test photographs to find the preferred camera settings for different films and ambient lighting. If you are fortunate enough to have an automatic 35-mm camera with a dedicated flash, the camera will adjust itself to make the necessary settings for you when taking visible light photographs, both in color and black and white.

Before approaching any photographic subject for close-up documentation of either a injury pattern or tool mark, remember to take an orientation shot. For example, in photographing a bite mark, typically a few preliminary photos would be taken at a distance which includes the location and orientation of the bite mark relative to its position on the body. This is to communicate to subsequent observers exactly where the injury occurred and its positional orientation. After the orientation photos, numerous close-up photographs using a macro lens should be taken, both with and without a scale in place. If the camera has a macro lens and is used for close-ups, be certain the scale is in the same focal plane of the object being photographed before exposing the film. This photographic protocol should be incorporated into the *standard technique* for the forensic photographer so that successful results will be assured case after forensic case.

Visible Light Color Photography

Advancements in design and manufacture of modern 35-mm cameras have greatly simplified color photography. These cameras have the capability to photograph objects with great accuracy and precise color detail. As discussed previously, the lenses have coatings and the flash units are filtered to direct only visible light to the film. Modern films record the images in brilliant colors and sharp detail. The most critical variables to consider when taking still photographs in color are (1) the type of the film and (2) the intensity of the light present when the film is exposed.

Color visible light photography is by far the most common type of photography used today. Modern cameras readily available today are manufactured and configured to take photographs using visible light. There are generally no special requirements or equipment needs assuming there is enough visible light energy available to properly record the image on the film.

When choosing the type of film, use the lowest speed film possible for the lighting available and proceed to take orientation exposures, gradually moving to the specific site of the injury. With routine color slide or print film illuminated by flash, a film of ASA 100 is generally adequate for close-up photography. Use the *standard technique* to completely record all aspects of the injury on color film. To insure color accuracy, it would be helpful to include a color correction guide in one or more of the exposures. One popular color correction guide is the Macbeth Color Chart, which is available in camera shops. Use of this guide will allow the film processing lab to correct the color temperature of the negative to the real color composition of the image before printing the photograph. Present the color guide used in the photographic session to the processing lab when dropping off the film for developing and ask that they verify the color composition of the image photographed before printing.

Visible Light Black and White Photography

Changing from color film to black and white film, the forensic photographer proceeds to re-photograph the injury. Use the same orientation and *standard technique* that was used when the color photographs were taken. In order to simplify this process, many photographers maintain two complete camera systems, with interchangeable bodies; one loaded with color film, the other with black and white. It may seem redundant to rerecord the injury with black and white photographs when color photographs of the same injury were just taken — or is it?

Remember that the human eye is very adept at seeing images in color. Because of the color information processed optically by the retina, other important details of the injury may be overlooked. When the injury is photographed in black and white, the eye is not distracted by the color composition of the injury and the normal surrounding areas. Consequently, this absence of color allows the viewer to see more detail in the injury.

When exposing film for black and white photographs, the same criteria for exposing color photographs are followed. These include film selection, bracketing, lighting, orientation, and close-up exposures, both with and without a scale. *One cannot take too many photographs!!!* In many situations there may only be one chance for photographs. If that is the case, take a minimum of three or four rolls of black and white and color photographs, bracketed widely, and illuminated from different angles.

Alternate Light Imaging and Fluorescent Techniques

The field of forensic investigation has seen a tremendous growth in the utilization of alternate light imaging for both locating and photographing latent evidence. Fingerprints,[7,8] serological fluids left behind at a crime scene[9] (blood, semen, saliva), types of ink used to counterfeit or falsify documents,[10] and bruises or other pattern injuries left on human skin that were sustained during violent crimes can now be more easily detected and also transformed into exciting and important exhibits with the utilization of fluorescence.[11] The application of this new technique has numerous titles. For simplicity, in this chapter it will be referred to as Alternate Light Imaging (ALI). The technique of photographing evidence with alternate light is called fluorescent photography.

"*Fluorescence* is the stimulation and emission of radiation from a subject by the impact of higher energy radiation upon it ... *Luminescence* is a general term for the emission of radiation that incorporates both fluorescence and phosphorescence, as well as other electro-chemical phenomena like *biolumi-nescence*."[12] An explanation of these definitions follows.

All of the physical reactions which occur during illumination with full spectrum visible light (reflection, absorption, transmission, and fluorescence) also occur for monochromatic light. Almost any object can be made to fluoresce, depending on the wavelength of light radiated upon it.[13] Although this filtered light is sometimes as much as 30 nm in width, it is called "monochromatic" (a misnomer), because very bright, full-spectrum light is filtered to only allow one color of visible light to be predominant. This is accomplished by the use of "band-pass" filters which are placed in the path of the light.

The technique requires an *alternate light source* which is capable of producing the monochromatic beam. Most alternate light sources are capable of emitting several frequencies of visible light by using different filters, but they are limited in purity since generally each color band is 30 nm in width. Some lasers, such as the 442-nm He-Cd (Figure 6.3) can be used as an

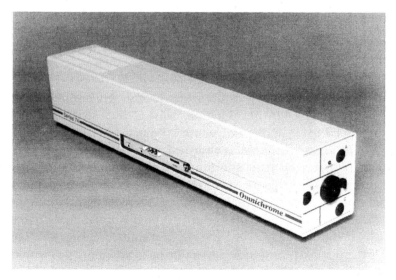

Figure 6.3   Helium/cadmium laser. (*Courtesy of Omnichrome Corp.*)

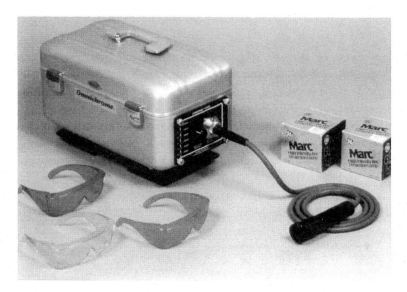

Figure 6.4 Omniprint 1000® forensic light source with fiber-optic cable and blocking filters. (*Courtesy of Omnichrome Corp.*)

alternate light source and it provides a pure, coherent, monochromatic light beam. However, lasers are not only bulky and require very specialized handling, they are also very expensive. Fortunately, there are a few less expensive, less complicated, and more portable light sources available that make photography at a remote location easy. One such forensic light source, the Omniprint 1000®, available from Omnichrome Corp., Chino, CA is in use in many crime labs throughout the world. It allows the user to individually tune several different frequencies of light, specific for each forensic application (Figure 6.4) The particular wavelength one tunes to depends upon what trace evidence the forensic investigator is seeking. There are optimal wavelengths for different applications; therefore the color (frequency) of the light and blocking filters will vary. Research and investigation of pattern injuries on human skin has shown that peak fluorescence of the epidermis occurs at 430 to 460 nm,[14,15] and is blue in coloration. Most of what strikes the surface of the skin is reflected.[16] Of the rest, about 30% penetrates below the surface. Some of it gets scattered, some is absorbed, and some is *remitted* as fluorescent light. The natural light-absorbing organic components of tissue are called chromophores.[16] Examples of chromophores are hemoglobin, bilirubin, and melanin. When illuminated with an alternate light source, the electrons of these excited molecules return to their normal state by releasing energy in the form of light. The light which is emitted during this transition is of a lower frequency and weaker than the incident light. The phenomenon causes the tissue to appear to glow or "fluoresce". The scientific explanation for this phenomenon was described many years ago by Professor Stokes and is referred to as "Stokes' Law" or the "Stokes' Shift". Since the fluorescent light is always less bright than the incident light, one must observe the fluorescence of an object with filters which allow only the fluorescent light through to the eye and block the more powerful reflected source light.

Principles and techniques previously described are used in fluorescent photography. Light returning to the film must be filtered to allow only the fluorescent image to be captured on the film emulsion. In documenting injury patterns, this filtration is accomplished with a yellow filter such as the Kodak gelatin #15 filter which blocks light transmission in the 400- to 500-nm range.

Fluorescent photography is best accomplished successfully in complete darkness, where all other sources of light are eliminated. One can imagine the difficulty in setting up and capturing this kind of photo, especially when the exposure times can range up to 2 to 4 s in length and the subject is alive and moving. Use of a tripod-mounted camera is mandatory. The light source optical output cable should also be mounted on a tripod and stabilized to illuminate the injury without moving (Figure 6.5). Exposure times should be bracketed at least two stops on either side of the indicated light meter reading through the lens. In fact, experience has shown that slightly under-exposing the film will produce better results than the actual metered exposure. This is true because during longer exposures even the fluorescent light coming back to the film is still bright enough to wash out some of the fine detail in the injury at the so-called "correct" exposure factor.

Figure 6.5 Typical tripod-mounted camera and light cable setup for fluorescent-light photography.

Several variables can influence the photographic protocol and parameters of exposure. Skin color (amount of melanin), skin thickness, wound healing response, light intensity, film speed, and location of the injury are but a few factors which affect the exposure times. Thick skin as found on the palm of the hand and sole of the foot fluoresces more than the thin skin covering the face. Darkly pigmented skin will require longer exposure times than lighter skin because more light is absorbed by the melanin pigmentation of the darker skin. Persons who bruise easily, such as the elderly, will produce injuries which may require shorter exposure times due to the thinness of the skin; but one can also expect longer exposures when greater hemorrhaging occurs beneath the skin since the blood absorbs light.

The primary advantage which alternate light imaging (ALI) imparts to the forensic investigator is improved detail and visibility of the subject matter. Fibers which are not easily located under normal light can become like beacons as they fluoresce under alternate light (Figure 6.6 and Plate 1). Gunshot residue on a dark background can be made to stand out as though it were photographed against a white background with the employment of ALI (Figure 6.7 and Plate 2). Illegal narcotic drugs such as rock cocaine (Figure 6.8 and Plate 3), or a latent fingerprint which may have otherwise gone undetected, can not only be located but may become crucial evidence by using ALI (Figure 6.9 and Plate 4). To the investigator who is responsible for documenting injuries to victims of violent and sexual crimes or human abuse, fluorescent photography using ALI will frequently provide more information about the actual pattern injury than one would observe under normal flash photography (Figures 6.10 to 6.12 and Plate 5).

Nonvisible Light Photography

The photographic requirements for recording injuries on film using nonvisible light become somewhat more complex. The appearance of the injury using nonvisible light illumination cannot be seen by the naked eye. Therefore, special techniques must be employed to record the injury on film and then print the image on photographic paper for viewing in visible light. Just as in ALI, these techniques require that band-pass filters be used. They are placed between the injury and the film, usually in front of the lens of the camera. The filters allow *only* the selected wavelengths of light to pass to the film. It is important that several factors be considered when attempting to photograph injuries in nonvisible light:

First, one must consider the type of film being used. The film's photoemulsion must be sensitive to the light wavelength the filter is allowing it to "see". Additionally, the light source must be strong enough to expose the film.

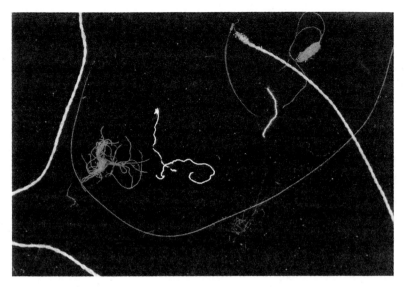

Figure 6.6 Fluorescence of fibers using alternate light imaging source (ALI). See also color Plate 1.

Figure 6.7 Fluorescence of gunshot residue around a central bullet hole in fabric using ALI. See also color Plate 2.

The camera's exposure settings (*f*-stop and shutter speeds) must be set to properly bracket for the type of light being used. The camera's ASA/ISO value must be correctly set for the film being used, and the lens must be focused correctly for the type of nonvisible radiation being used. It will take some

Figure 6.8   Fluorescence of illicit drugs (rock cocaine) using ALI. See also color Plate 3.

Figure 6.9   Identification and location of latent fingerprint using ALI and red-wop powder. See also color Plate 4.

experimentation with any camera to find the optimal settings. The forensic photographer, as a rule, will practice using his/her camera and establishing techniques before photographing actual cases. Suggestions of basic starting points are given in Table 6.3. Keep in mind that each camera is slightly different and these starting points may not work for every camera.

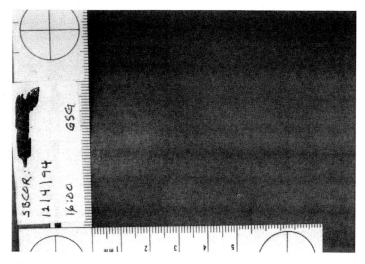

Figure 6.10A Bite mark located on deceased victim's abdomen using normal full-flash photography. See also color Plate 5A.

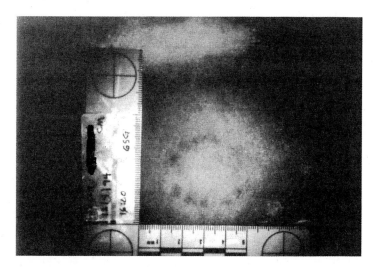

Figure 6.10B Same bite mark using ALI. See also color Plate 5B.

There are two major problems encountered with nonvisible light photography. First, it is difficult to acquire a predictable light source that emits enough of the desired wavelength to adequately illuminate the injury being photographed. Second, the exact amount of focal shift to produce a sharp photograph must be determined. Developing confidence and getting predictable results in nonvisible light photography will require some trial and error

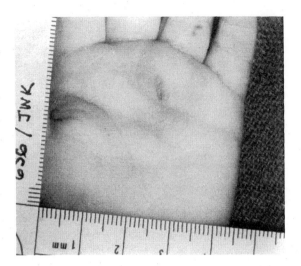

Figure 6.11A Normal "room light" photograph of palm side of two-month-old infant victim of child abuse; bite mark pattern is almost indiscernable.

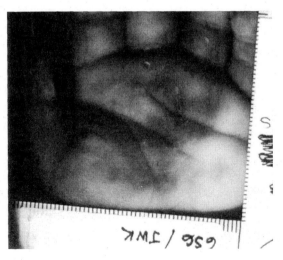

Figure 6.11B Same view using ALI; individual "tooth prints" now visible.

experimentation. Available and predictable sources of nonvisible lighting are listed below for both ultraviolet and infrared photography. This list is by no means totally inclusive and is intended to be a potential resource list. It is possible to find other sources of adequate nonvisible light than those listed here.

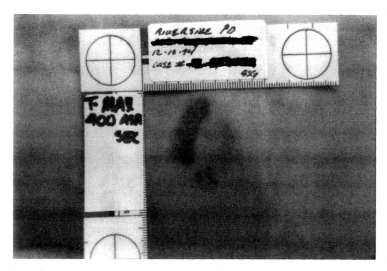

Figure 6.12A   Black-and-white view of abdominal bite mark exposed with full-spectrum room light.

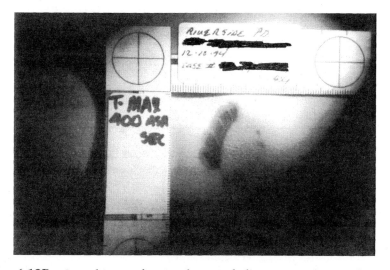

Figure 6.12B   Same bite mark using forensic light source at low-angle incident lighting. Note improved visualization of separations (striations) between teeth.

Ultraviolet (UV) light sources:

- *Sunlight*—A good source of long UV light but not practical for situations requiring indoor or nighttime exposures.
- *Fluorescent tubes*—Routinely used for indoor lighting; some useful UV emission. The best of these types of lights is known as a "black light", which emits good UV radiation; the brighter the better.

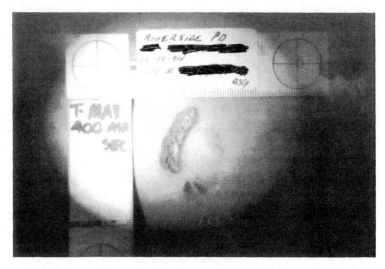

Figure 6.12C   Same bite mark with forensic light source at a 90° angle to surface of the injury. Note measurable and visible dimensions of lower incisors.

Table 6.3   Summary of Nonvisible Light Techniques

	Ultraviolet	Infrared
ASA/ISO range	ASA 100–400	ASA 25–64
f-Stop range	*f*-4.5 through *f*-11	*f*-8 through *f*-22
Shutter speed range	1/125 through 2 s	1/125 through 2 s
Filter (on lens)	Kodak Wratten 18A	Kodak 87 gel
Illumination wavelength (nm)	200–390 nm	700–960 nm

- *Mercury vapor lights*—Particularly useful in lighting small areas with intense UV light. Problems include long warm-up time for the light and limited availability.
- *Flash units*—Many older units provide adequate UV light emission. Some newer units emit a measurable amount of UV but will require experimentation to determine the correct output.
- *Combination fluorescent/black light*—This light combines the emission of the two light sources in one light fixture; commonly known as a Wood's lamp.

Infrared (IR) light sources:

- *Flash units*—Most commercial flash units emit sufficient IR light to be adequate, but require experimentation to determine their acceptability in infrared photography.

- *Tungsten lamps*—Used routinely in forensic investigations. The brighter the Kelvin value, generally the more IR output.
- *Quartz-halogen lamps*—Good source of IR radiation if unfiltered; more readily available and easy to use.

Focus Shift

After securing a source of predictable nonvisible light illumination, the problem of focus shift must be addressed. By definition, focus shift is "… the distance between the visible focus and either the infrared or ultraviolet focus …".[17] Focus shift is necessary because nonvisible wavelengths do not behave in the same way as visible light as they pass through a compound lens. The focal length of a lens is specific to a given wavelength of light. Most lenses are chromatically corrected to work within the 400- to 700-nm wavelengths (visible light). When the light energy falls outside of the visible spectrum, the optimal visual focus is no longer the optimally focused point for the nonvisible light energy used to expose the film.[17] While some manufacturers have developed achromatic lenses which act to bring two different wavelengths to a single coincident focus, many readily available chromatic lenses may require a focus shift for nonvisible light wavelengths. There are several published opinions concerning the correction of the focal point for nonvisible ultraviolet light photography. Kodak[18] has suggested the easiest method, and the one recommended to be tried first. It is their opinion that the focus shift required for ultraviolet photographs may be accounted for by simply increasing the depth of field. The recommendation is to decrease the lens aperture at least two stops if shooting from wide open. Since the construction of compound lenses used in 35-mm photography can be so different, Kodak[18] suggests that test exposures at various aperture settings be performed to determine the exact change for an individual lens.[18] Cutignola and Bullough[19] support Kodak's recommendation in correcting the ultraviolet focus by changing the depth of field. The downside to this modification is that it may significantly alter exposure times, lighting, and film speed.

Other authors have suggested small focus shifts by turning the focusing ring slightly from the visible focus position. Arnold et al.,[20] Lunnon,[21] Nieuwenhuis,[22] and Williams and Williams[23] have suggested shifting focus for UV photography in the *same* direction and amount as is done in infrared photography. The majority of modern high-quality achromatic compound lenses have a focus color correction to achieve sharp photos.

These authors have found that no focus shift has been required for ultraviolet photographs when using lenses designed specifically for UV. Extensive exposures using a Nikon Nikkor UV105 lens have produced very sharp ultraviolet photographs with no shift from the visible focus (Figure 6.13).

Figure 6.13 Nikon Nikkor UV105 lens. (*Photograph courtesy of* Nikon, Inc.)

Figure 6.14 Nikon camera setup with Nikon Nikkor UV105 lens, SB140 flash, and Nikon gelatin filter holder AF-1. (Photo courtesy of Nikon, Inc.)

Many of the focus shift problems can be eliminated by a commercial system such as that available from Nikon (Figure 6.14). This particular equipment is costly, but it is specifically designed for visible and nonvisible applications and it works predictably. It includes the following:

- Any Nikon 35mm camera body
- Nikon Nikkor UV105 lens (Note: the filter that comes with this lens works well with document examination but is inappropriate for UV photography of injury patterns in skin. See Table 6.3 for filter suggestions)[24]

Figure 6.15   Infrared focusing dot on Nikon Nikkor UV105 lens seen as the tiny dot adjacent to the infinity marking on the lens focusing ring. (Photo courtesy of Nikon, Inc.)

- Nikon SB140 flash and filters
- Nikon battery pack for the flash
- Shoe for the camera flash boot and cable from the boot to the flash
- Nikon gelatin filter holder AF-1 or Kodak 3-in. glass filter holder–#840449 with Kodak #18-A glass filter

The Nikkor UV105 is a special quartz-glass lens that has no fluorite coating and thus allows not only visible light to pass, but also 75% more energy throughout the UV range.[17] This lens has been chromatically corrected to have a coincident focus point for both ultraviolet and visible light. What this means to the photographer is that UV focus shift is eliminated. It also has a mark in the form of a small red dot on the lens for the focus shift when taking infrared photographs (Figure 6.15). The SB140 flash is an unfiltered flash, emitting a full spectrum of light (Figure 6.16). However, when purchased as a kit, included are three filters that can be used to limit the wavelength of light passing from the flash to the object to be photographed. One filter is for visible light, another for ultraviolet emission, and a third is for infrared light emission (Figure 6.17).

An advantage with the Nikon equipment listed above is that by adding a typical Nikon Nikkor 35–80 mm macro lens, the photographer has the ability to accomplish all visible and nonvisible light photographs with one camera, two lenses, and one light source (flash). For visible light photographs, one may use the Nikkor 35– 80 mm lens and clear flash filter on the SB140

Figure 6.16 Nikon SB140 electronic flash. (Photograph courtesy of Nikon, Inc.)

Figure 6.17 Nikon SB140 electronic flash with infrared, visible, and ultraviolet filters.

flash with the base camera body and proper film. For nonvisible light photography, one may use the unfiltered SB140 flash, the Nikkor UV105 lens, the appropriate band-pass filter in front of the lens with the base camera, and appropriate film. The unfiltered SB140 flash emits a very intense flash of light. Proper eye protection should be exercised if using this flash without filters. This camera setup will still require trial and error experimental sessions to refine the techniques and camera settings.

Additionally, band-pass filters are required for nonvisible light techniques for restricting the wavelength of light exposing the film. For reflective ultraviolet photography, the Kodak Wratten 18A filter is appropriate. This glass filter has a peak transmittance in the 365-nm band, which is ideal for long wavelength reflective ultraviolet photography. It also has a very small peak in the 700- to 840-nm band. While this is in the infrared band of the light spectrum, it does not allow enough infrared light to pass to properly expose the film.[25]

For infrared photography, the Kodak 87 gel filter is recommended. This "visibly opaque filter absorbs visible light"[26] and has transmittance in the 750-nm and higher wavelengths, which is ideal for infrared photography. Both the Wratten 18A and the 87 gel filters are placed in front of the lens *after* focusing with visible light. The ultraviolet technique *may* require a focus shift after the initial visible focus unless employing the Nikon Nikkor UV105 lens. The infrared technique *will* require a focus shift after the initial focus with visible light.

Finding the optimal camera setup, the correct focal point, and a dependable source of lighting may take many sessions of experimental trials. The photographer should exercise patience and remember to record the exposures and *f*-stops with every trial photograph taken in order to determine the optimal parameters.

Reflective Long-Wavelength Ultraviolet (UVA) Photography

Ultraviolet photography is used by the forensic photographer primarily for two reasons: the first is to increase the observed detail of the surface of the injury. The second reason is to recapture an injury on film after the injury has "healed" and is no longer visible to the human eye. This second use occurs because ultraviolet light is strongly absorbed by pigment in the skin. Any area of the injury having excess pigmentation when compared to the surrounding normal tissue will be recorded with excellent results using reflective ultraviolet photography.[27] Case reports suggest that it is possible to photograph a healed injury up to several months after the injury. Such a case, reported by Sobel and David,[28] illustrated a five-month-old injury recaptured using reflective ultraviolet photography where no injury pattern was visible to the eye.

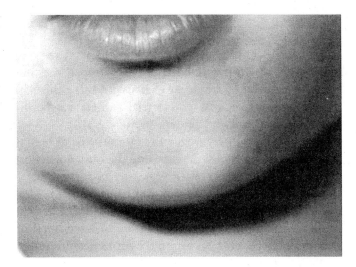

Figure 6.18A   Black and white photograph of canine puncture bite to chin after three months.

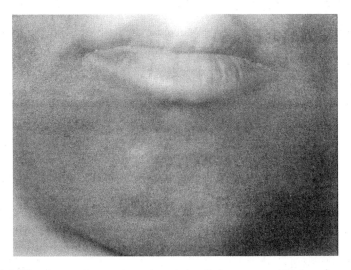

Figure 6.18B   Same view using ultraviolet light source. Notice the entire circumference of the bite is now visible.

The techniques for photography using reflective ultraviolet photography work to enhance surface detail (Figures 6.18A; 6.18B). Ultraviolet light does not appreciably penetrate the surface of skin, so photographs are taken using lower numbered *f*-stops that do not have too much depth of field at the focused distance. Bracketing exposures sequentially from *f-4.5* to *f-11*, at shutter speeds of 1/125 to 2 s for each *f*-stop with the Kodak Wratten 18A band-pass filter in front of the lens should be included in the standard

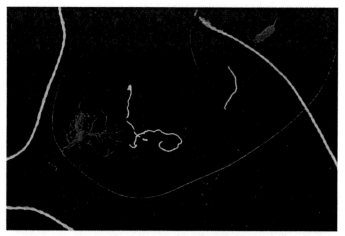

Plate 1   Fluorescence of fibers using alternate light imaging (ALI).

Plate 2   Fluorescence of gunshot residue around a central bullet hole in fabric using ALI.

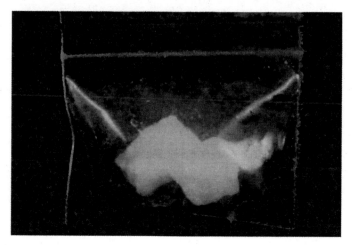

Plate 3   Fluorescence of illicit drugs (rock cocaine) using ALI.

Plate 4 Identification and location of latent fingerprint using ALI and red-wop powder.

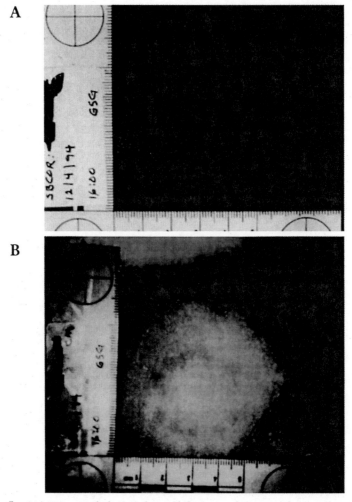

Plate 5 (A) Bite mark located on abdomen of deceased victim using normal full-flash photography. (B) Same bite mark using ALI.

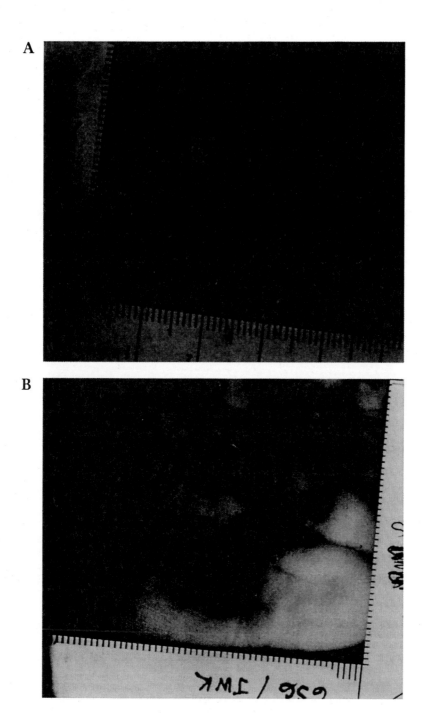

Plate 6 (A) Available light photograph of palm side of two-month old infant victim of child abuse; bite mark pattern is almost indiscernible. (B) Same view using ALI; individual "tooth prints" are now visible.

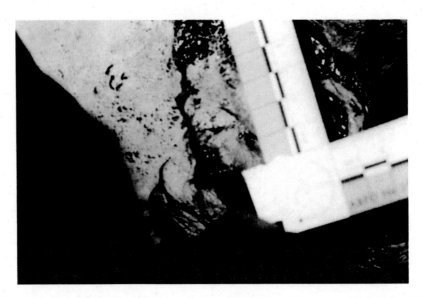

Plate 7 Photograph of a fatal gunshot to the left ear. This area of the wound has not been cleaned up in preparation of the autopsy.

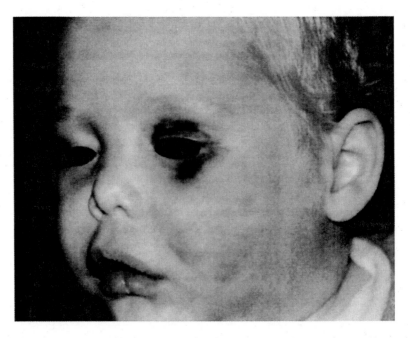

Plate 8 Bruises may change from reddish-blue or purple to green, yellow, then brown, over a period of 10 to 14+ days.

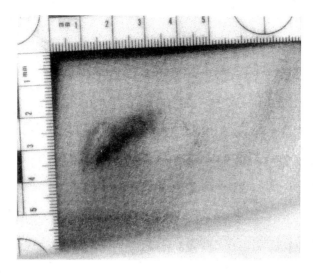

Figure 6.19A   Black and white photograph of a stab wound.

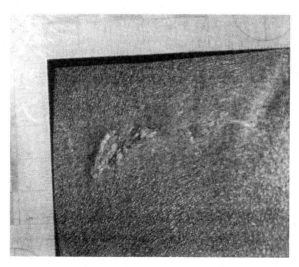

Figure 6.19B   Same view using ultraviolet light source. Notice the detail captured with UV defining the outline of the tool responsible for the injury.

technique. The resultant photographs will contain detail "seen" by ultraviolet light (Figures 6.19A; 6.19B). It is mandatory that the camera be mounted on a tripod before taking ultraviolet photographs due to the long exposure times. The UV-exposed film records the unseen information contained in the affected area of the injured skin which later becomes visible to the human eye on the photographic print, assuming that proper UV photographic techniques were applied to the injury.

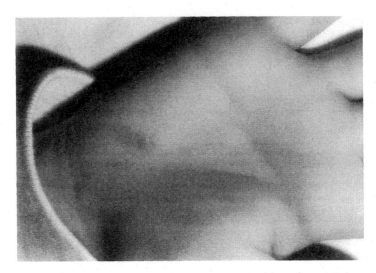

Figure 6.20A   Black and white photograph of a hand with a stab wound from a pencil. The point of the pencil was directed toward the finger tips. Notice lack of detail.

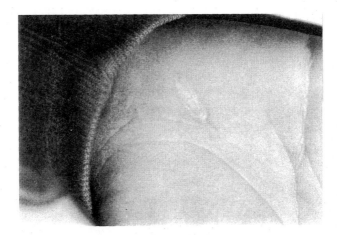

Figure 6.20B   Same view using infrared light source. Notice the detail of the injury, especially regarding the point of the pencil.

Changing the position (angle) of the UV light source relative to the injury, while keeping the camera perpendicular to the injury, will frequently allow surface details to be enhanced. Cutignola and Bullough[29] have stated that using the UV light source of two black lights (24″ General Electric F20 T12 BLB 20W) slightly elevated above the injury and offset at a 45° angle at a distance of 8 to 10 in. from the specimen provided the best surface detail. They go on to say "…when using ultraviolet light, the focal length of the chromatic lens is shorter than it would be with visible light." As previously stated, in order to correct the focus discrepancy they suggest decreasing the aperture of the lens, thereby increasing the depth of field.

Friar et al.[30] and Williams and Williams [31,32] recommend "push" processing reflective ultraviolet film to increase the film speed and thus the density of the image on the film. ("Push processing" is a term used to indicate a longer than normal time in the developer.) How long the development time is pushed depends upon just how much the operator underexposed the film.

Infrared Photography

Just as in reflective UV photography, infrared photography also requires special techniques. The infrared band of light is at the opposite end of the light spectrum from the ultraviolet band. Ultraviolet light is about one half of the wave length of infrared light. Because infrared is longer it penetrates up to 3 mm below the surface of the skin (Figures 6.20A; 6.20B). Since the depth of the injury recorded with the infrared technique is below the surface, the infrared focus point will not be the same as the visible focus point. Just as in UV photography, some allowance must be made for the differences in these focus points. After obtaining a through-the-lens focus, the lens must be moved slightly away from the injury. In other words, the lens-to-object distance must be increased (moved back) from the visible focus point, thereby making the correction. By using an aperture setting of f-11 or smaller to increase the depth of field, the discrepancy in focus points will be minimized.[33] Fortunately, many lenses are marked with a small dot (usually red) on the lens that indicates the infrared focus shift point. The photographer simply observes reference lines on the focusing ring of the lens which indicate the normal focus position, and moves the red dot to that location to acquire the correction.

Exposing infrared photographs requires several special considerations over conventional visible light photographs. The first is the camera setup. Unlike most films commercially available, Kodak high-speed infrared film does not come with a preset ASA/ISO speed rating. Each photographer's camera equipment should be tested in trial sessions to determine the optimum speed setting for the technique. Many cameras work best in the ASA/ISO range of 25 to 64. Whatever speed found best should be noted and marked on the surface of the canister containing the film so that it is processed correctly for developing and printing. Kodak[34] suggests that the infrared film "… can advantageously be developed for a 30 percent increase over the average time …. The additional fog is negligible and the resultant pattern is strengthened." What that means to the photographer is that the film can be "pushed" in processing for better results.

Figure 6.21A Photograph of a fatal gunshot inferior to the left ear. This area of the wound has *not* been cleaned up in preparation of the autopsy. See also color Plate 7.

Proper bracketing will usually give an opportunity to observe the best settings for infrared photographs. After setting a film speed, expose the film with multiple exposures beginning with *f*-8 and going sequentially through *f*-22. Use shutter speeds of 1/125 through 2 s for each *f*-stop. Remember to shift the focus point of the lens from the visible focus to the infrared focus point and to place the Kodak 87 gel filter in front of the lens just prior to exposures. The source of illumination (flash) must be strong enough to properly expose the film. Just as in the UV technique, infrared illuminated photography records the part of the injury "seen" with nonvisible light on a film emulsion, that when developed, will be viewable in the photographic prints (Figures 6.21A; 6.21B; 6.21C). Because of that fact, the injury documented with infrared technique will not appear the same as photographs taken using visible light. In Kodak Publication N-1, *Medical Infrared Photography*, this difference is discussed.

> It should not be overlooked that even when the lens is focused correctly, the infrared image is not as sharp as the panchromatic one. The reason is the lens aberrations have been corrected for panchromatic photography, so the anastigmatism is not as perfect in the infrared. The majority of biological infrared images are formed from details not on the outside of the subject. This accounts for the misty appearance of many infrared reflection records....[35]

Figure 6.21B   Same view using ultraviolet light source. Note no real change in the appearance of the wound.

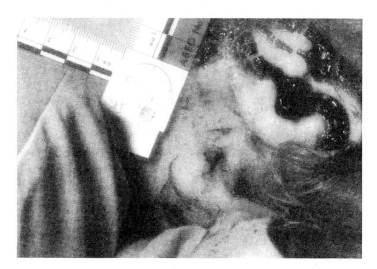

Figure 6.21C   Same view using infrared light source. Note the distinct entry site of the fatal wound. Because the infrared photograph records the injury below the surface of the skin, the dried blood associated with the wound *appears* to have been removed.

Successful infrared photography is a trial and error process, particularly when dealing with injury patterns. Since there is no way to know what injury detail is being recorded using this nonvisible light technique, wide bracketing and many exposures are highly recommended. If the injury did not cause sufficient damage to the deeper skin tissues, i.e., no bleeding below the surface of the injured skin, or if the surface of the injured skin is too thick for the infrared light to penetrate to find the site of the bleeding, there may be no infrared detail recorded in the photographs. No image appearing on the developed film and subsequent photographic prints should not be inter-preted as a failure of the technique. Expectations of 100% success with the technique are not realistic. One should not be discouraged as a result of a non-productive photo session. Nor should the lack of an image be interpreted incorrectly as though nothing was present. Additional sessions may be required to rephotograph the injury to successfully capture it on film.

Handling of Photographic Evidence

The photographs documenting a victim's injuries may become part of the legal system and, as such, are subject to *chain of evidence* rules. This requires an accountability as to what individuals had possession of the evidence from the time it was collected until it is marked and introduced into the legal system. As part of the standard technique, the forensic photographer should routinely mark each photograph with a categorizing system, usually consist-ing of numbers or letters which include the case number, as well as an identifying mark of the forensic photographer. This can be his or her initials or a signature, so that the photographs can be identified as originals and the *chain of evidence* maintained.

It is strongly suggested that the forensic photographer not part with the original negatives. Under no circumstances should both the negatives and prints be out of the possession of the photographer. If through carelessness they became "lost", there could potentially be no photographic evidence of the injuries and no way to recover from the mistake.

Photography is one of the most important applied protocols of forensic dentistry. The demands on the photographer can be great, especially in situations where an injury is the only evidence tying a suspect to the crime. Time, patience, and preparation in forensic photography are requirements for successful pattern injury documentation. While often frustrating and time consuming, when done properly the results yield good evidence, bringing with it a sense of accomplishment and satisfaction that the forensic dentist has made a significant contribution to the case. Developing the skills neces-sary to competently document these injuries with visible and nonvisible light is one of the great challenges in forensic dentistry.

References

1. *Kodak Guide to 35mm Photography*, Eastman Kodak Co., Rochester, NY; 6th ed., 1989.

2. Nuebart, J., *The Photographer's Guide to Exposure*, Billboard Publications, New York, 1988.

3. *Medical Infrared Photography*, Kodak Publ. N-1; 3rd ed., Eastman Kodak Co., Rochester, NY, 1973, pg. 6.

4. Kochevar, I. E., Pathok, M. A.; Parrish, J. A., Photophysics, photochemistry, photobiology; *Dermatology in General Medicine*, 4th ed., McGraw-Hill, New York, chap. 131, pg. 1632.

5. *Ultraviolet & Fluorescence Photography*, Kodak Publ. M-27, Eastman Kodak Co., Rochester, NY, 1972, pg.12.

6. Robbins, S. L., Angell, M., Kuman, V., Inflammation and repair; *Basic Pathology*, 3rd ed.; W.B. Saunders, Philadelphia, 1981, chap. 2, pg. 28.

7. Bramble, S. K., Creer, K.E., et al., Ultraviolet Luminescence From Latent Fingerprints, *Forensic Sci. Int.*, 59 (1993) 3-14.

8. Ray, B., Use of Alternate Light Sources for Detection of Body Fluids, *Southwestern Assoc. Forensic Sci. J.*, Vol. 14, No. 1, 1992, p. 30.

9. Stoilovic, M., Detection of Semen and Blood Stains Using Polilight as a Light Source, *Forensic Sci. Int.*, 51 (1991) p. 289-296.

10. Masters, N., Shipp, E., and Morgan, R., DFO, Its Usage and Results — A Study of Various Paper Substrates and the Resulting Fluorescence Under a Variety of Excitation Wavelengths, *J. Forensic Identification*, Vol. 41, No. 1, Jan/Feb, 1991.

11. Golden, G., Use of Alternative Light Source Illumination in Bite Mark Photography, *J. Forensic Sci.*, Vol. 39, No. 3, May 1994.

12. Williams, R., Williams, G., The invisible image — A Tutorial on Photography with Invisible Radiation. II. Fluorescence Photography, *J. Biol. Photog.*, Vol. 62, No. 1, Jan. 1994.

13. Guilbault, G., *Practical Fluorescence*, 1973, Marcel Dekker, New York.

14. Devore, D., Ultraviolet Absorption and Fluorescence Phenomena Associated with Wound Healing, *Thesis for Doctor of Philosophy*, University of London, Dept. of Oral Pathology, Oct. 1974.

15. Dawson, J.B., A Theoretical and Experimental Study of Light Absorption and Scattering by in Vivo Skin, *Phys. Med. Biol.*, 1980, Vol. 25, No. 4.

16. Regan, J. D. and Parrish, J. A., *The Science of Photomedicine*, Plenum Press, New York, 1982, p. 160.

17. Nieuwenhuis, G., Lens focus shift required for reflected ultraviolet and infrared photography, *J. Biol. Photogr.*, 1991, pg. 17.

18. *Ultraviolet & Fluorescence Photography*, Kodak Publ. M-27; Eastman Kodak Co. Rochester, NY, 1972, pgs. 6-7.

19. Cutignola, L., Bullough, P. G., Photographic reproduction of anatomic specimens using ultraviolet illumination; *The American Journal of Surgical Pathology*, Raven Press, NY, 1991, pg. 1097.

20. Arnold; Rolls: Stewart; *Applied Photography*, Focal Press, New York, 1971.

21. Lunnon, R., Reflected Ultraviolet Photography in Medicine; M. Phil., University of London, 1974.

22. Nieuwenhuis, G., Lens focus shift for reflected ultraviolet and infrared photography, *J. Biol. Photogr.*, 1991, pg. 19.

23. Williams, A. R.; Williams, G. F., The invisible image — a tutorial on photography with invisible radiation. 1. introduction and reflected ultraviolet techniques, *J. Biol. Photogr.*, 1993; Vol. 61; no. 4; pg. 124.

24. Personal communication with Dr. Thomas Krauss, DDS, San Antonio, TX, 1994; Mr. Robert Carruthers, Nikon, Inc., San Antonio, TX, 1994 and Nashville, TN, 1996.

25. *Ultraviolet & Fluorescence Photography*, Kodak Publ. M-27, Eastman Kodak Co., Rochester, NY, 1972, pg. 5.

26. Kodak Filters; Publication B-3A KIC, Eastman Kodak Co., Rochester, NY, pg. 3.

27. *Ultraviolet & Fluorescence Photography*, Kodak Publ. M-27, Eastman Kodak Co., Rochester, NY, 1972; pg. 9.

28. David, T. J., Sobel, M. N., Recapturing a five month old bite mark by means of reflective ultraviolet photography, *J. Forensic Sci.*, 1994; Vol. 36, no. 6, pgs. 1560-1567.

29. Cutignola, L., Bullough, P. G., Photographic reproduction of anatomic specimens using ultraviolet illumination, *The American Journal of Surgical Pathology*, Raven Press, NY, 1991, pgs. 1096-1097.

30. Friar, J. A., West, M.H., Davies, J. E., A new film for ultraviolet photography, *J. Forensic Sci.*, 1989, Vol. 34, no. 1, pgs. 234-238.

31. Williams, A.R., Williams, G.F., The invisible image — a tutorial on photography with invisible radiation. I. Introduction and reflected ultraviolet techniques. *J. Biol. Photogr.*, 1993, Vol. 61, no. 4, pg. 119.

32. Williams, A. R., Williams, G. F., The invisible image — a tutorial on photography with invisible radiation II. Fluorescence photography, *J. Biol. Photogr.*, 1994, vol. 62, no. 1, pg. 4.

33. *Medical Infrared Photography*, Kodak Publ. N-1, Eastman Kodak Co., Rochester, NY, 1973, pg. 26.

34. *Medical Infrared Photography*; Kodak Publ. N-1, Eastman Kodak Co., Rochester, NY, 1973, pg. 45.

35. *Medical Infrared Photography*; Kodak Publ. N-1, Eastman Kodak Co., Rochester, NY, 1973, pgs. 26-27.

36. Eastman Kodak Co., Personal communication with technical support department, Eastman Kodak Co., Rochester, NY, March, 1995.

37. *Professional Fujichrome, Fujicolor/Neopan Data Guide*, ver. A; Fuji Photo Film Co., Tokyo, 1994.

Bite Mark Techniques and Terminology

7

PAUL G. STIMSON
CURTIS A. MERTZ

Introduction

Once bite mark comparisons were accepted by the courts as a proper scientific procedure,[1] it became obvious in these early cases that we, as forensic dentists, had much work to do before the techniques of bite mark comparisons were to be considered scientific by our peers, the legal profession, and law enforcement overall. Following the formation of the American Board of Forensic Odontology (ABFO) in 1976, many diplomates of the board became concerned that the procedures used and accepted in the courtroom were more empirical than scientific. Individual dentists were using many various techniques that were being accepted in the courtroom, based on the precedence set forth in the *Doyle* case.[1] On closer review by these same concerned odontologists, many of these techniques were found to be lacking in scientific methodology, and instead were more an impression of the individual who had done the examination and experimental technique to gain the results about which she or he testified. Many early cases caused great consternation when they were reviewed by the entire forensic group at large. We refer to the description of the *Milone* trial[2] in the text by Moenssens et al.[3] where a mock trial using the evidence from *People v. Milone* is described:

> "In a mock trial the evidence in *People v. Milone* was read from the transcripts — though one proponent contends it was an edited and shortened version — several of the original experts who testified at the trial reading their own testimony. The visual evidence was also presented, and the leading proponents and opponents had an opportunity to comment after the presentation. The session was open to all Academy members. It was attended by several hundred forensic scientists. At the conclusion, upon leaving the hall, many of them expressed unabashed astonishment that a fact finder could possibly have believed that the defendant's identity had been positively established by the bite mark, upon the evidence presented."[3] (See Figure 1 in Appendix B.)

0-8493-8103-7/97/$0.00+$.50
© 1997 by CRC Press LLC

It was the text author's contention that this forensic event was probably a prime factor in causing the ABFO to form the bite mark study committee. The first studies by some members of this committee were bite marks applied from dental models mounted in modified vice-grip type pliers onto the abdomens of anesthetized dogs under controlled conditions. Phase two of the study occurred in Anaheim, California in 1977 where the diplomates, using the same or similarly mounted models caused bite marks on themselves. This was a most interesting experiment, as the instrument was given to one diplomate who then applied it to himself and applied as much pressure as his individual pain threshold could endure. Two diplomates were observing and ready to record time of application of force. After the artificial bite, a series of photographs was taken. It had been the author's contention for years that the use of the term "suck mark", implying negative pressure at the time the bite was made, was not scientifically founded. It is our belief there are differing capillary fragilities in the skin of each individual. In some individuals the capillaries are strong and unyielding, and in others rather friable. This was based on the observation that some women bruise easily during certain phases of their menstrual cycles. This was from personal observations as an oral pathologist (PGS) treating clinical cases. The bruising resulted from minimal injury. This type injury causes minimal or no bruising at other times in their menstrual cycles. There is a hormonal aspect to the increased bruising in females and a constitutional one in males.

After creating the bite-cast injury, many individuals began to get petechial hemorrhaging in the center of the bite area. No negative pressure had been applied to the injured area by the instrument. It was interesting to watch the variation in the degrees of bruising that occurred in the individuals involved in the study. Some formed a large hematoma and it spread rapidly under the skin surface, others formed little if any hematoma. Some variation was due to the differences in the pressure of the force applied by the instrument when individuals caused their own bite (probably due to varying degrees of pain threshold). This research effort culminated in the adoption in 1984 and publication of *The Guidelines for Bite Mark Analysis*, by the American Board of Forensic Odontology in 1986.[4]

The committee realized there were considerable differences in the interpretation by members of the ABFO of "pattern mark" injuries to the skin at the time of publication. At any meeting of the ABFO diplomates, when a bite mark was shown and discussed, there would be differences in opinion to catagorize the bite as a good, mediocre, or poor one. There were also, on occasions, differences in the interpretation of the bite mark when compared with the casts of the suspect(s). This is an honest difference of opinion, but is most disconcerting to attorneys and the triers of fact. Occasionally, there was a difference of interpretation due to the experience of the individual involved. Many years ago there was a suggestion that an impartial committee analyze the bite mark material and advise the court as to the admissibility of the bite mark.[5] This has not yet occurred, to our knowledge. The bite mark standards committee of the ABFO tried to systematize bite marks by publishing the first attempt at a scoring guide. The attempt was to get the individual analyzing the bite mark to ascribe a score to it. The score could then be understood by other odontologists or compared with his or her own score. After sending out a sampling of the controlled bite marks from the dog experiments and receiving the scores, much more work obviously had to be done in this area. The variance in the scoring method caused publication of a clarification and partial retraction of this portion of the initial bite mark publication.[4]

The ABFO realized the importance of trying to become more scientific about bite mark interpretation. A formal bite mark committee was then formed to continue the work that led to establishment of the previous workshop. Bite mark material was sent to selected diplomates for another attempt on scoring by the late Dr. Tom Krauss of the bite mark committee. Due to the formulation of the questionnaire in this attempt, unfortunately little actual useable statistical data were obtained. One thing that that is recalled is Dr. Krauss telling one of the authors, after receiving the initial return of the material, "it is obvious we have much work to do. We have to get people closer in scoring and evaluating bite marks." Dr. Krauss zealously championed the scientific method and justice. His work with Mr. Hyzer resulted in the ABFO scale[6] that is used today.

Another accomplishment was the reversal and freeing of an individual found guilty in a case caused by an improper evaluation of a bite mark in the trial using a microbiological method instead of the usual photographic method.[7] The board of directors of the ABFO then decided to have another bite mark workshop in San Antonio (Workshop #2) February 12 to 14, 1994. This was a most productive workshop and culminated in the ABFO Bite mark Terminology Guidelines.[8] The board of the ABFO has graciously allowed the authors to publish the material from this workshop in the text with the comment and feeling that it is important scientific and public information. This information was made accessible to all diplomates as a part of their notebook information and was sent to each of them by the ABFO secretary.

Nomenclature

The first term discussed in ABFO Workshop 2 was the term *bite mark* vs. the term *bitemark*. It was pointed out that language is a dynamic, living thing and is evolving constantly. The ABFO then decided that both terms are clear and there was no reason to endorse either one. The authors prefer the two-word term. Many other scientific terms are two words: suck mark, lacerated wound, tool mark, etc. The choice is obviously personal, and either is correct. The terms abrasion, contusion, laceration, ecchymosis, petechiae, avulsion, indentation, erythema, and punctures are associated with, or can be seen in bite marks. They are well defined in medical dictionaries and forensic texts and were not further defined. The workshop pointed out that an incision is made by a sharpened instrument, and cannot, therefore, be made by the anterior front teeth or incisors. The group also favored the term *latent* injury or wound over occult or trace wound when referring to an injury that is not visible to the unaided eye but can be brought out by special techniques such as infrared or ultraviolet photography.

Characteristics is a term introduced into bite marks from a similar field — that of tool marks,[9] by Dr. Lowell J. Levine[10] paraphrasing the Osterburg text. As Osterburg states, "There are two types of characteristics or details which are useful in the comparison of two objects. *Class characteristics* are the more obvious, gross features distinguishable in an object. In fingerprints they are the patterns that form a loop, whorl, or arch. With evidence involving impressions such as those left by shoes, tires, and some tools, their general dimensions, design, and contour of the imprint constitute the class characteristics (Id. p. 161). The minutiae of detail in the ridge formation on digital skin were used to illustrate the basis of fingerprint identity. The fine scratch marks, called *striations,* imparted to a bullet by a gun barrel, constitute the individual details that characterize a firearm. This is the concept of *individual, characterizing details*" (Id. p. 162).[9] A characteristic, when applied to a bite mark, is a distinguishing feature, trait, or pattern within the mark. These are further broken into two types, *class and individual* characteristics. A class characteristic is a feature, pattern, or trait that is usually seen in, or reflects a given group. The usual finding of rectangles or small box-like shapes or linear contusions in the midline of a bite mark is a class characteristic of human incisor teeth. The upper teeth would create larger patterns, due to their size. The value of this is that when seen in photographs, impressions or on the skin of a living or deceased individual they allow one to identify the group (here upper or lower teeth) from which they originated. An individual characteristic is a feature, pattern, or trait that represents a variation from the expected finding in a given group. An example of this would be a rotated tooth, or perhaps a misshapen, damaged, or broken tooth that would help to differentiate between two different dentitions to help in determining the dentition that caused the bite injury or mark. It is the summation of the individual characteristics that determine, when they are present in a bite mark, which dentition best matches these unique or different markings when present in the dentition of a suspect, when compared with other suspects in the case.

A bite mark is defined as a physical alteration in or on a medium caused by the contact of teeth. Another definition is that it represents a pattern left in an object or tissue by the dental structures of an animal or human. Bite marks are further described as a circular- or oval-patterned injury consisting of two opposing U-shaped arches separated at their bases by open spaces that, in life, represent the throat or posterior portion of the mouth. Along the outer edge or periphery of the impressions of the arches there is usually a series of abrasions, or contusions, with or without lacerations, that reflects the size, shape and arrangement of the class characteristics of the incisal or occlusal surfaces of the dentition that made the mark. Variations will be found in many bite marks. Central ecchymosis (or contusions), when found, can be caused by pressure of the teeth, with distortion, leakage, or rupture of the small vessels and capillaries present. It can also be caused by the application of negative pressure caused by sucking or negative pressure produced by the biter at the time of the bite. Linear abrasions, striations, and contusions can be caused by the movement of the teeth over the skin, or by imprinting of the inner surfaces of the teeth against the skin *(lingual markings)*. These have also been called *drag marks*. Occasionally a double bite pattern is seen, where two bites were done quickly in the same location or the skin slips and the teeth quickly contact a second time. Occasionally, the double pattern is done purposely by the biter, as in the Bundy case.[11] See also photos in Appendix B.

Patterns can be left on the skin by pressure against cloth or wire grates, or by cloth interposed between the skin and the teeth. Partial bite marks can be seen in situations where the victim moved during the bite (for example in an assault) so the bite was partial or incomplete. Only a few individual teeth marks show, which could be due to uneven pressure or a dentition with missing teeth. Bite marks change from the time they are made, both in the living and the dead. The longer the time intervals before bite marks are studied in the living, the less distinct the mark will be as far as individual teeth. The mark will be shown as two circular or horseshoe-shaped bruises with few other details. The ecchymosis will continue until there is a complete loss of identifying characteristics of the upper and lower areas that would be consistent with the upper and lower dental arches. The authors like to speak of these type marks as "consistent" with a bite mark. Of course, they could be consistent with a belt buckle, a brooch, or any other circular or semicircular object. Occasionally bites may be superimposed or there may be many multiple bites on the victim. Depending on the circumstances of the how and when they are made they may be very similar, or show irregularities due to movement, distortions, bruising, lacerations, etc. The most traumatic type bite, requiring considerable force, is that where a loss of tissue or avulsion actually occurs. This is more common in carnivore type animal bites, but is also occasionally seen in human bites. The avulsed bite implies extreme sadism, anger, or mental derangement of the biter. Note that these terms are only about the overall bite mark configuration. A detailed description would have to be done to show the unique features of each tooth in the dentition and the way they mark in the tissue.

As the general discussion of terms continued in ABFO Workshop #2, those terms used to describe bite marks and how best to categorize them for reports and testimony occurred. The diplomates were asked to submit their written suggestions from a list. After collection and some collation, the list was then discussed and pared down to some workable terms and definitions. Dr. Mark Bernstein from the nomenclature subcommittee led a very lively discussion and was able to get a general consensus on terms that can and should be used in bite mark reports and testimony. One term that generated much discussion was *unique*. This term, when applied to bite marks, means the bite mark is so distinct and unusual that **no other person** could have made an identical pattern with their dentition. This was the meaning to most of the ABFO diplomates present at the meeting. In the vast experience in bite marks of the diplomates present, it was felt that no bite mark studied to date meets this strict criteria. The term *unique* should be reserved for that bite mark that is still waiting to be studied; the one that odontologists and both the prosecution and defense attorneys agree is one of a kind, extremely rare and unusual: the individual characteristics are so unique that they are readily identifiable to both prosecution and defense experts and nonexperts. This explains the very limited and restricted use of the term *unique* in bite mark usage. The diplomates present who took a more liberal approach said that unique was the same as unusual or rare. If the term is properly defined, either in writing or testimony, it could be used either way. Another word critiqued was *distinctive*. This word was defined in bite marks as meaning highly specific, individualized, or a variation from normal, unusual, or infrequent. The consensus of the audience present felt that "unique" implies a greater degree of individual characteristics leading to identification than "distinctive."

A "possible bite mark" is a mark that could have been caused by teeth, but also could have been caused by other similar marking implements such as a brooch or belt buckle, etc. This type of mark lacks all of the characteristics that should be present to further categorize it as a "possible bite mark". This pattern has a stronger implication that it originated from teeth, but again could have been caused by something else. There are indentations that could be teeth in a pattern that is similar to the horseshoe-shaped exemplars usually found. To proceed further we now come to "definite bite mark", which means to the qualified forensic odontologist there is no doubt the mark was caused by teeth and other considerations have been appraised and eliminated. This phrase states that all of the classic features and characteristics that are typical to a bite mark are present in the injury. They have the class and individual characteristics of being caused by human or animal dentition and they are readily discernible in the bite mark. It should be understood that these terms represent opinions of the observer or odontologist and have no statistical or other measurements of the degree of probability. After closer study and use of other materials such as salivary amylase, DNA, or photographic enhancement techniques, the opinion can be shifted either stronger or lesser in degrees of match terminology.

The next portion of the workshop discussion concerned terms that could or do indicate that a visible injury represents a bite mark. The terms are in a ranking order from extremely positive or little doubt in the odontologists mind that it is a bite mark, to there being insufficient injury even to characterize it as a bite mark. The first set of terms are *definite* or *positively* and show that there is little doubt in the mind of the odontologist that it is a bite mark. The next set of terms are *reasonable medical/dental certainty* or *highly probable*, which suggests that it is a virtual certainty of being a bite mark but there is room for the possibility of another cause, although this is highly unlikely. The next set of terms includes *possible, similar to, consistent with, conceivable, may or may not be, cannot be ruled out, cannot be excluded*. These terms imply that the mark could have been produced by teeth, but it could have been created by something similar and give markings that look like a bite mark. There is no commitment at this time, using this nomenclature, that this is a definite bite mark. Continuing in descending order are the terms *unlikely, inconsistent, improbable*. Use of these terms gives a connotation that it is unlikely that this injury pattern is a bite mark. Lower on the scale are the terms *incompatible, excluded, impossible*, which imply there is no doubt in the mind of the examining odontologist that this is not a bite mark and represents something else. The final set of terms is *indeterminable, should not be used*, and *insufficient*. The pattern is such that it cannot be related to teeth or a tooth as a cause of the injury. Note that the above terms define the injury. They should not be used to describe the degree of certainty that a particular dentition caused the injury pattern.

Many terms can be used to describe a bite mark and to link the bite mark to the dentition of a suspect. First of these terms is *a point*. This is also called a match or a consistent point. This is a feature that is available for comparison or evaluation. The term is also used to count a feature seen in either what is being studied or the exemplar. This term is one used in reports or testimony and does not imply any degree of specificity and is not a characteristic. It represents a focus in a comparison. A *concordant point*, on the other hand, is a point of comparison seen in both the bite mark and the suspect(s') exemplars. It could also represent an area that can be linked to a particular tooth and an area of injury it could have caused in the bite mark. It is sometimes called a matching point or unit of similarity. The *area of comparison* is a specific region to be compared. It may also represent a pattern of several points or group of features and points that lend themselves to exact or nearly exact correlations. When the term *match* or *a positive match* is used it is a nonspecific term suggesting some degree of similarity between a single feature, groups of characteristics, or a majority of the entire case. This term implies a degree of similarity without any degree of probability or specificity. In other words, this is not a positive statement in a bite mark that all of the materials in a bite mark case match. It does not mean that the bite mark matches the suspect's teeth in all respects, as lay members of the jury might surmise from the use of the term. There are some points or similarities that match, but others do not. Use of these terms must be carefully considered so as not to portray some matching characteristics to be misunderstood as enough to make a complete match for evidentiary and trial purposes. Because points match, this does not mean the entire bite mark matches, which has been misinterpreted by juries, attorneys for one side of the case, or the media. As Professor Starrs states "the use of the word match to denote the outcome of a comparative analysis in odontology and elsewhere in forensic sciences should be banned as perniciously misleading. To the understanding of a lay person a match means an identification has been made to a particular person or object to the exclusion of all other persons or objects."[12]

The above comments came after a discussion of a case in this review by Professor Starrs. He quoted *State v. Cages*, 875 S.W.2d 253 Tenn. 1994 "in which one odontologist testified that a suspect's teeth molds matched a bite mark on the victim's breast 'to a reasonable degree of dental certainty that the defendant's teeth made the bite mark on the victim.'" Another odontologist said the defendant's teeth "could have made the bite marks on the victim". No defense odontologist was used since the trial court rejected a funding request for this purpose. The defendant appealed his conviction and death sentence and the Tennessee Supreme Courts gave no credence to the claim that the odontologists' opinions were too speculative or uncertain to be accepted as proof. The reviewing court credited the first odontologist as "matching the bite marks" and this precipitated the discourse on the word "match" by Starrs.[12] When writing opinions or testifying perhaps the terminology would be something like "there are a sufficient number of unique points in both the tooth models and the bite mark that are the same or similar that allow me, with a reasonable degree of dental certainty, to state that teeth as depicted in the model made the bite mark." Question, "could someone else with similar dentition have made the mark"? The odontologist would then state what the points of comparison were, how many there were, and if they were unusual.

The next term considered was *consistent with*. This means that there is a "match" between two or more things in a bite mark, but there is no degree of preciseness implied in the use of the term. When queried, the audience defined the term to suggest a "possible match" to a "match of absolute certainty." When used as proposed it means there are some similarities in the mark and the suspect's dentition, but there may be others with similar similarities in their dentition. *A possible biter* could have caused the bite, but she or he may not have. The teeth examined could have caused the bite, but other similar dentition could have as well. This is basically a statement implying similarity of class characteristics and no inconsistencies could exclude the suspect. We now progress to *a probable biter* that the suspect most likely made the bite. There is something unique in the dentition and mark that would not be present in the general population, or if it is present would be in a very small number. The odds of two individuals having the same unusual feature(s) being brought together in a place of occurrence of the injury is very unlikely, but still possible. The next higher order of terminology is *reasonable medical/dental certainty,* which implies that the odontologist (investigator) is extremely confident that the suspect made the bite. This also implies that any other expert with similar training, experience, and background, when evaluating the same evidence, would come to the same conclusion. It also implies that any other opinion would be unreasonable. The one word in this statement to keep in mind is reasonable. There is some latitude of proof here and it is based on what the investigator has to work with at the time of the examination. The use of terms such as "indeed, without a doubt," or "in my opinion, the suspect is the biter," or "no one else in the world could have made the mark" are unprovable and reckless. Occasionally, when pressed in testimony one could use the term "in my opinion the suspect is the biter" after they have shown in great detail the exact similarities between the bite mark and the dentition, but this statement must then be in the context of the entire testimony and not lifted out as the sole opinion. Keep in mind that lawyers have a way with words because their profession is words and the use of them. We, as odontologists and investigators, use words to convey concepts and ideas and sometimes do not realize their exact meaning when words or terms are closely scrutinized or taken out of context.

In working with bite marks, time is of the essence. This type of injury in either the living or the dead begins to change from the time it was made. In the living, bruising occurs. In the dead, the body begins to decompose, first on a cellular level and then more body wide. Gravity also plays a role in the changes that occur in the mark depending on the final position of the body of the deceased after death. Gravity may place fluid into the bite or cause it to leave the bitten area. The "standard" protocol should include photographing the evidence, first without scales then with them, and with a location photograph to show where on the body the mark is found. Next step would be salivary swabs for blood group trace evidence and the presence of amylase to show the presence of saliva. Next step would be making an impression of the mark. In the living individual a biopsy could be considered if there were sufficient scientific reason and some contributions to the case could be gained. Removal of the bitten area in a deceased individual should be considered for transillumination and other studies and for long-term preservation and storage of the injury in the tissue of the victim.

We will now turn to recovery of bite mark evidence from the victim. Photographs should be taken of the overall area where the mark is found and then close-up photographs should be taken. As Hyzer and Krauss point out,[6] it is vitally important to get the scale as close to the bite marks as possible. They state "The single most important consideration in using the scale is in positioning it relative to the bite mark or that portion to be depicted." The object of this is to prevent any parallax distortion from occurring (Id. p. 501). This topic is covered in Chapter 6.

After proper photographs are taken, salivary swabs should be done. We strongly recommend wearing gloves in bite mark examinations to prevent contamination of evidence. We each secrete the ABH blood groups in saliva, seminal fluid, tears, and perspiration. In 80 to 85% of most individuals the levels are high enough for routine testing to be effective. In the remaining approximately 15% the agglutinins are present but in such small amounts the techniques to detect them are expensive and time consuming. We have been told by a forensic serologist that the results are somewhat questionable after a tremendous amount of work was done to concentrate and obtain them. The finding of amylase suggests that saliva is present near the injured area and implies that it was a bite mark or that the mouth or lips were in contact with the skin or other surface tested. It might also imply that the individual has been spat upon. There are various techniques to test for ABH blood groups and each has some limitations. One limitation is that sometimes by the time a bite mark has been determined to be present, the body has been autopsied and probably washed to be more presentable for transportation to the funeral home. This is the custom of most medical examiner offices. Ask if this has been done to save yourself some unnecessary work.

Two techniques are generally used to test for ABH groups: cotton swabs and cigarette paper samples. If moistened cotton swabs are used, they must be refrigerated immediately after the samples are obtained. The bacteria on the skin surface can generate enzymes and these enzymes break down the blood groups found on the swab and render the test ineffective. To prove this to yourself immerse a cotton swab in your own saliva. Place it in a sealed plastic bag kept at room temperature for a day or two and then open the bag and smell the swab. We have used cadaver blood with saliva-tinged swabs and in a day or two there is visible hemolysis of the material. Before doing the swabbing technique check with your forensic serologist to find out how they would like the samples taken and how quickly they can get to them once you deliver them.

Another technique that works equally well and is simpler to do is to use white cigarette rolling paper like that used to make cigarettes with loose tobacco. Cut the paper squares into various shapes and they will serve as visible reminders of where the sample was taken. Moisten the paper in the same manner as the swab with either normal saline or tap water. Gently swab the area of concern with the cotton or the paper. Pressing too hard will distort the bite, but you must press hard enough to moisten and obtain some agglutins. With the swab, identify the area and write it on the outside of the plastic bag or glass or plastic tube, insert it, and refrigerate immediately. If possible the swabs can be allowed to air dry, but this will take up to an hour depending on the weather conditions where they are being used. The swabs can be propped against a test tube rack or some similar stand. Be careful when swabs are done in this manner and dried that no contamination occurs. Taking them to another environment might be better than the one you are working in, especially if it is a morgue or funeral home preparation room that is a semicontaminated area to begin with. With the paper disc use a small square for the bitten area, a similar round paper for the same area not bitten (square on right bitten breast, circle on similar area on left breast) so that you have normal controls to see if the individual living or dead was a secretor. You should also do rectal, oral, and vaginal smears in deceased individuals. These smears are done should blood group determinations be forgotten, overlooked in the autopsy, or the blood type specimen is contaminated or lost. It is also possible the results were not given to you or perhaps they are questionable in the case. On living victims, oral smears should be taken in addition to the skin smears. Knowing the blood type of the victim to validate the test is necessary. This test is not very productive if both the victim and the suspect have the same blood type. With the paper technique, allow the paper to air dry and then insert in plastic envelopes with the necessary information written on the outside with a Sharpie® pen to keep the chain of evidence intact. Because the samples are dry there is no breakdown of the blood group agglutins.

It has been reported the deoxyribonucleic acid (DNA) determinations can be done on the sloughed epithelial cells of the salivary gland ducts and the cells lining the inner surfaces of the lips and oral mucosa and the leukocytes from the gingival tissues and fluids. In a recent report,[14] it was shown that saliva from an individual placed on cadavers could be tested for DNA. The study showed a minimal recovery of 57.6% and a maximal recovery of

78.8%, depending on the DNA locus being tested. This study strongly supports the use of salivary trace evidence and the possibility of suspect identification with greater significance than blood types alone.

Impressions

Skin surface impressions are very useful in either living or dead individuals with bite marks. One thing that is missing in a photographic representation of a bite mark is that of the normal curvature present. Some odontologists feel impressions are not necessary, but they do add another dimension to the final product. The first impression taken should not be used, but put in a safe place for a court exhibit. We feel it is best not to pour a model of the first impression made of the mark. If the impression is distorted, or produces a model with bubbles in it, one critical piece of evidence in the case is distorted. It could be argued in trial that the impression technique possibly changed the place from where it was obtained when performed. The second impression will differ from the first, or will it? No research in this area has been done except with metal or acrylic models that are different from impressions on body tissue. Models can be poured creating a positive model from the second or subsequent impressions. They should be consecutively numbered as they are made and poured for future reference. Most surfaces of the body have some degree of curvature and this becomes even more marked in areas like the inner thigh or the female breast. Many dentists are very familiar with the use of various dental impression materials and their usage.

Because a bite can change as the position of the area changes, the impressions should be done in the same anatomical setting in which the bite was made, if possible. To prove this, use any kind of rubber-stamp mold with an address, an animal, etc. on it. Flex your arm so the deltoid muscle is retracted. Impress the stamp of the mold on the skin of the retracted muscle. Straighten the arm and look at the picture or address. It has changed. If the object is circular, it becomes somewhat oblong. This is the argument for taking the impression as close as possible to the position in which the bite was made. This may cause some difficulties as the material may flow away from the bite. A small dam of some type can be used with wax or similar material to keep the material in the desired area. If the skin surface is hairy, it should be gently clipped so the material will not adhere to the hair. Shaving the area could cause other artifacts by causing a nick in the skin or perhaps removing a scab or blood clot if one is present.

One of the better impression materials to use is a vinyl polysiloxane (VPS) such as Exaflex®, President®, Cinch-vinyl®, Mirror-3®, and Reprosil® or similar low to medium viscosity material. These materials contain palladium or a similar agent to modify hydrogen gas production so no errors are introduced in the setting phase. Earlier products produced small amounts of alcohol as a by-product and this introduced small but critical errors in the impression. Handling any of these materials is easy and they clean up well without staining. They will reach final set under some unusual temperature situations. If the body is cold the setting time will be prolonged. If warm, the setting time will accelerate. This setting time must be tested before the final impression on an area on the body or material away from the bitten area. VPS and polyethers or polysulfide impression material have been found experimentally to be extremely accurate as shown by Ciesco et al.[15] and Lacey et al.[16] The use of stiffer mixtures, such as heavy-body or more firm type materials, should be avoided as this tends to distort the injured area due to the pressure used to apply the materials. The vinyl polysiloxanes have good shelf life and is an additive-type reaction without any product produced so other errors are not produced by use of the material. The type and brand of material used is the choice of the odontologist and is usually what they are using in their practice and are familiar with. When using impression material, as with all forensic tests and procedures, make sure that you record the lot number and the expiration date placed by the manufacturer. Inject a small amount of the mixed material on a site away from the injury area and time the setting reaction. Record the time of set. The materials are designed to set at normal body temperature in approximately 7 to 10 min. If the body is cold from refrigeration, or warmed from being in a warm environment and undergoing some partial decomposition, this will affect the setting time of the VPS material. Do not attempt to accelerate the setting time of the material as this will probably change the usual properties of the material being used. The use of a hair dryer or lamp for heat may affect the stability of the material in an unknown fashion. As usual in these situations, these are "one shot" procedures and if done incorrectly or poorly will distort the injury site. Practicing on sites other than the critical area is one way to lessen errors. The stability of the mixed finished product is very long term so the studied materials can last while awaiting the ultimate trial in the case. New dispensing systems that can deliver properly premixed amounts of the base and catalyst pastes are now available and should be used whenever possible to facilitate the taking and accuracy of the impressions (Figure 7.1). It should be kept in mind that dental impression materials are designed to work on hard tissues and against some resistance, as they are when used in the oral cavity. Using the premixed materials in a syringe with a small orifice tip, they are injected directly onto the injured site (Figure 7.2). The small tips used on the conventional impression syringes by dentists work very well. The material is injected slowly so that it flows into the lower areas of the mark and does not trap air that will create a bubble or void in the finished negative impression.

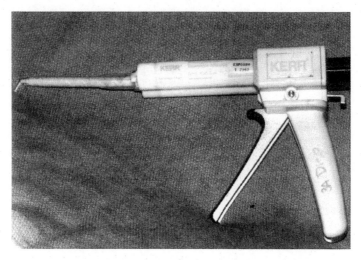

Figure 7.1 Mixing gun for dispensing mixed polyvinylsiloxane impression material.

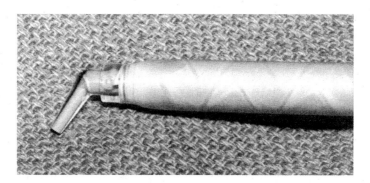

Figure 7.2 Smaller tip on mixing gun for dispensing mixed polyvinylsiloxane impression material.

VPS materials, even the most heavy-bodied types, are flexible when done in a thin sheet as would be used in a bite mark impression. Therefore, some material must be used to support and reinforce the impression material, to diminish the risk of distortion. The curvature of the body area bitten will now be maintained as well. Various materials such as dental laboratory stone, acrylic dental impression tray material, thermoplastic dental tray or fracture material, and an orthopedic thermoplastic mesh material (Hexcelite®), as favored by Sperber,[17] have and are being used for backing the impression material. Materials like Hexcelite® can be softened in a hot solution, such as coffee, and then molded into place. These were originally designed for use by physicians to temporally or permanently immobilize bone fractures. When

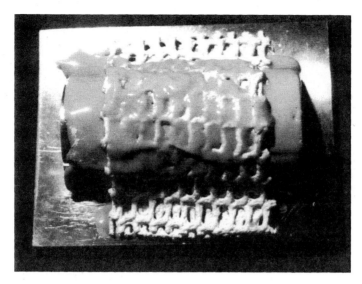

Figure 7.3 Vinylpolysiloxane material injected onto Hexcelite® (gauze-like) material placed on metal study mold.

the mesh is placed over the injected material, another layer of impression material is injected over the material to lock it into place as the VPS material will bond to itself (Figure 7.3). This material was tested against using a dental stone backing and was found to be as accurate.[18] Dental stone is also used for a backing. To insure a mechanical locking of the stone and the impression material, staples are dipped into extra impression material and placed on end in the impression material on the injury site (Figure 7.4). When set, the staples stand on end and provide a right angle mechanical anchor for the stone to prevent separation. A stone cap that is moderately thin is then poured over the impression material with the staple locks in it and allowed to set. Acrylic tray material is also used. The acrylic dental tray material is mixed according to the manufacturer's directions and molded when still pliable to the approximate shape of the area where the impression is to be taken. This can be done on the bitten area or a similar area on the opposite side of the body. A tray adherence material can be painted on the underside of the mold for retention of the impression material, or holes can be made in the impression tray to allow the impression material to exude out and mechanically lock itself into place. Before removal of the finished impression in any of the above techniques, the necessary anatomical location, date, time, and initials of the individual(s) doing the work is written on it with a Sharpie® pen (Figures 7.5 and 7.6).

Techniques using hot-water-soaked materials or autopolymerizing materials that have an exothermic reaction must be used with care in living

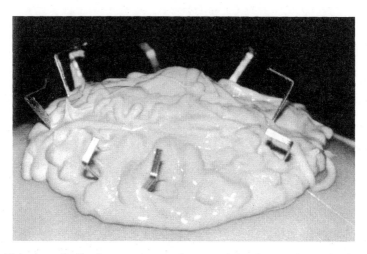

Figure 7.4 Vinylpolysiloxane material injected on skin with staples for locking stone cap.

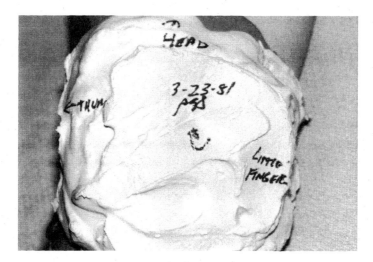

Figure 7.5 Anatomical landmarks, date, and initials on set stone cap locked onto impression prior to removal.

individuals who might suffer a burn as the material sets or is molded. The heat generated in the setting of the impression tray material might change the bite mark area in a deceased individual. A technique advocated by Dailey et al. is described as atraumatic, does not generate heat, and is not too difficult.[19] In this technique a low-viscosity impression material is injected upon the bite mark without bubbles in the impression. The periphery of the impression is extended approximately 1 cm beyond the mark area. After final set, the material is painted with the appropriate tray adhesive for the material

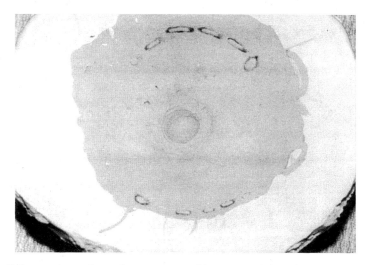

Figure 7.6 Undersurface of impression of breast model with teeth marks accentuated for illustration. Material on perimeter of impression is dental stone.

used. The authors then use Easy Tray® material (Anson International, distributed by Block Drugs, Jersey City, NJ) which is a thermoplastic material that softens under heat and cools to form a solid without a chemical reaction. The wafers are molded in warm water at a minimum of 170° for 20 to 30 seconds and then removed from the water and molded to the desired size and thickness. The authors state the wafers are still moldable at body temperature and may have to be heated and contoured two to three times to get the final desired result. A suitable size overlaps the impression material and is approximately 2 mm thick. A gauze is then lightly pressed into the material creating a textured surface for adhesion to the impression material. The impression and the backing are then joined, and after a final set of the impression material, is removed. Again, a test of setting time with the material used should be done on the victim away from the area in question and the setting time recorded.

When approval is obtained from the medical examiner or the coroner, tissue can be removed and stored for future reference and study. The odontologist **must** obtain the necessary medical or legal clearance before removal of any tissues from a deceased individual. We work under the authority of the medical examiner or coroner, who under law can collect or obtain any tissue, body fluid, or other substance necessary to assist in the solving of a criminal or civil case. If the odontologist has a relationship with either the medical examiner or coroner who is a member of the team, and is deputized as a certified deputy and is doing what is necessary in a scientific examination, there is usually no question. Keep in mind that this area could be grounds to keep an exemplar out of evidence so **always** obtain permission and show it in your written records, even if it is verbal. Obtaining written permission or a court order is always prudent if there is any doubt in the mind of the examiner.

There are no fixatives used in medicine and pathology that do not have some element of shrinkage. The best method for preserving tissue is to obtain a specimen with wide margins in all directions, immediately place it in a plastic bag, and freeze it. There will still be some changes due to the formation of ice crystals in the tissue, but it will and can be preserved for a considerable length of time in this manner. One technique, as advocated by Dorion,[20,21] is to use a custom-fabricated acrylic ring made of a proper mixture of monomer and powder according to the manufacturer. He gives a very short and concise method about preserving, storing, and transporting excised skin and transillumination of bite marks in the recent issue of the *Manual of Forensic Odontology*.[22]

Another technique is to use rings of acrylonitrile butadiene styrene (ABS) or similar pipe called polyvinyl chloride (PVC) cut from water or sewer pipe. The material chosen should be of the proper dimension to fit over the bitten area with some clearance on both sides. One problem with this technique is that the anatomic curvature of the skin area will be lost. The thickness of the pipe or acrylic ring should be about 3/8 in. The acrylic ring can be placed directly on the skin before final set and obtain some anatomic contour. The other materials can be heated in a salt bath or a water bath to allow them to be contoured to the skin surface around the injury site. In either case the rings are then permanently attached to the skin surface using a combination of cyanoacrylate ("crazy glue") and an interrupted suture combination. After the skin is permanently attached to the ring, the portion of the ring above the skin surface is filled with vinyl polysiloxane (VPS) impression material to maintain the correct anatomic curvature. The upper surface of the impression material is then marked with the necessary date, anatomic orientation, and time. After the impression material is thoroughly "set" and properly polymerized in the ring, the backing and skin are dissected free from the body. The dissector must make sure that the full thickness of the skin down into the underlying fatty tissue is taken to insure that the skin surface is removed intact. The entire specimen is then placed in 10% buffered formalin and allowed to remain for 10 to 12 h for proper fixation. After fixation the VPS can be gently removed. If the technique was successful, the correct anatomic curvature should be present as the skin was then fixed in this position by the action of the formalin. Distortions can and possibly will occur on separation of the two media so extreme care is advised when taking them apart. If the material is distorted on separation, it must be used for study with extreme caution. If the odontologist is working for the prosecution, the specimen will be available to the other experts representing the defense.

Under the Federal Rules, and in some states, all material must be shared with both the prosecution and the defense. If the case notes reflect any untoward or unexpected happenings, they can be defended under extensive questions in trial. When these notes are missing or overlooked, and the opposing experts discover what has occurred, the testimony will be tainted or circumspect, no matter how well the rest of the examination was done. When things are accidentally or purposely left out, this leads to questions like "What else have you overlooked or conveniently left out in this case, sir"? "Is it not the function of a true scientist to record all observations, not just the favorable ones"?

The advocates of this technique further state that the fatty tissue can be gently dissected free from the under surface of the skin and discarded. Dr. Dorion has used similar techniques and later could transilluminate and blacklight the specimen to study the outline and other aspects of the bite injury. He has stated that he has observed no appreciable change over a period of up to five years.[23] One of the authors (PGS) received a bite mark specimen that was dissected free from the body and pinned to a board. Photographs were available with scales before the removal and the resulting specimen had shrunk considerably (more than 20%) because the specimen was small and thin and the peripheral margins away from the bite mark were only 2 cm. Additional photographs were taken with more contrast to help outline and orient the injury. Histopathologic sections showed that the bite injury occurred before death. Critical measurements or other studies were not warranted due to the shrinkage of the resected specimen.

Photographic overlays are useful in the study of bite marks. Some odontologists prefer to use warmed aluwax or styrofoam for their studies. No one technique is preferred above any of the others as each works well for the individual odontologist. There are several methods of producing overlays. One method is to place a thin glass or plastic sheet over the occlusal surfaces of the study casts and trace the outlines of the anterior teeth back to the level of the first premolar. It is a very unusual bite mark that has teeth indentations beyond the first premolar. In a severe prognathic or retruded chin case other premolars and molars are possible. The sketching of the occlusal outlines takes time and patience. One possible problem with this technique is that of examiner bias. The tracings should be done on all suspects and labeled prior to any use of them on the life-sized bite mark photographs. A line of questioning that will be asked on the witness stand is "Doctor, you are very concerned about the rotation of this certain tooth, are you not? It is very critical in the examination and tends to point to the suspect does it not? Is it possible, knowing that, that when you sketched the teeth you could have accentuated it just a little, to make it fit better"? To counter that problem and produce overlays that can have multiple copies a photographic method is preferred by the authors.

A Sharpie® pen is used to outline the incisal and occlusal surfaces of the anterior teeth and the first premolar (Figure 7.7). The entire occlusal surface of one posterior molar on either the right or left side of both the mandibular and maxillary study cast is darkened. This will later be used to orient the overlays and prevent one of them from being inadvertently reversed. All overlays should be marked to prevent reversal and aid in their usage. Some odontologists also like to mark the duplicated casts with their choice of tooth-numbering system. A scale is placed at the incisal edge of the anterior teeth and a photograph is taken to produce a black and white negative (Figure 7.8). This can be done in a 135-mm format or in actual life size. Once the negative is obtained, the background scatter is removed, being careful to avoid the critical areas of the incisal and occlusal surfaces. This is brought back to life size in the darkroom and multiple copies in either sheet film or overhead projection type prints are then produced. The overlay represents an exact photographic representation of the surfaces of the teeth in the study casts. The overlays are then used to place over the life-sized photograph to judge the relative size, rotations, and fit of the suspect's dentition. Another method used to produce overlays is to use a copy machine with clear laser print film. When doing this technique it is imperative that two ABFO #2 scales are used at right angles, or four small scales used at right angles in the upper and lower opposite corner of the resulting copy of the occlusal surfaces. The study cast occlusal surfaces can be highlighted with the Sharpie® as before. The reason for the double set of rulers is to determine the accuracy of the product produced by the photocopy machine, as discussed by Dailey.[24] The actual rulers used must stay with the case to prove that life size was achieved in the technique. Substitution of other rulers will detract from the accuracy.

Other methods of making study aids include resin casts, aluwax impressions filled with a radiopaque material, and cast occlusal outlines. McKinstry[25] describes two techniques for the fabrication of resin casts. One technique produces visible-light-cured dental casts in approximately 30 min. This technique is useful for rapid screening of suspects in a bite mark case. The second technique fabricates "crystal clear" epoxy resin casts of the suspect's dentition. The dental casts are translucent and thus permit visualization through the teeth when comparisons are made to bite marks or to tracings or life-sized photographs of bite marks. The author states that the resin casts are less brittle than stone casts and are better for storage. They also make excellent educational tools for use by a jury in trials involving bite marks.[25]

Aluwax or pink baseplate wax can be heated and pressed against the incisal and occlusal surfaces of the teeth, or a stone model. The indentations can then be filled with amalgam fillings or any other radiopaque substance

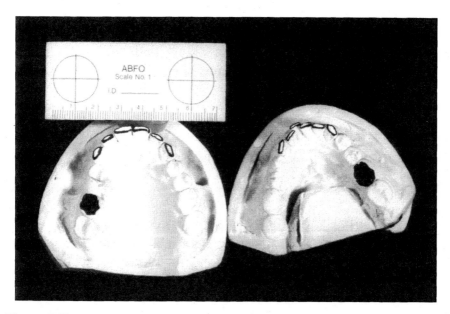

Figure 7.7 Outlines of incisal surfaces of the anterior teeth on a dental stone study model. Note blackened occlusal surface of posterior right molars to insure proper alignment when using finished overlays.

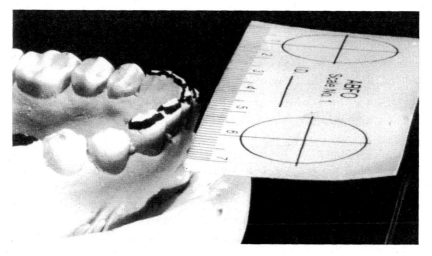

Figure 7.8 Scale at height of incisal edge of teeth for producing photographic negative. This helps to diminish distortions in the finished overlay.

and a radiographic image taken. This produces a black film with a white outline of the teeth. The film can be trimmed to provide the outer or inner edge of the teeth and their relative spacing and placement in the mandible or maxilla. This can then be used as a template for use studying a bite mark.

A few years ago, one of the authors (PGS) used orthodontic wire to outline the outer edges of a suspect's dentition to study a bite mark. The outlines were used for photographic purposes and ultimately were taken to court. While being viewed by the jury, one juror happened to bend the wire frame. After the study casts are duplicated (which should be done in every case to prevent breakage of critical evidence), cast metal outlines of the outer surfaces of the dentition are then produced. Instruct the laboratory to cover the surface of the first premolar tooth and to polish this surface very well. When used by attorneys or juries, the instructions to them are "place the shiny side of the horseshoe-shaped metal frames down on the picture." This insures that the proper orientation of the metal frame will be used for study or comparison. (See also photographs in Appendix B.)

Duplicated study casts can be placed over the life-sized photograph of the bite mark for comparisons. This is somewhat difficult as close details are lost due to the type of material that the study casts are made from. The crystal-clear cast[25] would be a distinct advantage in this situation. The angle of the photographic image is very critical when dental casts are placed over a photograph and must be used with caution. When presented with this type of evidence always ask to have the original material, or duplicates, to make the match on your own. The clear cast would be helpful, but there will be artifacts in it due to the thickness of the material and the shape of the teeth.

References

1. *Doyle v. State,* 263 S.W.2d. 779 (Tex. Crim. App. 1954).

2. *People v. Milone,* 43 Ill. App. 3d 385, 365 N.E. 2d 1350, 1358 (1976).

3. Moenssens et al., *Scientific Evidence In Civil and Criminal Cases,* Foundation Press, Westbury, New York, 1995, p. 983.

4. American Board of Forensic Odontology, Guidelines for bite mark analysis, *J. Am. Dent. Assoc.,* 112:383-6, 1986. Comment: Vale, G.L., Rawson, R.D., Sperber, N.D., Herschaft, E.E., Reliability of the scoring system of the American Board of Forensic Odontology for Human Bite Marks, letter, *J. Forensic Sci.* 33:1;20, 1988.

5. Hale, A., *Southern Calif. Law Review,* Vol. 51:309:257-284, 1978.

6. Hyzer, W.G., Krauss, T.C., The Bite Mark Standard Reference Scale — ABFO No. 2, *J. Forensic Sci.* 37:4;115-24. 1992.

7. *Wilhoit v. State,* 809 P.2d 1322 (Ct. Of Crim. App. Of Okla.) (April 16, 1991) 816 P.2d 545 (same opinion with appendix).

8. American Board of Forensic Odontology, *Manual of Forensic Odontology,* pp. 334-353, American Society of Forensic Odontology, Chicago, 1995.

9. Osterberg, J., *The Crime Laboratory,* 2nd ed. Boardman, New York, 1982.

10. Levine, Dr. Lowell J., Personal communication.

11. *Bundy v. State,* 455 So.2d 330 (Fla. 1984), cert. denied 476 U.S. 1109 (1986).

12. Starrs, J.E., Bite Marks in the Courts, a Review of 1994's Appellate Court Decisions, *Sci. Sleuthing Rev.,* 184:4;4 Winter, 1994.

13. *State v. Cazes,* 875 S.W.2d 253 (Tenn. Supp. Ct.) (Feb. 14, 1994).

14. Sweet, D., Forensic Identification of Stains of Human Saliva Using DNA Analysis (Abstr. F4), Am. Acad. Forensic Sci. Meet., Nashville, TN, 1996.

15. Ciesco, J.N., Malone, W.R.P., Sandrik, J.L. and Mazur, B., Comparison of Elastomeric Impression Materials Used in Fixed Prosthodontics, *J. Prosthet. Dent.* 45:88-94, 1981.

16. Lacy, A.M., Fukui, H., Bellman, T., and Jendresen, M.D., Time-Dependent Accuracy of Elastomer Impression Materials. II. Polyether, Polysulfides, and Polyvinylsiloxane, *J. Prosthet. Dent.,* 45:329-33, 1981.

17. Sperber, N.D., Bite Mark Evidence in Crimes Against Person, *FBI Law Enforcement Bull.* pp. 16-19, July, 1981.

18. Stimson, P.G., Collard, S.M., A comparison study of two bite mark impression techniques. abstr., *Am. Acad. Forensic Sci.,* 1987.

19. Dailey, J.C., Shernoff, A.F., Gelles, J.H., An improved Technique for Bite mark Impressions *Manual of Forensic Odontology,* Printing Specialists, Vermont, 1995.

20. Dorion, R.B.J., Preservation and Fixation of Skin for Ulterior Scientific Evaluation and Courtroom Presentation, *Can. Dent. Assoc. J.,* 50:2; 129-30, 1984.

21. Dorion, R.B.J., Transillumination of Bitemark Evidence. *J. Forensic Sci.* 32:3; 690-97, 1987.

22. Dorion, R.B.J., Impression of Bite Site. Excision of Bite Marks. Transillumination of Bite Marks, *Manual of Forensic Odontology,* Printing Specialists, Vermont, pp. 159-163, 1995.

23. Dorion, R.B.J., Personal communication.

24. Dailey, J.C., A practical technique for the fabrication of transparent bite mark overlays, *J. Forensic Sci.* 36(2);565-70, 1991.

25. McKinstry, R.E., Resin dental casts as an aid in bite mark identification, *J. Forensic Sci.,* 40(2);300-2, 1995.

Dentistry's Role in Detecting and Preventing Child Abuse

8

GERALD L. VALE

"Ladies and gentlemen, we are all screwing up. As a result, children are dying."
— Los Angeles Police Detective
Santa Monica Child Abuse Conference

Introduction

With the above terse statement, a seasoned police officer expressed his horror and frustration at society's failure to deal with a 240% increase in child homicides in his jurisdiction. He cited the case of a child who was repeatedly beaten at home and was brought to the hospital four times in a period of three months. Yet nothing was done to change the situation, and the child was ultimately beaten to death. This author has witnessed similar tragedies in the coroner's office.

From 1985 to 1994, the number of children reported abused nationwide has increased every year and there has been a 63% increase during this period[4,13] (Figure 8.1). In 1994, an estimated 3,140,000 cases of suspected child abuse and neglect were reported, and 113,960 cases of sexual abuse were served by child welfare agencies. Significantly, the rate of confirmed fatalities has increased 48% between 1985 and 1994. In 1994, an estimated 1,271 children died from abuse or neglect.[1]

Child abuse may be defined as any act of commission or omission that endangers or impairs a child's physical or emotional health and development. Such acts include physical, sexual, or emotional abuse, as well as physical neglect, inadequate supervision, and emotional deprivation. Child abuse is second only to SIDS (Sudden Infant Death Syndrome) as the leading cause of death in children under one year of age. In older children it is second only to accidents.[2]

It is now widely agreed that an absolutely crucial factor in the fight against child abuse is early recognition of the problem so that effective intervention can be undertaken.[4,5] It has been reported that 35% of children who have

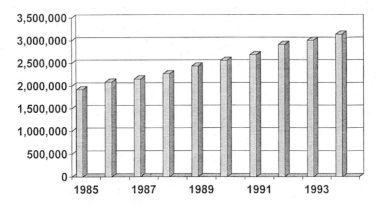

Figure 8.1 Between 1985 and 1994 the number of children reported abused increased from 1,919,000 to 3,140,000.

been abused will be seriously reinjured if returned to the parent or guardian without intervention. Indeed, 5% will be killed.[5]

It is important to realize that all members of the dental team have a unique opportunity — and a legal obligation — to assist in the struggle against child abuse. This special opportunity exists because a high proportion of abused children suffer injuries to the face and head, including the oral and perioral regions. These injuries may be observed during the course of dental treatment — and in some cases even before the child is seated in the dental chair.[6]

This chapter, then, is dedicated to helping dental health care workers and others fulfill an important mission — the detection and reporting of child abuse. It will also touch on the use of dental evidence in crimes against children. The ultimate goal is to save children's lives.

Our mission involves (1) knowing the signs of child abuse and neglect, and (2) fulfilling the legal and moral obligation to prevent further abuse by documenting the injuries by photographs or other means and reporting the matter to the police or social welfare agency. In addition, the individual who has studied the techniques of forensic dentistry may have the opportunity to participate in the investigation of crimes against children and to testify as an expert witness. Whether called by the prosecution or the defense, the expert's goal should always be the same — to assist the trier of fact (the judge or the jury) in the effort to seek the truth.

Incidence of Orofacial Lesions

Perhaps because crying or speaking emanates from the mouth, this area is frequently the focus of attack in cases of violent child abuse.[8] Studies have shown that oral or facial trauma occurs in about 50% of physically abused children. Thus Cameron et al., studying 29 fatal cases, found that approximately half had facial injuries.[9] Similarly, Becker et al. reported orofacial trauma in 49% of 260 documented cases of child abuse;[10] 65% of the abused children had injuries to the face, head, or mouth — 61% of these injuries were to the face, 33% were head injuries, and 6% were intraoral.

In general, any evidence of severe or repeated trauma to a child suggests the possibility of abuse.[11] This should precipitate not only a particularly thorough oral and physical examination, but also a careful history and observation of the child and parents.

Detecting Child Abuse in the Dental Office

History

When a child presents for examination, particularly if there is an injury involved, the history may alert the dental team to the possibility of child abuse. Indeed, the history may be the single most important source of information.[12] Because legal proceedings could follow, the history should be recorded in detail.

While one should always realize that there are other possible explanations, the possibility of child abuse or neglect should be considered whenever the history reveals the following:

- The present injury is one of a series of injuries that the child has experienced.
- The family offers an explanation that is not compatible with the nature of the injury. For example, the author recalls a case in which an effort was made to explain away a clearly identifiable human bite mark as a scrape caused by the edge of a diving board.
- There has been an extraordinary delay in seeking care for the injury.
- The family does not want to discuss the circumstances of the injury.

While the above findings are by no means conclusive, they should cause the examiner to look further for possible signs of abuse, and to consider this among the possibilities to be confirmed or eliminated.

General Physical Findings

Before examining the mouth, alert members of the dental team may note general physical findings that are consistent with child abuse or neglect:

- The child's nutritional state is poor and growth is subnormal.
- Extraoral injuries are noted. They may be in various stages of healing, indicating the possibility of repeated trauma (Figure 8.2 and Plate 8).

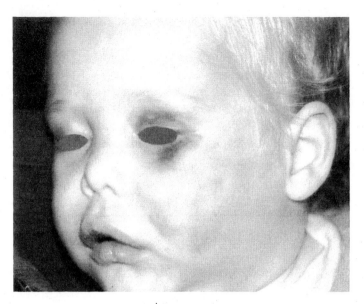

Figure 8.2 Bruises may change from reddish-blue or purple to green, yellow, then brown over a period of 10 to 14+ days. See also color Plate 8.

- There may be bruises or abrasions that reflect the shape of the offending object, e.g., belt buckle, strap, hand (Figures 8.3, 8.4, and 8.5).
- Cigarette burns or friction burns may be noted, e.g., from ligatures on wrists, gag on mouth.
- There may be bite marks, bald patches (where hair has been pulled out), injuries on extremities or on the face, eyes, ears, or around the mouth (Figure 8.6).

As always, the examiner must remember that there may be explanations other than child abuse for some of these findings.

Findings on Dental Examination

Examination of dental injuries includes thorough visual observation, radiographic studies, manipulation of the jaws, pulp vitality tests, and percussion. Transillumination may also be helpful.

Typical Oral Lesions

Both oral and facial injuries of child abuse may occur alone or in conjunction with injuries to other parts of the body. The oral lesions associated with child abuse are usually bruises, lacerations, abrasions, or fractures. Suspicion of child abuse should be particularly strong when new injuries are present along with older injuries. Thus scars, particularly on the lips, are evidence of previous

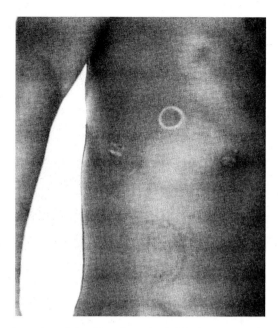

Figure 8.3 Right side of fatally abused child shows marks consistent with cigarette lighter (above) and belt buckle (below).

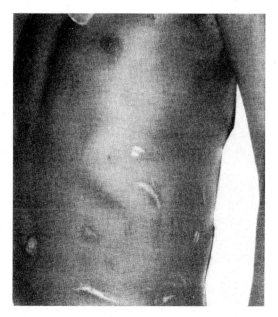

Figure 8.4 Multiple scars on body of victim seen in Figure 8.3 demonstrates that there was a history of physical abuse before the fatal beating occurred.

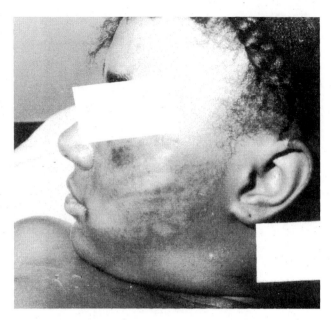

Figure 8.5 A hard slap to the face left marks of four fingers of attacker's right hand on this victim's cheek.

trauma and should alert the investigator to the possibility of child abuse. As noted earlier, further investigation is required when the explanation for the injuries does not justify the clinical findings.

Tears of the labial or lingual frenula

Tears of the frenula, particularly the labial frenum, are frequently seen in child abuse cases. These injuries may result from blunt force trauma. For example, the labial frenum may be torn when a hand or other blunt object is forcibly applied to the upper lip to silence the child (Figure 8.7). Injuries of this type may also occur in forced feeding, as a result of the bottle being forced into the mouth.[13]

Oral mucosa torn from gingiva

Blunt force trauma to the lower face may also cause the mucosal lining of the inner surface of the lip to be torn away from the gingiva. A forceful slap, for example, may have this effect. The location and extent of the injury will depend on the magnitude of force and the location and direction of the blow (Figure 8.7).

Loosened, fractured, or avulsed teeth

Severe trauma to the lower face may loosen teeth, completely displace them from their alveolar sockets, and/or cause dental fractures (Figure 8.8). It is

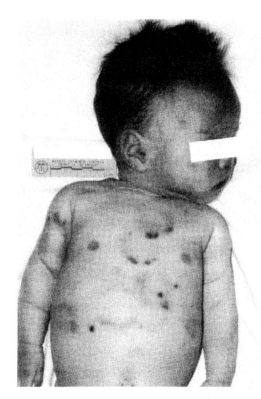

Figure 8.6 Multiple bite marks on fatal victim of child abuse.

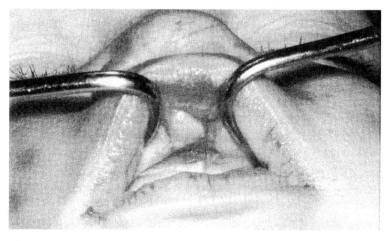

Figure 8.7 Classical child abuse injury in maxillary frenum area apparently caused by heavy blow to upper lip.

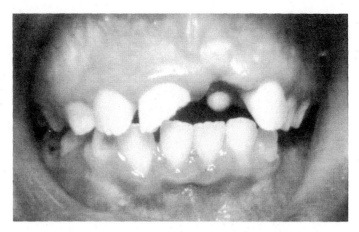

Figure 8.8 Traumatic injuries should be assessed to determine whether the injury is compatible with the explanation, and whether there is evidence of earlier trauma.

not uncommon for root fractures to occur, but this finding may be missed unless the radiographs are examined carefully.

These injuries, as well as most other traumatic injuries, may be accidental rather than abusive. Therefore, one must always determine whether the injury is compatible with the explanation given. If the dental injuries resulted from a fall, for example, one would usually expect to also find bruised or abraded knees, hands, or elbows. When these additional injuries are not present, further inquiry is appropriate.

In evaluating and reporting dental injuries, it may be helpful to use Andreasen's classification, based on a system adopted by the World Health Organization.[14] It is summarized below:

Crown infraction — incomplete fracture (crack) of enamel with loss of
  tooth substance
Uncomplicated crown fracture — confined to enamel or enamel and
  dentin, pulp not exposed
Complicated crown fracture — involves enamel and dentin, pulp is
  exposed
Uncomplicated crown-root fracture — involves enamel, dentin, and
  cementum, but does not expose pulp
Complicated crown-root fracture — involves enamel, dentin, cementum, and exposes pulp
Concussion — injury to supporting structures without abnormal loosening or displacement of the tooth, but with marked reaction to
  percussion

Subluxation (loosening) — injury to supporting structures with abnormal loosening, but without displacement of the tooth

Intrusive luxation — tooth displaced into alveolar bone, injury accompanied by comminution or fracture of alveolar socket

Extrusive luxation — tooth partially displaced out of its socket

Lateral luxation — tooth displaced in a direction other than axially, with comminution or fracture of alveolar socket

Exarticulation (complete avulsion) — tooth completely avulsed from socket

Comminution of alveolar socket — crushing and compression of alveolar socket, found with intrusive and lateral luxation

Fracture of alveolar socket wall — fracture confined to the labial or lingual socket wall

Fracture of mandible or maxilla — involves the base of mandible or maxilla and often the alveolar process, may or may not involve alveolar socket

Laceration of gingiva or oral mucosa — shallow or deep wound in mucosa resulting from tear, and normally produced by sharp object

Contusion of gingiva or oral mucosa — bruise usually caused by blunt object, no break in mucosa, usually causes small submucosal hemorrhage

Abrasion of gingiva or oral mucosa — superficial wound produced by rubbing or scraping mucosa, leaving raw, bleeding surface

Darkened and/or nonvital teeth

The tissues of the dental pulp receive their primary blood supply through the apical foramen. When the tooth receives a concussion, the apical blood vessels may be severed, or hematoma or edema may occlude the blood vessels as they enter the tooth.[15] As a consequence, the pulp may become necrotic and nonvital. Necrosis of the previously pink pulp tissues will usually cause a noticeable darkening of the tooth.

In some cases of dental trauma, the dental pulp's response to the injury may be to deposit additional secondary dentin in the pulp chamber. This may continue until the entire pulp chamber is filled in, or obtunded. Again, the loss of the hollow pulp chamber with its normally pinkish contents is likely to cause a change in the color of the tooth.

It is important to remember that both of the processes described above occur over a period of weeks, or even months. Consequently, when a child presents with current dental trauma and also has one or more dark teeth unrelated to caries, it is probable that the child has experienced previous trauma. Further inquiry to determine the nature of the trauma should be undertaken.[16]

Previously missing teeth
In examining a child who has experienced recent trauma, it may be noted
that one or more teeth has been lost prior to the present incident. The etiology
of this earlier tooth loss should be investigated. If it was due to "an accident",
a pattern of repeated trauma has been established. This pattern needs to be
evaluated, and child abuse is one of the possibilities to be considered.

Trauma to the lip
It is not uncommon to find contusions, lacerations, burns, or scars on the
lips of abused children. Bruises to the lip may result from forced feeding.
Burns on the lip, as well as burns on the face or tongue, may be signs of
physical punishment.[13] Bruises at the angles of the mouth may result from
efforts to gag or silence a child.

Trauma to the tongue
The tongue of an abused child may exhibit abnormal anatomy or function
due to scarring.[17] This may result from a burn or other trauma.

Other soft tissue injuries
Trauma to the mouth may also cause ulceration of the palate or uvula.
Additionally, lacerations are sometimes found in the floor of the mouth,
which may be caused by forced bottle feeding.

Fractures of jaws and associated structures
Fractures of the maxilla, mandible, and other cranial bones may be found in
cases of child abuse. If the radiologic study shows signs of old as well as new
fractures, a pattern of repeated trauma has been found, and needs to be
investigated with reference to possible child abuse.

The examination for maxillofacial fractures is performed within the concept
of overall patient care, including airway maintenance, control of hemorrhage,
and neurologic examination. In a significant number of jaw fractures there is
also damage to associated structures, including the cribriform plate, nasal, and
zygomatic bones. Intracranial lesions and skull fractures may also be present.

The diagnosis of fractures of the jaws is made primarily on the basis of
clinical and radiographic findings.[18] The clinical examination includes both
extraoral and intraoral palpation. Bilateral palpation is helpful to detect
asymmetry.

Swelling or ecchymosis in the lower face is suggestive of fractures of the
mandible. Fractures should also be suspected if there is an abrupt change in
the occlusal level of the teeth. This may be associated with open bite, difficulty
in opening the mouth, and facial asymmetry. Other signs and symptoms

include abnormal mobility of bony structures, or the ability to move the mandible beyond its normal excursion in any direction. Dingman and Natvig suggested supporting the angle of the mandible and pressing the anterior mandibular region up and down to detect fractures of the body of the mandible.[18] Crepitation and deviation of the midline on closing may be diagnostic signs, as well. Pain in the area of the temporomandibular joints may suggest fractures in this region.

The medical practitioner who observes dental trauma is well advised to seek consultation with a dentist experienced in dental injuries to children. This might be a pediatric dentist, oral and maxillofacial surgeon, or general dentist. This added expertise is important, not only to care for the present injury, but also to help evaluate previous trauma.

General neglect of the mouth

A child with rampant, untreated dental decay and poor oral hygiene is suffering from significant neglect. The consequences may be pain, infection, and a threat to the child's general health and well-being. The medical or dental practitioner who observes this condition, particularly if it continues after having been brought to the attention of the parents, should realize that the situation is no different than having parents neglect any other important medical condition. Moreover, this may be a sign of a more generalized problem in caring for the child. Indeed, Blain reports that a preliminary study supports the high correlation between dental neglect and CAN (child abuse and neglect).[19]

Health professionals faced with the need to decide when a case of dental neglect justifies reporting may be interested in guidelines developed by the California Society of Pediatric Dentistry. As reported by Blain, the following conditions should be considered reasons for reporting if the caretaker consciously fails to follow treatment recommendations in potentially life-threatening situations:

- Failure to provide prescribed antibiotics.
- Failure to seek treatment for cellulitis and its associated infections.
- Failure to seek treatment for any acute or chronic infection, including dental caries, when underlying life-threatening system conditions are present such as subacute bacterial endocarditis, glomerulonephritis, or juvenile-onset diabetes.

In addition, consideration should be given to reporting the following conditions if the dental situation is deteriorating to the point where irreversible harm will be done, leading to pain, discomfort, or a decrease in health or welfare:

- Diagnosed caries or periodontal diseases which have been referred for treatment and caretakers have failed to keep appointments.
- Presence of untreated traumatic injuries as indicated by nonvital teeth, avulsed permanent teeth, and injuries to soft tissues, including signs of scarring.
- Failure to seek recommended treatment for diagnosed severe malrelationships of the maxilla and mandible, including craniofacial anomalies, which may result in deficient speech, esthetic deformities, and psychological disturbances.

Relative Frequency of Lesions in Suspected Child Abuse

In a survey of 1155 primarily pediatric dentists, it was found that the principal dental injuries in cases of suspected child abuse, in descending order of frequency, were fractures of the teeth (32%), oral bruises (24%), oral lacerations (14%), fractures of the mandible or maxilla (11%), and oral burns (5%).[20] However, other authors report that lesions in which the oral mucosa is torn away from the gingiva may be the most common injury to the face, and may occur in as many as 50% of child abuse cases.[21]

Becker et al. reported that of the 14 cases in their series with **intraoral injuries**, 43% were contusions and ecchymoses, 28.5% were abrasions and lacerations, and 28.5% were dental trauma.[10]

Associated Facial Lesions

Becker et al. found that in their series of **facial injuries** in abused children, 66% of the injuries were contusions and ecchymoses, 28% were abrasions and lacerations, 3% were burns, 2% were fractures, and 1% were bites.[10]

Knowledge of the color changes associated with bruising may be important in determining when the injury occurred, and in determining whether other injuries occurred during the same event or at different times (See Figure 8.2 and Plate x). Kessler and Hyden point out that after the injury occurs, the area is usually tender and swollen, but the bruise may not be visible as a contusion or ecchymosis for 24 to 72 hours. A reddish-blue or purple color may be visible immediately or within the first 5 days. This initial color may change to green in 5 to 7 days, then to yellow in 7 to 10 days, then to brown in 10 to 14+ days, before clearing in 2 to 4 weeks.[12]

Injuries to the face may include trauma to the eyes, ears, and nose, as well as to the oral cavity. Blunt force trauma to the eye may cause periorbital bruises (black eyes), acute hyphema (blood in the anterior chamber of the eye), retinal and subconjunctival hemorrhage, ruptured globe, dislocated lens, optic atrophy, traumatic cataract, and detached retina.[12]

Direct trauma to the nose may cause deviated septum due to cartilage injury or hematoma formation. Such trauma may also cause nasal fractures, with accompanying bilateral periorbital ecchymosis. Injuries to the ear may be associated with twisting and bruising, while repeated blows may eventually result in a "cauliflower ear". Blows to the ear can also rupture the tympanic membrane or cause hemorrhage and hematoma formation.[13]

Bruises from hand slapping are not uncommon. In such cases the bruise may reproduce the outline of the hand in startling detail (Figure 8.5). As noted earlier, other cutaneous injuries may also take the shape of the object used to inflict the injury, such as a belt buckle or looped electric cord.[13]

It has been suggested that whenever bruises occur on both sides of the mouth or face at once, or if there is scarring of the lips, abuse should be suspected. Also, the presence of injuries on multiple body surfaces suggests abuse. McNeese and Hebeler point out that such multiplanar injuries would occur accidentally only as a result of tumbling falls (e.g., falling down stairs) or trauma incurred during automobile accidents.[13]

As noted earlier, the lips and corners of the mouth may show contusions, lacerations, burns, or scars due to the frequency of attack to the mouth in abused children. In the author's experience, bite marks on the face of children are most commonly found on or around the cheeks. However, they may occur on the ear, nose, chin, or elsewhere.

Documenting and Reporting Child Abuse

When one suspects child abuse, it is important to document the findings thoroughly. This record of the evidence is crucial for whatever legal proceedings may follow. Documentation may involve written notes, photographs, and radiographs. In some cases videotapes or audiotapes may be helpful. It is important that critical photographs of injuries include a ruler or scale held adjacent to the injury and on the same plane as the injured surface. When possible, 35-mm photography should be used.[22] Fortunately, cameras equipped for dental photography are ideal for photographing most body injuries.

It the child requires medical attention, referral should be made to the proper resource. Even if immediate medical care is not required, if a pediatrician is readily available the dentist may wish to consult regarding the suspected child abuse prior to reporting. However, the absence of consultation does not relieve the dentist from the responsibility to promptly report suspected abuse.

In the great majority of states, dentists, as health professionals, are required by law to report suspected cases of child abuse and neglect, and a penalty is provided for failure to report. All 50 states have child abuse legislation granting immunity to mandated reporters.[21]

To illustrate the reporting requirement, California law requires that any child-care custodian, health practitioner, nonmedical practitioner, or employee of a child protective agency who has knowledge of, or who observes a child whom he or she suspects has been the victim of child abuse, report to a child protective agency immediately or as soon as possible and send a written report within 36 hours of learning of the incident. The definition of health practitioner includes dentist resident, dental hygienist, and other licensed individuals, which includes the registered dental assistant. Also, the Penal Code provides that failure to report is a misdemeanor punishable by up to 6 months in jail or a fine not to exceed $1000, or both.[24]

The report can be made to the local police agency or welfare department. Persons desiring further information on the agency to call can phone the National Child Abuse Hotline at (800)422-4453 for referral to a local agency or for other supportive information.

In addition to criminal liability for failure to report, the practitioner could also face a civil lawsuit if there is subsequent injury to the child.[25]

In general, most states provide broad legal protection for health care practitioners who report child abuse. In the California example, the mandated reporter shall not be "civilly or criminally liable for any report required or authorized by this article."[24]

While lawsuits can still be brought against the reporter, they are likely to be dismissed under the immunity statutes. Considering the legal obligation to report and the statutory protection provided for the reporter, there would seem to be a greater risk from failing to report than from reporting.[26]

Problems in Dental Reporting of Child Abuse

It is generally agreed that the true number of child abuse cases is probably far in excess of the number of cases actually reported. Since a substantial number of abused children have injuries in or around the mouth, it would seem likely that dentists would be a significant source of child abuse reporting.[6,26] However, this has not been the case historically.

Blain reviewed the records of three large metropolitan hospitals and the state and local police reports of child abuse and neglect (CAN). Of the 1276 cases diagnosed as suspected or confirmed CAN, only one had been referred by a dentist.[17]

In a survey of general dentists and specialists in Massachusetts, with 537 responses, 95% of oral surgeons and 90% of pediatric dentists reported seeing cases of orofacial trauma. More than 8% of all dentists surveyed saw cases of orofacial trauma of a suspicious nature. The percentages were much higher for oral surgeons (22%) and pediatric dentists (18%) than for other dentists.

Although 22 cases of confirmed child abuse were noted in the responses, only 4 cases (18% of the suspected cases) had been reported to the appropriate agency.[10]

Malecz reported a survey of 155 dentists, 75% of whom practiced pediatric dentistry full or part time. Only 9% had ever filed a report, and 7% stated that under no circumstances would they do so. The most common reason given for unwillingness to report was uncertainty about the diagnosis, fear of litigation, unfamiliarity with symptoms of child abuse, possible effect on the practice, reluctance to believe one could inflict cruelties on one's offspring, and uncertainty about the reliability of the child's account of the injury. Significantly, the overwhelming majority felt they had inadequate training in the diagnosis of child abuse, and many who were surveyed stated that they would be interested in obtaining additional information on the subject.[20]

Blain has suggested that dental professionals may be negligent in their legal and social roles of preventing and intervening in cases of CAN.[17] He noted that, "This failure to report cases of child abuse violates state reporting laws; not reporting cases may, in effect, allow the continuation of child abuse, and more importantly, prevent both the child and his family from getting the social welfare and medical aid that they may need." However, Becker and co-workers pointed out that the low rate of reporting among dentists is similar to the low rate of physicians reporting confirmed abuse cases, as indicated in other reports.[10, 12]

It should be noted that in recent years efforts have been made to educate the dental profession and encourage appropriate reporting. New York State, for example, requires all dentists and dental hygienists to complete a two-hour course in the identification and reporting of child abuse as a condition of relicensure. Also, publications of the American Dental Association and material and presentations developed by the P.A.N.D.A. Coalition (which can be contacted through Delta Dental Plans) have played a significant role in heightening the dental profession's awareness of its responsibilities in this area.

Overdiagnosis of Child Abuse

While the importance of reporting suspected cases of child abuse and neglect cannot be overemphasized, the thoughtful practitioner should also consider the other side of the coin. When a child's problem is thought to be child abuse and it is not, considerable harm may be done to the child, the parents, and the doctor-patient relationship. Kaplan reviewed 15 cases that were misdiagnosed as child abuse. They included a child whose generalized bruises were later found to be related to cystic fibrosis.[27] McClain et al. reported on another supposedly abused child who was found to have acute lymphoblastic leukemia of childhood.[28] Kaplan concluded that overdiagnosing the battered child syndrome can be as harmful as failing to consider it.[27]

In an interesting recent case, physicians noted vaginal discharge in a nine-year-old girl. They suspected sexual abuse. The child was taken from the parents that same day and placed in protective custody for seven weeks. It was later determined that the discharge was due to chicken pox, rather than child abuse. The parents then sued the physician, hospital, and others.

Not surprisingly, the California appellate court held that the claims for malicious prosecution, defamation, and civil rights violation could not be maintained. They were consequences of the reporting and were barred because of the immunity provided by the Child Abuse Reporting Act. However, the court held that the claims for malpractice, false imprisonment, and intentional and negligent infliction of emotional distress could go forward. In so ruling, the court made it clear that the plaintiffs would be permitted to allege, if possible, only facts that may have occurred "outside the reporting process". Immunity under the Act extends only to the reporting and all results flowing from it.[29]

As a related matter, it is important for the dental team to be familiar with certain cultural practices that may produce lesions similar to those of child abuse. For example, children from Vietnamese families may present with ecchymotic lesions involving not only the back, but the face as well. These lesions may be produced by pinching the skin, or by rubbing it with a coin or cloth. This is part of the practice of *cao gio* (literally, "scratch the wind"), intended to free the body of "bad winds", believed responsible for various illnesses. The practice has been described as "pseudobattering" because the intent is to help rather than harm the child.[30]

Case Reports

As noted at the beginning of this chapter, dentists not only have the opportunity to report suspected cases of child abuse, they may also be in a position to assist the justice system in the investigation of crimes related to child abuse. Two such cases are presented here.

Case1: Identification of Murder Victim

On a college campus north of Los Angeles County, a boy was playing with his dog on an autumn day. He threw a stick into a clump of brush and trees, expecting the dog to retrieve it. Instead, the dog returned with a human hand and arm. Searchers ultimately recovered additional, mostly skeletonized remains of a young child.

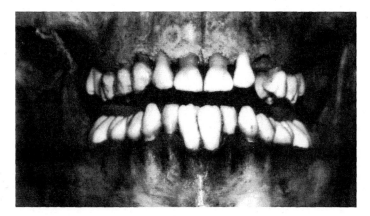

Figure 8.9 Case 1. Skull of child homicide victim shows crowding and overlap in mandibular incisor region.

The authorities suspected the body might be that of a six-year-old boy who had disappeared approximately three months earlier. With other methods of identification unavailable, the sheriff's department transported the skull to Los Angeles to see if dental evidence could be helpful (Figure 8.9).

A problem in this case was that no dental records of the suspected victim were available for examination. The youngster was reportedly caries-free and had never been to a dentist. The only dental information was in the form of two smiling photographs taken of the boy about ten weeks before he disappeared.

Dental radiographs were taken of the skull to assess dental and chronologic age (Figure 8.10). From the stage of development of the dentition, it was determined that the skull was consistent with that of a youngster approximately six years of age. In the absence of restorations or unique dental findings, it would be much more of a challenge to attempt to individualize the skull.

The photographs of the boy's face were enlarged as much as possible to enhance the visibility of the teeth without losing all detail (Figure 8.11). These photographs documented that the suspected victim's erupting mandibular central incisors were slightly crowded. This caused some rotation of the left central incisor, with the mesial surface turned labially and overlapping the right central incisor slightly. With allowance for some additional eruption since the photographs were taken, these findings of crowding and rotation matched the condition of the skull.

The author and the director of a large pediatric dental program then closely examined each tooth visible in the photograph and compared it to the corresponding tooth in the skull. The examiners looked at relative size and shape of the crown (including morphology of the incisal edge), height

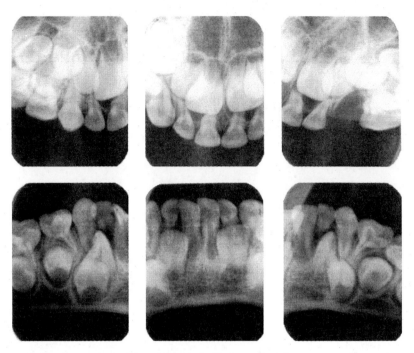

Figure 8.10 Case 1. Radiographs of skull show development and eruption pattern consistent with child approximately six years old.

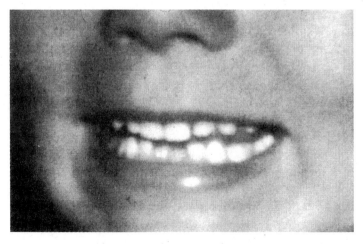

Figure 8.11 Case 1. Extreme enlargement of smiling photograph shows crowding and overlap of mandibular central incisors. Additional eruption occurred prior to death.

of the tooth and angular relationship to adjacent teeth, size and shape of embrasure, etc. This study yielded 14 variable features that matched, including 2 that were considered distinctive.

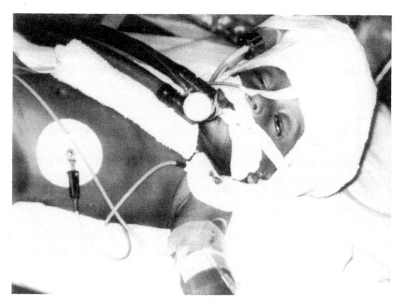

Figure 8.12   Case 2. Child abuse victim when examined in hospital. Bite mark is on left arm with portion of mark visible through tape.

The author reported his conclusion that the skull was that of the young boy in the photograph. Because the dental evidence was somewhat limited, the author suggested that the police also attempt to use other methods (if possible) to corroborate the dental findings. He was later informed that efforts to match friction ridges on the mummified soft tissues of the victim's extremities had succeeded, and had produced the same conclusion as the dental investigation. A suspect was arrested, tried, and convicted of the child's murder.

Case 2: Identification of Murder Suspect

A local police agency asked the author to examine a child abuse victim in the intensive care unit of a university hospital. The child appeared to have been severely beaten and was being maintained on life support systems (Figure 8.12). Although there were multiple contusions, the only area that could be clearly identified as a human bite mark was on the upper left arm, close to the axilla.

The bite mark appeared to be of poor evidentiary value (Figure 8.13). It included a faint, diffuse crescent-shaped arc that was consistent with a well-aligned human dental arch. The opposing arch left a small registration that lacked detail. In addition, there were three sets of striated contusions (scratches) that appeared as if they could have been caused by human teeth with rough edges. The child died several days after being examined at the hospital.

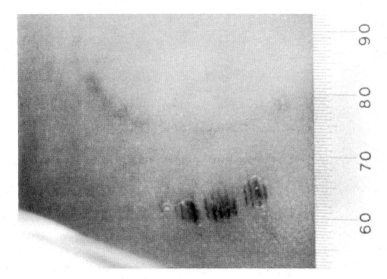

Figure 8.13   Case 2. Lower portion of bite mark showing faint mandibular arch and three sets of striated contusions or bruises.

The suspect in the case denied involvement in the crime and suggested that any bite marks would have been caused by the child's sister. Accordingly, the sister was bought in for examination. It was quickly determined that it would have been impossible for her very narrow deciduous dental arch to have caused the broad bite mark found in this case.

Further attention was then given to the casts of the suspect's teeth. It was noted that his mandibular teeth were well aligned and made a rather flat arch. When the cast of his mandibular arch was placed over a life-sized (1:1) photograph of the bite mark, it fit exactly as to size and shape. However, this only made the suspect a member of the class of people whose mandibular arch would be similar to the bite mark under study.

In evaluating individual characteristics of the suspect's teeth, it was noted that the mandibular right central incisor had a very slightly chipped incisal edge. In addition, the adjacent incisal portions of the tooth on each side also had slight chipping (Figure 8.14). However, it seemed very questionable that such slight irregularities would account for the distinct striated contusions or bruises found on the victim's body.

To evaluate this question, the author enlisted the assistance of a criminalist, with the intent of utilizing comparison microscopy. The plan was to compare the tooth irregularities with the scratch marks in the same manner that a tool mark examiner compares scratch marks on a damaged surface with features of a suspect tool. Ultimately, however, the criminalist made a series of test scratch marks in baseplate wax, using casts of the victim's teeth

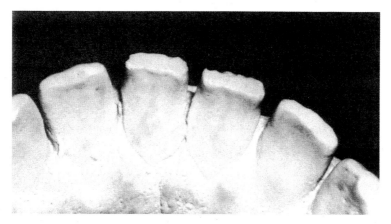

Figure 8.14 Case 2. Slight chipping is present on labial incisal edge of mandibular right central incisor and to a lesser extent on adjacent teeth.

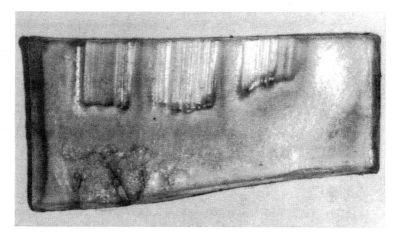

Figure 8.15 Case 2. Marks in wax produced experimentally, using mandibular cast of suspect's teeth.

(Figure 8.15). This made it possible to compare marks made by a known source (the suspect's teeth) against the striated marks found on the victim's body. The author made further tests and was able to replicate the criminalist's findings.

When the scratch marks in wax (made by the suspect's dental casts) were compared to the photographed scratch marks on the victim's body, it was noted that there was a high degree of correlation. There were similarities as to the spacing between the incisor teeth and to the nature of the striations caused by the irregular tooth surface. There was also correlation as to size of the teeth and their lack of rotation (Figure 8.16). Coupling these observations

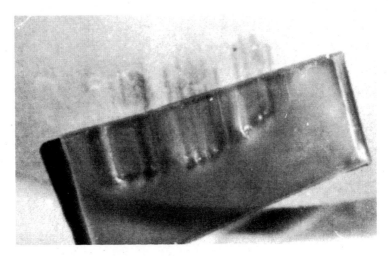

Figure 8.16   Case 2. Marks in wax produced by cast of suspect's teeth compared to marks on child's body.

with the matching dental arch form and size, it was the author's opinion that the suspect had bitten the child.

The results of the dental examination were then presented to the suspect. Although he had previously insisted on his innocence, he now decided to change his plea to guilty and was subsequently convicted in the child's death.

Summary and Conclusion

It is the author's view that there is no worthier goal than to save the life of a child. The dental team that is alert to the fact that many children are being abused, and that many of these abused children have injuries to the head and around the mouth, may be able to identify an abused child and institute steps that might save the child's life. Moreover, the dental team may also be in a position to assist in the apprehension and conviction of the individual responsible for abusing or killing a child.

In conclusion, the author wishes to emphasize the need to fulfill these obligations in a thoughtful and responsible manner. The practitioner should remember that incorrect or irresponsible accusations of child abuse can have a devastating effect upon the life of an innocent individual. With regard to expert testimony, the practitioner should remember that his or her obligations are the same, whether retained by the prosecution or the defense. The expert's role is not to act as an advocate for one side or the other. The expert's role is to assist the judge or jury in the search for truth.

Acknowledgments

The author expresses his appreciation to Drs. Richard Mungo, Joseph Anselmo, Betty Hoffman, and Mr. Steven Dowell for their valued participation in the cases presented. Sincere thanks is also given to Dr. Hugh Kopel, who provided Figure 8.8.

References

1. Wiese, D. and Daro, D., Current trends in child abuse reporting and fatalities: the results of the 1994 annual fifty state survey, National Committee to Prevent Child Abuse, Working Paper 808, April, 1995.

2. Fain, D. B. and McCormick, G. M., Unusual case of child abuse homicide/suicide, *J. Forensic Sci.*, 33, 554, 1988.

3. American Humane Association, Child Protection Leader, December, 1, 1991.

4. McDermott, R. F., Abused children need you, *Aide*, 12, 8, 1992.

5. Sanger, R. G. and Bross, D. C., Implications of child abuse and neglect for the dental profession, *J. Am. Dent. Assoc.*, 104(1), 55, 1982.

6. Croll T. P. et al., Primary identification of an abused child in a dental office: a case report, *Pediatr. Dent.*, 3(4), 339, 1981-82.

7. Silverstein, H., Child abuse I.D. and reporting in New York, *Forensic Odontology News*, Winter, 2, 1992

8. Schwartz, S., Oral manifestations and legal aspects of child abuse, *J. Am. Dent. Assoc.*, 95(3), 591, 1977.

9. Cameron, J. M. et al., The battered child syndrome, *Med. Sci. Law*, 6, 2, 1966.

10. Becker, D. B. et al., Child abuse and dentistry: orofacial trauma and its recognition by dentists, *J. Am. Dent. Assoc.*, 97(7) 24, 1978.

11. Sperber, N. D., The dual responsibility of dentistry in child abuse, *J. Calif. Dent. Assoc.*, 3, 31, 1980.

12. Kessler, D. B. and Hyden, P., Physical, sexual, and emotional abuse of children, *Clin. Symp.*, 43(1), 4, 1991.

13. McNeese, M. C. and Hebeler, J. R., The abused child: a clinical approach to identification and management, *Clin. Symp.*, 29(5), 1, 1977.

14. Andreasen, J. O., *Traumatic Injuries of the Teeth*, W. B. Saunders, Philadelphia, 1981, chap. 1.

15. Finn, S. B., *Clinical Pedodontics*, W. B. Saunders, Philadelphia, 1973, chap. 11.

16. Hamilton, J., Child abuse: the dentist's responsibility, *Chicago Dent. Soc. Rev.*, 83 (9), 19, 1990.

17. Blain, S. M., Child abuse, *Pediatric Dentistry; Scientific Foundations and Clinical Practice*, Stewart, R. E. et al., C. V. Mosby, St. Louis, 1981, chap. 64.

18. Dingman, R.O. and Natvig, P., *Surgery of Facial Fractures*, W. B. Saunders, Philadelphia, 1964, chap 3.

19. Blain, S. M., Abuse and neglect as a component of pediatric treatment planning, *J. Calif. Dent. Assoc.*, 19(9), 1991.

20. Malecz, R. E., Child abuse, its relationship to pedodontics: a survey, *J. Dent. Child.*, 46(3), 193, 1979.

21. Council on Dental Practice, *The Dentist's Responsibility in Identifying and Reporting Child Abuse*, American Dental Association, Chicago, 1987, p.5.

22. Reiter, C., Crimes against children, *RDH*, Apr. 16, 1990.

23. Carpenter, C., Child abuse recognition and reporting: putting an end to a destructive cycle, *NY State Dent. J.*, 3, 37, 1991.

24. California Penal Code, Secs. 11166, 11172(c),11172(a).

25. *Landeros v. Flood*, 17 Cal.3d, 399, 1976.

26. Tennenhouse, D., Legal forum, *Nursing Review*, May, June, 26, 1988.

27. Kaplan, J.M., Pseudoabuse — the misdiagnosis of child abuse, *J. Forensic Sci.*, 31, 1420, 1986.

28. McClain, J.L., Clark, M. A., and Sandusky, G. E., Undiagnosed, untreated acute lymphoblastic leukemia presenting as suspected child abuse, *J. Forensic Sci.*, 35, 375, 1990.

29. *Cream v. Mitchell*, CA2d, 264 Cal Reporter, 876.

30. Primosch, R. E. and Young, S. K., Pseudobattering of Vietnamese children (cao gio), *J. Am. Dent. Assoc.*, 101(1), 47, 1980.

Mass Disaster Management

9

WILLIAM M. MORLANG II

Introduction

The world has experienced a plethora of mass disasters in recent years — hurricanes, earthquakes, floods, typhoons, mud slides, transportation mishaps, aircraft accidents, fires, volcanic eruptions, industrial accidents, terrorist acts, and armed conflicts.[1-9] In addition to naturally occurring disasters, as the world population increases technology expands and life becomes more complicated. As a result, we may anticipate more untoward events generated by people. The role that forensic dentistry and the forensic science community plays in such disasters varies with the jurisdiction throughout the world.[10-20] The response to a disaster may also differ. Society, religion, government structure, laws, and resources are some of the response-determining factors.[21-32] The identification of human remains in mass disasters allows surviving family members to go through the grieving process; place legal, business, and personal affairs in order, and continue with the processes of life. Formal documentation of death requires positive identification and is essential to the collection of life insurance, the settlement of estates, actions in wrongful death suits, remarriages, and in some cases, federal intelligence issues. The lack of a death certificate, in most jurisdictions, results in extensive legal problems for surviving family members which may span many years. The investigation into the cause, the manner and the mechanism of the death allows for improvements in safety, design, health care, wellness, and life in general.

The goals of this chapter are (1) to provide an overview of disaster management, (2) to detail the role of forensic dentistry in the identification of human remains in mass disasters, and (3) to provide a protocol that integrates the forensic science sections into an Identification Center. The

---

* The views expressed in this article are those of the author and do not reflect the official policies or position of the Department of Defense or the U.S. Government.

protocol presented is not the only approach to human remains identification in mass disasters. It has, however, been developed in response to and utilized in some of the largest disasters in modern history. The protocol can be scaled up or down in size and scope to meet the local need. If your jurisdiction does not already have an Identification Center plan, it offers a starting point. For those with an established response plan, it is food for thought and a plan enhancement tool.

Disaster Assistance

When the magnitude of a disaster overpowers the local jurisdiction, one must remember that public law provides for assistance. The local authorities formally request assistance from the county and then from the state government. The State Governor may request assistance from the Federal Government through the President and the Federal Emergency Management Agency (FEMA). Once support is approved, federal agencies can lend assistance. Military Services in the local area can help with immediate life-saving activities in the civil sector, but once that is accomplished, their efforts must stop until federal approval of support is gained. The Federal Bureau of Investigation (FBI) has a disaster fingerprint team on call that can respond rapidly to a mishap such as an aircraft accident with a known population. They respond with fingerprint data from their files on persons listed on the airline manifest or believed involved. A telephone point of contact for this team is (202) 324-5401. The Federal Aviation Administration (FAA) and National Transportation Safety Board (NTSB) are also immediately available for aviation and transportation mishaps. These three federal agencies are governed by a different series of public laws that permit their direct response to a request for assistance by a local jurisdiction without FEMA involvement, or are required to act in the event of aircraft or transportation mishap.

Disaster Site Management

In the recovery phase of the disaster, a 500 to 2000-ft security cordon should be established outward from the disaster site. An entry control point for the cordon is placed upwind of the site. An access list is developed and all personnel within the cordon must wear identification badges. These actions are necessary to protect disaster evidence, staff, and bystanders. Once the site has been declared safe by fire department and safety personnel, an overlapping ground search should be undertaken by a specially trained recovery team. The team carefully searches the site for human remains or fragments.

Fragmentation and commingling of remains will be a major problem with high g force mishaps. The integument will be the organ system most often found in such cases. The training of this recovery team is critical to the success of the Identification Center. The Identification Center staff is limited by the evidence recovery expertise of the staff in the field. Professional staffing on the recovery team pays a big dividend in successful team action and facilitates the gross identification of human material in the field. As the recovery team accomplishes its task, it should mark the locations where human remains or fragments are found. A body recovery tag should be placed on each specimen. The numbering system should be as simple as possible ... 1, 2, 3, ... Tags can be prenumbered prior to the disaster to avoid duplication and errors in the field. If multiple recovery teams are working, again, keep the system simple ... Team A, Team B, Team C. Tags should read: A-1, A-2, A-3 ... B-1, B-2, B-3 ... C-1, C-2, C-3. The use of computers and bar code readers can be most helpful from the beginning in remains/fragment tracking, documentation, and management. A grid chart or map should be developed that graphically relates the remains to the site and other evidence points. Remains exposed to fire require special attention prior to movement. Normally, dental identification may be the only identification methodology available in severe burn cases. The heads of severe burn cases should be wrapped in elastic bandage and then in plastic prior to movement to protect dental evidence that could otherwise be dislodged or lost. Once the body has been prepared, it is placed in a recovery bag for transport to the identification center. The On-Site Command Post must carefully track the movement of bodies from the site. Each jurisdiction must ensure they have an adequate supply of recovery bags and be aware of a rapid replacement source. Dealing with human remains without recovery bags is traumatic and labor intensive. The remains should be removed to the Identification Center and refrigerated to approximately 37°F as soon as possible. Refrigerated trailers and railroad cars are efficient means to deal with this task in time of disaster: 50 to 75 bodies can be stored per trailer, depending on size. Once all the remains have been removed from the site, it is wise to repeat the overlapping ground search. You will be surprised at the large volume of body fragments and personal effects that will be located with the second effort.

Disaster Management

Preplanning, organization, coordination, and disaster response exercises are the keys to successful disaster management.[33-37] In reviewing mass disasters to date, the problems haven't changed. The major problems facing a forensic identification center in time of mass disaster are

1. Large numbers of human remains
2. Fragmented, commingled, and burned remains
3. Difficulty in determining who was involved in the disaster
4. Acquisition of meaningful medical and dental records and radiographs
5. Legal, jurisdictional, organizational and political issues
6. Internal and external documentation and communications problems.

In most jurisdictions, there are three or four legally admissible methodologies used to identify human remains: (1) visual identification, (2) fingerprints or footprint identification, (3) dental identification, and (4) DNA evidence. The visual methodology is the least reliable due to subjective factors and the stressful situation in which a relative or friend is placed. The fingerprint mode is long respected, but is subject to the availability of antemortem prints on file or retrievable latent prints from personal effects. Trauma and fire associated with mass disasters sometimes destroy postmortem fingerprint and footprint evidence. Most military aircrew members have footprints on file and routinely wear flying boots that protect their feet. Additionally, many military flyers also wear a "dog tag" in their boots. The dental structures are highly resistant to destruction, but dental identification is also subject to available antemortem dental records and radiographs. Dental radiographs afford abundant objective evidence when antemortem and postmortem radiographs are compared. Full mouth dental and panoral radiographs detail unique and individual anatomy for comparison even in the absence of dental restorations. The Department of Defense (DOD) has established a backup file of panoral radiographs for all military members in the event their dental records are destroyed or are not available. These panoral radiographs remain on file indefinitely, even after the individual has left the armed forces. The telephone point of contact for this DOD Panoral Radiograph Repository in Monterey, California is (408) 646-1010. The dental insurance industry utilizes dental radiographs extensively, therefore, dental radiographs are far more available from private providers and insurance companies in time of contingency. In recent years, dental record keeping has also been enhanced. The unique and individual patterns of palatal rugae may play a positive role.[38]

DNA comparison is legally admissible in a growing number of jurisdictions, but is somewhat limited due to the availability of antemortem comparison data.[39-42] The Armed Forces Institute of Pathology and the Armed Forces Medical Examiner have proposed that a blood sample for all military members be maintained on file for DNA comparison.[43] If immediate relatives of the victim are available, the genetic makeup may be established without an antemortem DNA record of the victim being on file.

Medical records, both inpatient and outpatient, with associated radiographs also give the pathologist and anthropologist a wealth of antemortem information for postmortem comparison. Medical and dental records of persons with prior federal service are retired to the National Records Repository in St Louis. A telephone point of contact for this agency is (314) 263-7261.

It is important to recognize that there are no acute emergencies in the forensic sciences. Time is required and must be provided for quality work. If postmortem material is available, one should make identifications in multiple modes for confirmation purposes. If the identification is questioned in court, the availability of multiple modes of positive identification is beneficial, especially if one mode is not admitted to the court. A case should be signed out only after all sections in the Identification Center have completed their efforts and the findings jointly evaluated. Discrepancies and conflicts are easiest to resolve at this point. Each jurisdiction must establish the forensic forms to be used in time of disaster. It is wise to make this selection in advance and to store a supply of the required forms. At a minimum the following forms are needed:

1. Anatomic pathology
2. Anthropology
3. Personal effects
4. Fingerprint/footprint
5. Antemortem/postmortem/summary dental
6. Identification/death certificate.

Completing these forms during training exercises prepares the staff for their use when needed.

Forensic Identification Center Organization

Experiences with the Big Thompson Canyon Flood, the Pan Am/KLM Tenerife mishap, the Jonestown Guyana tragedy, the LOT Polish Airline accidents, the terrorist explosions in Beirut, the Arrow Airways mishap in Newfoundland, the Battleship Iowa explosion, and other disasters have shown that a multidisciplinary disaster Identification Center (Figure 9.1) with a forensic sciences processing line (Figure 9.2) is highly effective in the identification of large numbers of human remains. Each section noted (Figure 9.1) should have a team chief responsible to the Identification Center team chief. The success of this organization is keyed to preplanning, cooperation, and smooth communications between all sections. Daily staff meetings are a necessity at two levels: between the center chief and the section chiefs, and within the various forensic sections. In the early stages of operation,

DISASTER IDENTIFICATION CENTER ORGANIZATION SCHEME

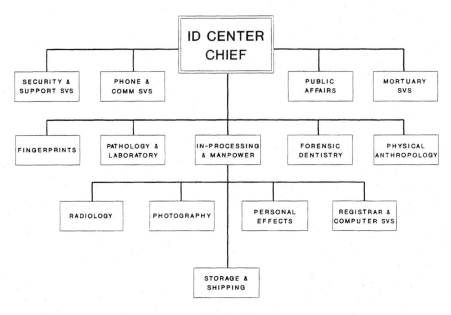

Figure 9.1

IDENTIFICATION CENTER PROCESSING SCHEME

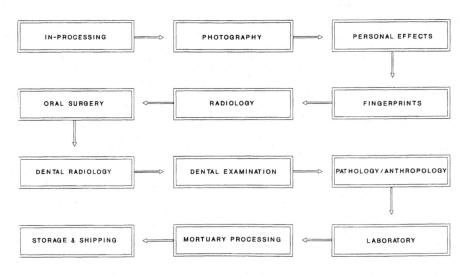

Figure 9.2

multiple daily meetings are essential for problem identification and resolution. Data flow between all sections must be orderly to enable each section
to capitalize on what other sections have learned (Figure 9.3). For example,
time can be saved if the Forensic Dentistry Section knows that the Personal
Effects Section has found a name in an article of clothing or a military
identification tag on a particular body. Time can be saved for the FBI in
fingerprint data review if the dental section forwards to them the name
discovered on a dental appliance. The FBI is then able to do a direct comparison, saving countless hours in postmortem print classification. The
golden rule in the Identification Centers must be SUCCESS = TEAMWORK!
Positive identification should be pursued by all sections and the cases should
be signed out by the Identification Center chief after all sections have completed their investigation and a positive identification is confirmed in as many
modalities as is reasonably possible. Remember, most courts recognize only
three or four evidence modes for the identification of human remains. Sup-
press the urge to make positive identifications based upon personal effects
such as a "dog tag", tattoo, or item of jewelry, or by association or exclusion.
View these latter factors as clues in the antemortem/postmortem comparison
process. In working jewelry clues, a jeweler on your staff can be most helpful
in working descriptions of high-cost postmortem jewelry evidence against
insurance policy descriptions. Remember to log and safeguard high-value
items recovered. One individual responsible for such tasks establishes
accountability. In all cases, rely on objective scientific evidence for positive
identification.[44,45] The status of human remains may be thought of in three
categories: (1) positive identification, (2) findings consistent between antemortem and postmortem records, and (3) unidentified.

Registrar, computer services, communication services, public affairs,
mortuary service, security, and support services are critical sections supporting the Identification Center chief and the various forensic science sections.
The source of information emanating from the Identification Center must
be either the Identification Center chief or the Public Affairs officer. A manpower bank and storage/shipping section are also vital. In a large disaster,
the forensic processing line (Figure 9.2) is best implemented by placing each
set of human remains on a gurney cart. Each case is then moved from section
to section in the forensic processing line by a volunteer attendant from the
manpower section. The attendant should only move the body to the next section
and should not accompany the body through the entire processing line.

An Identification Center processing checklist (Figure 9.4) accompanies
each case, is carefully maintained, and is signed by each forensic section/sub-
section chief. This keeps the process orderly and aids in passing significant
data between the forensic sections in the processing line. The processing
begins with the In-Processing Section which maintains a log (Figure 9.5) on

FORENSIC DATA FLOW

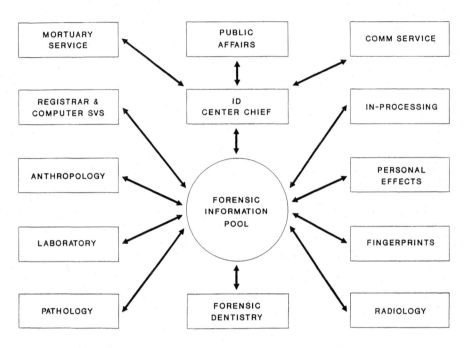

Figure 9.3

each case and is responsible for the whereabouts and storage of each case. It is essential that this section catch any remains numbering problems generated in the field and resolve them before the body begins its journey down the processing line. The prenumbered log will also serve to catch any duplicate case numbers received at the Identification Center from the disaster site. If the bodies were recovered from an armed conflict, terrorist act, or a mishap associated with hazardous materials, it is essential that the In-Processing Section conduct a search for hazards. To locate explosives, the use of an E Scan, explosive ordnance personnel, and chemical detectors may be indicated. Remember that life support systems for military aircrew members may contain explosive devices. Seek expert aid in this regard. The presence of a bioenvironmental engineer on the staff can be highly valuable to the Identification Center chief, the On Site Command Post, the In-Processing Section and all Radiology Sections.

Each section should be somewhat redundant in their professional procedures and record keeping to address mistakes as they occur, since people working under Identification Center stresses may make more mistakes than might normally be expected.

```
IDENTIFICATION CENTER PROCESSING CHECKLIST


IDENTIFICATION NUMBER: _____

SECONDARY NUMBER: _____

FACILITY: _____ LOCATION: _____

MISHAP: _____



        SECTION                DATE              SIGNATURE

1.   IN-PROCESSING

2.   PHOTOGRAPHY

3.   PERSONAL EFFECTS

4.   FINGERPRINT

5.   RADIOLOGY

6.   ORAL SURGERY

7.   DENTAL RADIOLOGY

8.   DENTAL EXAM

9.   PATH/ANTHROPOLOGY

10.  LABORATORY

11.  MORTUARY PROCESSING

12.  STORAGE

        STORAGE LOCATION: _____

SIGNIFICANT FINDINGS/REMARKS: _____

_____

_____

_____
```

Figure 9.4

General Medical Considerations

Jurisdiction in time of mass disaster is a pivotal issue. Jurisdiction can be viewed as local, county, state, or federal, and can be exclusive or concurrent. Most deaths of U.S. citizens overseas are in the jurisdiction of the State Department, (202-647-1512), although some military-associated deaths may be governed by Status of Forces Agreements. Agreements made in advance between area agencies with overlapping concerns speed disaster response operations and avoid or limit disputes during a crisis situation.

In mass disasters, the application of sound forensic science procedures is essential. Sometimes, because of the magnitude of the mishap, there is the

IN-PROCESSING HUMAN REMAINS LOG						
NO.	REFRIGERATOR LOCATION	TEMPORARY LOCATION	DATE RECEIVED	DATE PROCESSED	REMARKS	DISPOSITION
1						
2						
3						
4						
5						
6						
7						
8						
9						
10						
11						
12						
13						
14						
15						
16						
17						
18						

Figure 9.5

tendency among some nonforensic managers to shortcut established scientific procedures. When possible, this should be avoided. Take the time to do the proper procedure correctly from the outset. One never knows where a mishap investigation will lead, such as in the case of the explosion aboard the U.S.S. Iowa. Well-established forensic medical and dental procedures were a key in the final resolution and drew praise because they were well indicated and precisely accomplished. Positive identifications established duty stations within the turret that day. Injury patterns reflected what each sailor was doing at the time of the explosion. Type and severity of injury helped detail the location and forces of the explosion.

The medical-legal autopsy is indicated in accidental, unexpected, or unattended death. Homicide, suicide, and death in confinement are other reasons for this procedure in most jurisdictions. The medical-legal autopsy is a special procedure directed by legal authority normally within 24 hours of death before the body is embalmed.

Identification of the deceased is a prime task in this autopsy procedure. The reason for this postmortem examination is to determine cause, manner, and mechanism of death. Particular attention is devoted to injury patterns, time of death, scene evidence, and circumstances surrounding the death. Time of death can usually be estimated by core body temperature change, insect activity, or the onset of rigor. The autopsy report includes, in addition to the above concerns, an extensive external description, comments regarding evidence of health care, results of organ system examination, results of radiographic, microscopic tissue, and toxicology studies in addition to a summary listing cause and manner of death. Manner of death may be listed as accidental, homicide, suicide, natural, or undetermined. Perhaps more undetermined deaths could be resolved with expanded toxicology studies. Basic toxicology studies will screen for carbon monoxide, lactic acid, volatiles, drugs, and chemicals.[46] The following specimens are usually required: blood, urine, vitreous humor, and major organ tissue samples. If the specimens cannot be immediately delivered to the laboratory they may be preserved by refrigeration or freezing, as indicated. The Armed Forces Institute of Pathology Forensic Toxicology Laboratory is able to screen for over 35,000 substances.

Captain Glenn N. Wagner, MC, USN, a friend and well-respected forensic and aerospace pathologist, has a series of Forensic Pathology Rules that apply to disaster management:

1. Never assume anything.
2. You can never have too much evidence.
3. Don't get caught with insufficient evidence if you can avoid it.
4. When in doubt: "Max Out".

Aircraft accidents are the disaster with which we are most frequently confronted. Principles of aerospace pathology are generally relevant to other disaster situations. Investigation of aerospace accidents includes mishap reconstruction to determine the cause, with the secondary aim of how to prevent future accidents and make flying safer for everyone.[47-49] Design of aircraft, equipment, instruments, aircraft seats, interiors, materials, life support systems, restraint systems, and egress systems are impacted by these investigations. Presently, aircraft mishaps are caused by a variety of factors. The leading causes, approximately 70%, are human factors. This is followed by mechanical and environmental factors in equal proportions. Human factors are obviously the major player and are hopefully of the greatest interest to health care professionals. We have a great opportunity, as we investigate these accidents, to benefit safety, survivability, and preventive medicine. In the evaluation of human factors, three components are considered: physiological, psychological, and pathological. Issues pursued in the physiological component are hypoxia, hypoglycemia, dehydration, hypo/hyperthermia, disorientation, and fatigue. Mental health, crew rest, and interviews with family and friends are issues reviewed under the psychological component for contributory input. The pathological component delves into preexisting disease, the environment, and postcrash trauma. Development of new entry-level medical standards for flyers, in addition to enhanced wellness and physical fitness programs, have been offshoots of such data collection.

Injury patterns tell the story of the mishap.[50,51] Thermal, blast, blunt force, decelerative, impact, intrusive, or combined injuries afford evidence of the event. Injuries give insight to the g forces developed in the mishap: vertebral injuries: 20 to 30 g, tears in the aorta: 50 g, transected aorta: 80 to 100 g, pelvic fractures: 100 to 200 g, and body fragmentation: 300+ g. Time is a determining factor in the g forces the human body can survive. The body may withstand a 40-g pulse over a very short period, but not survive a 10-g load over a longer period. Another indicator of g forces involved may be the aircraft itself. Some aircraft have g force indicators which may be recovered. As a rule of thumb, if the aircraft is generally intact and recognizable, probably less than 20-g forces were involved. Air speed, angle of attack, impact forces, dispersal patterns of the wreckage, occupiable space, restraint systems, environment, energy absorption, and post-crash environment are reviewed. The mishap report includes sections on survivability, injuries, preexisting conditions, psychological factors, physiological factors, personal equipment, and egress.

Examples of positive results from mishap reconstruction and injury analysis include a 20-g aircraft seat, improved restraint systems, crash-worthy fuel tanks, flexible fuel lines with force limit disconnects, new cabin materials that do not produce toxic fumes in fires, improved egress patterns, and superior egress lighting systems. The collection of data over the life span of an aircraft type clearly aids future technology.

It is valuable for all Identification Center professional personnel to understand the "Big Picture" associated with mishap or disaster investigation so that all may constructively contribute to the forensic process.

A last medical consideration is the safety and well-being of the Identification Center staff. Occupational Safety and Health Administration (OSHA) guidelines on radiology, hazardous materials, and bloodborne pathogens apply to the Identification Center. Protective procedures and equipment are essential. Disposal of contaminated waste is of concern. These factors are critical in preplanning, training, and logistics.

Mental Health Considerations

Working to identify human remains is a difficult task which will be stressful to the staff, both from a physical and a mental standpoint.[52-56] Each individual will react differently to stress. All are at risk — especially the young assistants and technicians who have not been gradually exposed to trauma, gross anatomy, and death. The majority of health care providers have been afforded time in professional schools to adapt to these issues. The forensic team member is exposed to visual and olfactory distress and is forced to come face to face with his or her own mortality. Each person's background, experience, and religious beliefs provide the mental tools for dealing with this stress. The positive knowledge that they are helping the deceased person and the deceased person's family to progress with life is paramount.

Stress is cumulative and is dose related. It is a product of work in the Identification Center and at the disaster site. It is the summation of the work, the sights, the sounds, the odors, the hours, and the environment combined with the disruption of their normal way of life, their normal work patterns, and family activities.

The Identification Center staff will develop adaptive mechanisms that will allow them to cope, such as humor, escape mechanisms, altruism, perspective, and support modalities. One chief area of concern is the clear possibility that some of the staff may develop maladaptive coping mechanisms such as the "macho male routine", denial, substance abuse, numbing, and impulsive behavior. Consequently, you must actively look after the mental health status of the Identification Center staff very carefully. This area was neglected in several of the world's largest disasters and staff members are still undergoing professional care for posttraumatic stress disorder, adjustment problems, substance abuse, and depression. Be careful not to repeat the mistake. Symptoms of problems might include flashbacks, dreams, insomnia, apathy, avoidance, and dysphoria.

As you keep a watchful eye on the professional family within the Identification Center, you will note that the warning signs may either be quite subtle or more easily recognized, such as hysterical crying. The withdrawal mechanism is more common but more difficult to recognize. This may range from gradual withdrawal to a blank, glazed expression. After Identification Center activities are completed and the team has returned to their homes, families, and normal day-to-day life, many things may linger — sadness, recollections, dreams, lack of enthusiasm, chronic fatigue and the desire to avoid deep feelings about anything. Recognizing these issues is the first step to avoiding mental health problems. There are many things you can do to help your staff cope:

- Use volunteers
- "In and Out" briefings on mental health ... "what to expect" ... "what's normal"
- Good training and exposure to problems in advance during exercises
- Know your staff well, know their normal behavior and note change
- Good work areas, good equipment, proper support
- Reasonable work hours — 12 hours maximum
- Rotation of staff between subsections when possible
- Don't permit volunteers to push a case to all processing line stations
- Don't identify with remains, concentrate on professional aspects
- Observe the staff carefully each day, especially at start and end

- Encourage friendship, support, and quality teamwork
- Watch for substance abuse and excess alcohol use
- Good quarters and full hot meals
- Good work clothes and full, rapid laundry support
- Clean rest rooms, showers, and break room
- Good ventilation
- Unwind together at the end of the day
- Have dinner together
- Gain adequate sleep and rest
- Encourage chaplains to be in the work area
- Have mental health providers available but not in immediate work area
- Encourage humor
- Play reasonable music in the work area
- Keep perspective, keep in touch with family by phone
- Praise the staff and reward excellence
- Limit criticism, be constructive, keep such actions in private
- Recognize the humanitarian actions being accomplished.
- Care for each other
- Lead by example, be devoted to quality

Forensic Dentistry Considerations

A Forensic Dentistry Section should be an integral part of the organization of the disaster Identification Center. The Forensic Dentistry Section (Figure 9.6) should be divided into three subsections and should be headed by a team chief responsible to the Identification Center chief. The role of the chief of the Forensic Dentistry Section is that of manager, facilitator, coordinator, and spokesperson for the section. Each subsection of the Forensic Dentistry Section should have a person designated as being responsible for the activities of that subsection.

The role of the postmortem dental examination and dental radiology subsection is perhaps the most straightforward and uncomplicated of the three subsections, and is the actual part of the dental section that is within the forensic processing line. A forensic photographer should be available to provide photographic support during the postmortem examinations. In a large mass disaster where severe burning of the victims has occurred, the postmortem dental examination team should be further divided into three parts. As the remains are received in the dental section portion of the processing line (see Figure 9.2), the first part of the dental team, made up of oral surgeons, accomplishes the necessary facial dissection to allow the oral cavity to be visualized and radiographed. In large mass disasters, the practice of

FORENSIC DENTISTRY SECTION

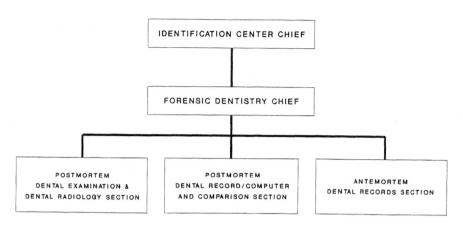

Figure 9.6

removing the maxilla and mandible is not encouraged due to time, resource, and legal considerations.

A facial dissection technique described in Appendix 9.1 provides access for examination, radiology, and photography. Dissection is undertaken on nonviewable remains. In general, dissection can be legally accomplished to the degree necessary to identify the body, but should be undertaken in concert with the guidance of the Identification Center chief. Facial dissection is absolutely essential in severe burn cases. After the facial dissection has been accomplished, the remains are moved to the next area within the postmortem dental examination subsection for dental radiographs.

A full-mouth postmortem dental radiographic series is accomplished utilizing a portable dental X-ray unit. A 50-kVP dental radiographic instrument is quite adequate since normal exposure factors can generally be reduced by one quarter to one half when working with severely burned victims because of water loss from the body. Adequate shielding of the radiology area is important as well as an X-ray dose film badge system for monitoring personnel working in the dental radiology area. The use of automatic dental X-ray film processors with daylight loading hoods is recommended. This avoids the requirement for a darkroom. The film processor should produce dry films ready for mounting. Only one case at a time should be introduced into the film processor to avoid commingling of dental radiographs. A dentist must review film quality and mounting at this point and retake radiographs where indicated. Once the body departs the dental section, retakes of radiographs become a significant problem. The use of dental radiology in forensic dentistry is an absolute necessity. Dental radiographs provide objective evidence that is essential within the scientific community and in court. The comparison of antemortem and postmortem dental radiographs allows for the positive identification of victims by radiographic visualization of the anatomy of oral structures, existing restorations, materials, pathology, root canal therapy, previous surgical procedures, fractures and prosthetic devices. In those cases where a normal dentition exists and where no previous restorations are present, the unique character of the individual's dental apparatus viewed radiographically will usually permit an identification to be made if antemortem radiographs are available. Radiographs usually permit identification of dental fragments containing as little as one tooth if a restoration or unique anatomic characteristic is present.

Flat plate radiographs of the entire body, although expensive, provide significant medical and anthropological evidence and are an excellent tool for locating personal effects and dental fragments in commingled, charred remains.[57-59] Normally, the only bottlenecks in the forensic processing line are in the dental radiology section or the medical radiology section.

Cataloging of personal effects is also time consuming, but does not normally slow the processing line. With adequate staffing and proper equipment these bottlenecks can be avoided. The well-planned forensic processing line can complete 75 to 100 cases per day. After a full-mouth postmortem dental radiographic series has been taken, the case is then moved on for a dental examination.

After a thorough cleaning of dental structures with a dilute bleach solution, a team of three dentists, or two dentists and a dental hygienist or assistant, charts all dental evidence on a postmortem dental record form (Figure 9.7). The entire dental team must agree to be consistent in the charting methods. Dental charting methodology is presented in Appendix 9.3. You may use any good charting system, but you must be consistent in its use in the Identification Center. Examples of the selected charting format should be provided for reference to all team members. The universal numbering system is preferred because it is simple in nature and is easily computerized. The use of a fiber-optic light is invaluable in the examination process. The examiner begins by evaluating tooth #1 and associated radiographs. The second dentist on the examination team evaluates tooth #1 and confirms the findings of the first dentist. The recorder charts the finding of tooth #1 and all three team members confirm the charting. Tooth #2 is examined and the process repeated until all 32 teeth have been charted. The approach is redundant, but errors are corrected as they are made. Charting should be done in pen, not pencil. Errors should be corrected in a legally acceptable fashion. Sometimes it is effective to begin a new form in order to present an error-free form in court. Findings to be recorded during the postmortem examination

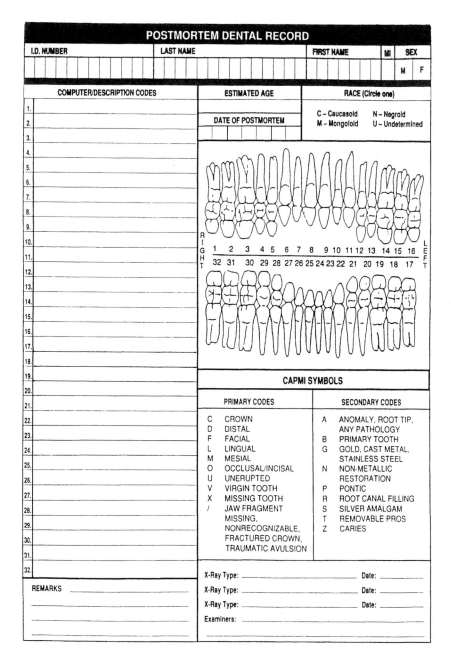

Figure 9.7

are dental restorations, missing teeth, prosthetic appliances, pathology, unique anatomy, age estimate, and references to possible gender and/or racial group. Teeth missing due to the trauma of the mishap should be specifically noted to avoid confusion over extracted or congenitally missing teeth. A prosthodontist should be available to examine and describe dental prosthetic appliances.[60,61] In some cases, the appliance may have been specifically marked for identification. It is wise to solicit, from the victim's dentist or family, study models or extra prosthetic appliances which may be available. Such evidence is important in providing antemortem data regarding ridge shape/size, rugae patterns, and general oral anatomy. Techniques used in the post-mortem examination and the Dental Radiology Section have been extensively described in the literature.[62-68] The team should be watchful for identification microdots placed on teeth, especially in children and young adults.[69]

Another major subsection in the forensic dentistry area is the antemortem dental record subsection. Dentists, hygienists, skilled dental assistants, and dental investigators can effectively operate this subsection.[70] The task of personnel in this section will always be the most difficult in the entire forensic dentistry arena since they will be required to determine who was involved in the disaster, locate and procure antemortem records and radiographs, arrange for the delivery of these materials, and undertake the process of developing a composite antemortem record for each victim from the evidence supplied. The quality, quantity, and variety of dental record documentation of this antemortem evidence present the major obstacles to this section.

It is clearly necessary to reduce all antemortem dental evidence to a single antemortem dental record form (Figure 9.8) in order to provide a composite antemortem picture. The latter may easily be compared to the postmortem findings recorded on a postmortem dental record of similar format. It is almost an impossible task to compare dental records sent directly from dental offices with the postmortem dental record. At least two members of the antemortem dental record staff should review each composite antemortem dental record as a quality control mechanism. The completed antemortem composite form should also be quality checked against antemortem dental radiographs. It is important to note the time elapsed between the time when the antemortem evidence was established and the time of the disaster. The potential of multiple providers in that elapsed time must be considered. You may not have all existing antemortem records. This may lead to discrepancies in the antemortem record and postmortem record comparison.

Photographs of possible fatalities are often received by this subsection. They may be of value in demonstrating malocclusions and other facial and dental anatomy. The anthropologist and forensic artist will also find these photographs of value. Remember to share this evidence. Carefully mark the reverse of these photographs with the name and address of the provider. More likely than not, this photograph will be the last or best of the victim. When possible, demonstrate compassion for the family of the victim by returning the photograph to them.

ANTEMORTEM DENTAL RECORD

SSN	LAST NAME	FIRST NAME	MI	SEX
				M F

DATE OF BIRTH / ESTIMATED AGE

RACE (Circle one)

C – Caucasoid   N – Negroid
M – Mongoloid   U – Undetermined

COMPUTER/DESCRIPTION CODES

DATE OF RECONSTRUCTION

I.D. NUMBER

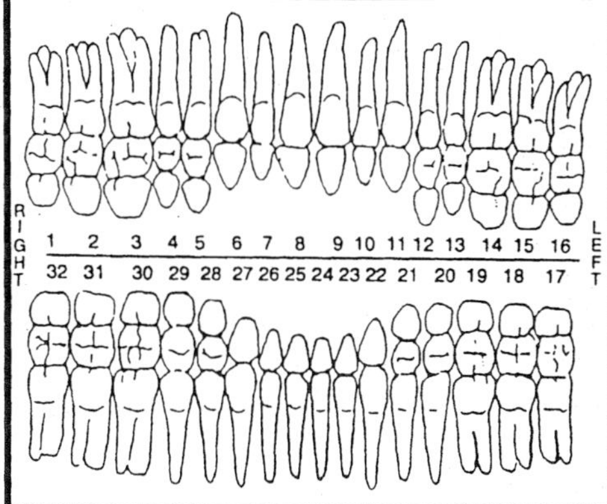

R I G H T

1 2 3 4 5 6 7 8 9 10 11 12 13 14 15 16

32 31 30 29 28 27 26 25 24 23 22 21 20 19 18 17

L E F T

CAPMI SYMBOLS

PRIMARY CODES		SECONDARY CODES	
C	CROWN	A	ANOMALY, ROOT TIP,
D	DISTAL		ANY PATHOLOGY
F	FACIAL	B	PRIMARY TOOTH
L	LINGUAL	G	GOLD, CAST METAL,
M	MESIAL		STAINLESS STEEL
O	OCCLUSAL/INCISAL	N	NON-METALLIC
U	UNERUPTED		RESTORATION
V	VIRGIN TOOTH	P	PONTIC
X	MISSING TOOTH	R	ROOT CANAL FILLING
/	JAW FRAGMENT	S	SILVER AMALGAM
	MISSING,	T	REMOVABLE PROS
	NONRECOGNIZABLE,	Z	CARIES
	FRACTURED CROWN,		
	TRAUMATIC AVULSION		

Computer/Description Codes numbered 1. through 32.

X-Ray Type: _____ Date: _____
X-Ray Type: _____ Date: _____
X-Ray Type: _____ Date: _____
Examiners: _____

REMARKS _____

Figure 9.8

The postmortem dental records/computer and comparison subsection is the third part of the Forensic Dentistry Section. Postmortem dental records and completed antemortem composite dental records are forwarded to this section. The task of this section is to compare all postmortem examination and radiographic findings with the completed composite antemortem dental records and radiographs. This section must also keep abreast of the findings of all forensic sections within the Identification Center and apply their findings in the dental comparison process. Normally, all the postmortem dental examination and radiographic work will be completed before even half of the antemortem composite dental records are available for comparison. The dental comparisons can be accomplished with the assistance of a computer or can be managed in a manual fashion. Experience has shown that a combination of both techniques is realistic.

If the subsection operates without a computer, the size of the section is dependent on the number of fatalities, since there is a requirement to place all postmortem dental records face-up on tables in numerical order for a comparison with the antemortem composite dental records. After all postmortem dental records have been placed on tables as described, the staff can systematically compare the antemortem dental composite records as they are received with the postmortem dental records placed on the table. This is done by hand, carrying the composite antemortem record and walking alongside the tables viewing the postmortem dental records looking for a significant point of comparison, such as a crown on a tooth #30. Once significant points of comparison are noted between the antemortem and postmortem dental record forms, the radiographs of the respective records can be reviewed and a possible identification established. Time is a major consideration. If you have 900 postmortem records and take 2 minutes to compare one antemortem record to each postmortem record, it will take you 30 hours to complete the process. Similarly, a 15 seconds look at each record will take 4 hours. In this manual mode, if it is possible to determine the gender of the disaster victims, it is possible to reduce the manual comparison task by placing the postmortem records in numerical order on tables by gender. Postmortem records of children may also be individually managed.

To provide quality control, the chief of the Forensic Dentistry Section should be provided the antemortem and postmortem dental records of potential positive identifications established by the staff. He or she must reconstruct the positive dental identification. A dental identification form which summarizes the identification data can be completed at this time. Several varieties of these forms are available (Figures 9.9 and 9.10). This form is a tool in the decision-making and documentation process. It is used to provide rapid answers to questions when the chief of the Forensic Dentistry Section meets with the Identification Center chief, at which time evidence regarding each case is presented. Only after all sections have presented their evidence and all inconsistencies have been explained or addressed should the Identification Center chief sign the case out as a positive identification. As indicated previously, it is advantageous to identify human remains in more than one specialty area in order to be adequately prepared should a court rule one form of evidence as inadmissible based on a legal or professional technicality.

DENTAL IDENTIFICATION FORM

IDENTIFICATION NUMBER: _____

ARMED SERVICES TAG NUMBER: _____

DATE OF EXAMINATION: _____

PLACE OF EXAMINATION: _____

EXAMINER: _____

EXAMINER'S ORGANIZATION: _____

ACCIDENT & AIRCRAFT TYPE: _____

PRELIMINARY IDENTIFICATION DATA:

EST. AGE: _____ SEX: _____ RACE: _____ COLOR HAIR: _____ COLOR EYES: _____

LOCATION OF BODY: _____

POSITION OF BODY: _____

POSITION OF BODY: _____

PHOTOGRAPHS: _____

FINGERPRINTS & FOOTPRINTS: _____

PERSONAL EFFECTS: _____

TYPE OF EXAMINATION: _____

CONFIRMED IDENTIFICATION: NAME OF DECEASED

LAST   FIRST   MI   RANK

ORGANIZATION: _____

SSAN: _____

SIGNATURE: _____ IDENTIFICATION DATE _____

Figure 9.9

After the case has been signed out as a positive identification, the antemortem and postmortem dental records and associated evidence should be combined with the summary sheet into a single completed file. The antemortem composite dental record should be placed in the completed file only if the full dentition was present with the remains or if all dental/oral fragments have been recovered. If this is not the case and an additional oral fragment is recovered, the postmortem fragment may go unidentified since the necessary antemortem dental record was placed in the completed file.

**DENTAL IDENTIFICATION
SUMMARY REPORT**

NAME OF DECEASED: _____   RECOVERY NUMBER _____

RANK: _____ SEX: _____ RACE: _____ AGE: _____   SSN: _____

EXAMINERS: _____ DATE: _____   PLACE: _____

COMPARISON OF ANTEMORTEM AND POSTMORTEM DENTAL RECORDS AND RADIOGRAPHS REVEAL CONCORDANCE ON

TEETH NUMBER (DESCRIBE FEATURE):

1._____	9._____	17._____	25._____
2._____	10._____	18._____	26._____
3._____	11._____	19._____	27._____
4._____	12._____	20._____	28._____
5._____	13._____	21._____	29._____
6._____	14._____	22._____	30._____
7._____	15._____	23._____	31._____
8._____	16._____	24._____	32._____

REMARKS: _____

_____

_____

FINDINGS (CIRCLE ONE):   POSITIVE IDENTIFICATION   CONSISTENT WITH   UNIDENTIFIED

SIGNATURE OF EXAMINERS: _____

FINDINGS CONFIRMED BY: _____   (DENTAL TEAM LEADER)

Figure 9.10

This mistake is made in almost every disaster. Please avoid it! In this consolidation process, the antemortem and postmortem dental radiographs that provided the conclusive evidence of the positive dental identification should be photographed. These photographs or slides are indispensable for record-keeping purposes and provide a superior method of displaying the evidence in court.

If the computer is to be utilized in the comparison process, the postmortem dental records/computer comparison subsection can be smaller in size than in the manual operation mode. Also, the dental records can be maintained in a file cabinet under the control of the dental section registrar. Computers reduce staffing requirements, costs, and save time. They increase the effectiveness and accuracy of the staff. They enhance fragment processing and provide useful management information.

The computer is properly utilized in the Forensic Dentistry Section to eliminate the tedious and time-consuming manual sorting of dental records by the professional staff. It is a method of bringing together the antemortem and postmortem dental records that have the greatest probability of containing a positive dental identification.[71-75] It is the forensic dentistry staff who, after comparing the records and the radiographic evidence, makes the positive dental identification using their professional expertise. Computers have been utilized most successfully in a number of mass disasters. When utilizing the computer in the Forensic Dentistry Section it is necessary to create antemortem and postmortem record files within the computer memory. The computer is programmed to provide a product that allows for the reduction of manual sorting of data and increases the efficiency and the accuracy of the staff. The computer products provide a list of antemortem and postmortem records for comparison based upon probability. Instead of walking around tables, the professional staff can be seated at tables with dental radiographic view boxes. A clerical crew utilizing the computer products, provides the staff with records and radiographs to compare. The computer can also be programmed to make specific inquiries into either the antemortem or postmortem dental record files. It can also be programmed to retain significant forensic data such as physical descriptions and background information. Computer technology combined with dental radiology provides the forensic odontologist a means for dealing with dental fragments as easily as the full dentition. Time is required to code the dental findings from the antemortem and postmortem records in most computer systems. Consequently, the computer approach is most effective when 100 or more fatalities or fragments are involved. The exception to this is the Northwestern University/Desk Top Solutions system which loads a database while providing an odontogram as the antemortem and postmortem record.

A Computer-Assisted Postmortem Identification System (CAPMI) designed by Colonel Lewis Lorton and Mr. William H. Langley, represents the latest development of an identification system utilizing today's technology.[76] The system provides efficient management of the antemortem and postmortem dental and physical data and rapid sorting of this data. It permits the professional staff to concentrate on comparing statistically significant and related antemortem and postmortem records. The purpose of the system is to increase the efficiency of the investigators by culling out the least likely identities and presenting the investigators with a list of the most probable matches. The system will reduce Identification Center costs by reducing the number of forensic dental staff needed and by optimizing their time. The system will compensate for changes in the database caused by unrecorded dental work and will facilitate fragment identification. Due to its inherent high selectivity, it can also overcome many human errors in the database.

The CAPMI system has been successfully tested and employed in several aircraft mishaps including the Arrow Airways tragedy in Newfoundland. This computer program is compatible with most computer systems and is available to public nonprofit organizations. The CAPMI system, combined with a proposed computerized military dental record and digitally stored dental radiographs could represent a major worldwide milestone in the postmortem identification process. The use of teleradiography and digital data transmission could speed the flow of critical identification information to the Identification Center.[77,78] This would clearly streamline the process whether one is attempting to identify a single body in a mortuary or thousands of battlefield remains at a central identification laboratory. It will also create a significant dental database in the U.S. of well over several million computerized dental records. The CAPMI system, Northwestern University system, and the Mertz and Purtilo System are examples of available computer programs in forensic dentistry.

Anthropology Considerations

Forensic physical anthropology is of sterling assistance to the identification process. The ability to accurately work the issues of race, gender, and age are essential.[79-86] The Identification Center should have reference skeletons of each major racial group that also demonstrate gender indicators. The ability to provide good physical descriptions of disaster victims is vital to managing a disaster where a large unknown population may be involved, such as in the Big Thompson Canyon Flood.[87] In that case, over 500 persons were listed as missing and a little over 100 bodies recovered. Those individuals filing missing person's reports, more times than not, failed to notify authorities when the missing person was located alive and well. Consequently, the Identification Center continued to deal with a large population group. Antemortem and postmortem physical descriptions were compared using computer files. Antemortem records and radiographs were requested only when the postmortem physical description comparison merited.

Anthropologists are quite knowledgeable in dentistry. Both professions are expert in postmortem age estimates. A study of cranial sutures, ossification centers, epiphyseal union, dental eruption patterns, dental histology, periodontal status, dental wear patterns, pubic symphysis, and osteon aging give a meaningful estimate of age. Gender is suggested by a study of the pelvis noting the morphology of the pubis and ischium, sciatic notch, and sacrum. Metric analysis of the pelvis also adds insight. The skull also offers suggestions of gender. The superior orbital margins, mastoid process, temporal and nuchal lines, mental protuberance of mandible and gonial angle are indicators.

Discriminant function analysis of the skull is also utilized to determine sex as well as race. Other indicators of race include craniofacial morphology and unique dental features. Several statistical methodologies are available for stature determination. Cultural effects are sometimes noted on the skull, femur, tibia, and teeth. Cranial defects, squatting facets, dental restorations, filing of teeth, and oral habits such as pipe chewing and hairpin opening wear are sometimes seen. Antemortem radiographs provide the anthropologist with a multitude of unique and individual features for comparison. Facial reconstruction may be of value in unidentified cases.[88] This process can be done by the forensic artist or the anthropologist with facial sculpturing. Photographic/radiographic superimposition may be another useful technique. Fragments are always a problem in mass disasters. The anthropologist can be the facilitator in resolution of this problem. Serology, DNA studies, and autoantibodies are laboratory capabilities in this regard. The significant insights of the anthropologist must be integrated with those of the medical and dental sections of the Identification Center team.

SUCCESS = TEAMWORK!

Planning Considerations

In writing plans for a Forensic Dentistry Section, it is helpful to first define a concept of operation and then to develop individual annexes regarding personnel, equipment, supplies, and facilities. These latter sections of the plan can be subdivided based on the proposed size of an operation. For example, the plan might include an annex for personnel, equipment, supplies, and facilities for dealing with up to 50 fatalities, 50 to 150 fatalities, 150 to 300 fatalities, and 300 or more fatalities. A general listing of dental equipment and supplies is provided (Figure 9.11) to stimulate planning. Appendix 9.2 offers a quantified listing of supply, equipment, and facility start-up requirements for an Identification Center of various sizes. A good plan and knowledge of a place where supplies and equipment can be rapidly procured can make a forensic dentistry team very responsive without a significant initial financial outlay. Facility requirement preplanning is essential. The size and composition of the forensic dentistry team is driven by the concept of operations and the magnitude of a disaster. If a concept of operations can be established, a core of team members can be trained and utilized to staff key positions. This core of personnel can then be augmented to address the size of a particular disaster (Figure 9.12).

FORENSIC DENTISTRY KIT

Reference material	35mm camera
Tape recorder	35mm film
Recording tape	Modeling clay
Paper pads	Boxing wax
Manilla envelopes for case	Fiberoptic lights or
records	flashlights
Identification forms	Striker saw or hand saw
Tags with string or wire	Straight & curved retractors
Masking tape	Scalpel handles
Staplers with staples	Scalpel blades
Felt tip pens	Large scissors
Large felt tip markers	Large hemostats
Plastic denture bags	Mouth props
Pencils	Tongue blades
Clip boards	Cotton applicators
Plastic cups	Mouth mirrors (front surface)
Fatigues/work clothes	Explorers
Boots	Periodontal scalers
Work gloves	Cutting pliers
Scrub suits	Straight pliers
Rubber aprons or surgical gowns	Straight chisel (large)
Surgical gloves	Mallet
Surgical masks	Millimeter rule
Portable dental X-ray	Disclosing solution
Dental X-ray	Hydrogen peroxide solution
Film badge monitor system	Sodium hypochlorite solution
Automatic film processor	4 x 4 sponges
with daylight loading hood	Toothbrushes
Dental X-ray film mounts	Computer/equipment
Dental X-ray film envelopes	Computer paper
X-ray light view boxes	Computer forms
Processor chemicals	File cabinet
Lead shielding	Batteries

Figure 9.11

Training Considerations

Training and exercises make a polished team with high potential for successful outcomes in time of need. The Armed Forces Institute of Pathology (AFIP) offers an annual course in forensic dentistry that is open to all. It includes a wide range of forensic topics including mass disaster management. "Hands On" laboratories in dental identification radiology and a mock aircraft mishap are an integral part of the course. Follow-on courses in forensic pathology, oral pathology, aerospace pathology, and advanced forensic pathology are offered by the AFIP and the FBI Academy. Numerous courses are available in the civilian sector. Continuing education in this area is available through the American Society of Forensic Odontology, the American Academy of Forensic Sciences, and many colleges and universities. Disaster planning

FORENSIC DENTISTRY SECTION STAFFING				
STAFF	FATALITIES			
	1 - 50	50 - 150	150 - 300	300 +
CHIEF (FORENSIC DENTIST)	1	1	1	1
DEPUTY (ORAL PATHOLOGIST)	1	1	2	3
ORAL SURGEONS	1	2	3	4
GENERAL DENTISTS	4	6	10	12
PROSTHODONTIST	1	1	1	1
OFFICE MANAGER	1	1	1	2
DENTAL X-RAY TECHNICIANS	2	4	6	8
DENTAL ASSISTANTS	4	8	10	10
COMPUTER ANALYST	1	1	1	1
COMPUTER OPERATORS	1	1	2	3

Figure 9.12

booklets are normally available from some of these organizations.[89,90] Board certification in forensic dentistry is gained through the American Board of Forensic Odontology under the sponsorship of the Forensic Sciences Foundation. The role of forensic dentistry in mass disasters has been explored by the American Dental Association.[91] Increased emphasis by dental schools and support by the American Dental Association of forensic dentistry greatly benefit the forensic science community and help keep dentistry a great national asset.[92,93]

Conclusion

It is only a matter of when and where the next mass disaster will occur. Hopefully, this chapter will help make you ready to meet the needs of your community and exceed the expectations of your colleagues.

References

1. Barsley, R. E., Carr, R. F., Cottone, J. A., Cuminale, J. A., Identification via dental remains: Pan Am Flight 759, *J. Forensic Sci.*, 30(1):128, 1985.

2. McCarty, V. O., Sohn, A. P., Ritzlin, R. S., Gauthier, J. H., Scene investigation, identification, and victim examination following the accident of Galaxy 203: disaster preplanning does work, *J. Forensic Sci.*, 32(4):983, 1987.

3. Piercy, J. H., Memories of the crash of Delta Flight 191: the reflections of a forensic dentist, Tex. Dent. J., 104(11):6, 1987.

4. Smith, G. A., Palian, C. W., Dental identification and the P-3 crash in Hawaii, *Mil. Med.*, 150(2):59, 1985.

5. Smith, J. H., Dental identification at Dover, *USAF Med. Service Digest*, Winter, 9, 1991.

6. Thompson, R. L., Postmortem findings of the victims of the Jonestown tragedy, *J. Forensic Sci.*, 32(2):433, 1987.

7. Vale, G. L., Anselmo, J. A., Hoffman, B. L., Forensic dentistry in the Cerritos air disaster, *J. Am. Dent. Assoc.*, 114(5):661, 1987.

8. Wagner, G. N., Clark, M. A., Koenigsberg, E. J., Decata, S. J., Medical evaluation of the victims of the 1986 Lake Nyos disaster, *J. Forensic Sci.*, 33(4):899, 1988.

9. Warnick, A. J., Dentists aid in identification of crash victims, *J. Mich. Dent. Assoc.*, 69(10):553, 1987.

10. Barsley, R. E., Forensic dentistry's importance to practitioners, *La. Dent. Assoc. J.*, 41(3):9, 1983.

11. Bell, G. L., Forensic odontology and mass disasters, *NY State Dent. J.*, 55(3):25, 1989.

12. Halik, F. J., New York State dentists respond to disasters, *NY State Dent. J.*, 57(4):23, 1991.

13. Hill, I. R., *Forensic Odontology — Its Scope and History*, Alan Clift Assoc., Solihull, England, 1984.

14. Jakush, J., Forensic dentistry, *J. Am. Dent. Assoc.*, 119(5):586, 1989.

15. Kirkland, G., Tatum, R. C., Soni, N. N., Perez, R. S., Forensic dentistry: solving the mysteries of identification, *Gen. Dent.*, 35(2):120, 1987.

16. O'Reilly, P., An overview of forensic dentistry, *Clin. Prev. Dent.*, 8(1):16, 1986.

17. Profilio, L., Wisconsin's disaster identification team helps set the pace for other states, *Wis. Dent. Assoc. J.*, 68(4):206, 1992.

18. Tillis, B. P., Forensic odontology serving modern society, *NY State Dent. J.*, 55(3):5, 1989.

19. Vale, G. L., The role of the practicing dental professional in forensic dentistry, *Calif. Dent. Assoc. J.*, 14(3):12, 1986.

20. Wolfe, R. R., The role of the Forensic dentist, *La. Dent. Assoc. J.*, 46(4):8, 1988.

21. Churton, M. C., Dental identification: Some problems and solutions, *J. Forensic Odontostomatol.*, 3(1):13, 1985.

22. Clark, D. H., Dental identification problems in the Abu Dhabi air accident, *Am. J. Forensic Med. Pathol.*, 7(4):317. 1986.

23. Clark, D. H., The British experience in mass disaster dental identification, *Acta Med. Leg. Soc.*, 40:159, 1990.

24. Dorion, R. B., Disasters big and small, *J. Can. Dent. Assoc.*, 56(7):593, 1990.

25. Doyle, C. T., Bolster, The medical-legal organization of a mass disaster-Air India crash 1985, *Med. Sci. Law*, 32(1):5, 1992.

26. Fischman, S. L., Role of the general practitioner in data collection and cross matching, *Int. Dent. J.*, 37(4):201, 1987.

27. Hill, I. R., Howell, R. D., Jarmulowicz, M., Identification in the Manchester air disaster, *Br. Dent. J.*, 165(12):445, 1988.

28. Jakobsen, J., Utilization of forensic dental experts from a visiting victim identification commission in mass disasters: A Scandinavian design, *J. Forensic Odontostomatol.*, 9(1):29, 1991.

29. Kraft, E., Liebhardt, E., Lindemaier, G., National characteristics of dental treatment in disaster victim identification, *J. Forensic Odontostomatol.*, 9(1):32, 1991.

30. Mason, J. K., The importance of autopsy examination in mass disasters, *Ann. Acad. Med. Singapore*, 13(1):12, 1984.

31. Paul, D. M., The coroner's role in mass disasters, *Ann. Acad. Med. Singapore*, 13(1):16, 1984.

32. Whittington, B. R., The importance of adequate antemortem dental records for postmortem identification, *NZ Dent. J.*, 87(387):17, 1991.

33. Clark, M. A., Clark, S. R., Perkins, D. G., Mass fatality aircraft disaster processing, *Aviat. Space Environ. Med.*, 60, A64, 1989.

34. Daily, J. C., Forensic odontology task force organization, *Mil. Med.*, 53(3):133, 1988.

35. Hollander, N., Air crash disaster planning, *Am. J. Forensic Med. Pathol.*, 8(2):183, 1987.

36. Hooft, P. J., Noji, E. K., Van de Voorde, H. P., Fatality management in mass casualty incidents, *Forensic Sci. Int.*, 40(1):3, 1989.

37. Morlang, W. M., Mass disaster management update, *Calif. Dent. Assoc. J.*, 14(3):49, 1986.

38. English, W. R., Robison, S. F., Summitt, J. B., Osterle, L. J., Brannon, R. B., Morlang, W. M., The individuality of human palatal rugae, *J. Forensic Sci.*, 33(3):718, 1988.

39. Haglund, W. D., Reay, D. T., Tepper, S. L., Identification of decomposed human remains by DNA profiling, *J. Forensic Sci.*, 35(3):724, 1990.

40. Sajantila, A., The polymerase chain reaction and postmortem identity testing, *Forensic Sci. Int.*, 51(1):23, 1991.

41. Schwartz, T. R., Mieszerski, L., McNally, L., Kobilinsky, L., Characterization of DNA obtained from teeth subjected to various environmental conditions, *J. Forensic Sci.*, 36(4):979, 1991.

42. Werrett, D. J., DNA fingerprinting, *Int. Crim. Police Rev.*, INTERPOL, September, Vol. 21, 1987.

43. Weedn, V., DNA identification, *AFNS*, 11 July, #436, 5, 1991.

44. Rawson, R. D., Ommen, R. K., Kinard, G., Johnson, J., Yfantis, A., Statistical evidence for the individuality of the human dentition, *J. Forensic Sci.,* 29(1):245, 1984.

45. Keiser-Nielsen, S., Dental Identification: certainty vs. probability, *Forensic Sci.,* 9, 87, 1977.

46. Hill, I. R., Toxicological findings in fatal aircraft accidents in the United Kingdom, *J. Forensic Sci.,* 7(4):322, 1986.

47. Clark, M. A., Wagner, G. N., Wright, D. G., Ruehle, C. J., McDonnell, E. W., Investigation of incidents of terrorism involving commercial aircraft, *Aviat. Space Environ. Med.,* 60(7):A55, 1989.

48. McMeekin, R. R., Aircraft accident investigation, in *Fundamentals of Aerospace Medicine,* Lea & Febiger, Philadelphia,1985, 762.

49. McMeekin, R. R., An organizational concept for pathologic identification in mass disasters, *Aviat. Space Environ. Med.,* 51(9):99, 1980.

50. Guill, F. C., What aircrew escape system and life support system designers need from investigating medical officers and pathologists, *Aviat. Space Environ. Med.,* 60, B1, 1989.

51. Hill, I. F., Mechanism of injury in aircraft accidents, *Aviat. Space Environ. Med.,* 60, A18, 1989.

52. McCarrol, J. E., Ursano, R. J., Wright, K. M., Fullerton, C. S., Psychiatric and psychological aspects of the management of catastrophic incidents, *J. U.S. Army Med. Dept.,* Sep/Oct, 36, 1990.

53. Galle-Tessonneau, J. R., Psychopathology and air force flight safety, *Med. Aeronaut. Spatiale,* 26, 328, 1987.

54. Murphy, S. A., Perceptions of stress, coping and recovery one and three years after a natural disaster, *Issues Ment. Health Nur.,* 8(1):63, 1986.

55. Ursano, R. J., McCarroll, J. E., The nature of a traumatic stressor: handling dead bodies, *J. Nerv. Ment. Dis.,* 178(6):396, 1990.

56. Williams, C. L., Solomon, S. D., Bartone, P., Primary prevention in aircraft disasters: Integrating research and practice, *Am. Psychol.,* 43(9)730, 1988.

57. Lichtenstein, J. E., Madewell, J. E., McMeekin, R. R., Feigin, D. S., Wolcott, J. H., Role of radiology in aviation accident investigation, *Aviat. Space Environ. Med.,* 51(9):1004, 1980.

58. Lichtenstein, J. E., Fitzpatrick, J. J., Madewell, J. E., The role of radiology in fatality investigations, *Am. J. Roentgenol.,* 150(4):751, 1988.

59. Mulligan, M. E., McCarthy, M. J., Wippold, F. J., Lichtenstein, J. E., Wagner, G. N., Radiological evaluation of mass casualty victims: Lessons from the Gander Newfoundland accident, *Radiology,* 168(1):222, 1988.

60. Ligthelm, A. J., Van Niekerk, P. J., Forensic odontological contribution to the identification of a denture wearer, *J. Forensic Odontostomatol.,* 2(1):25, 1984.

61. Woodward, J. D., Denture marking for identification, *J. Am. Dent. Assoc.,* 99, 59, 1979.

62. Cottone, J. A., Standish, S. M., *Outline of Forensic Dentistry,* Yearbook Medical Publishers, Chicago, 1982.

63. Gustafson, G., *Forensic Odontology,* Elsevier, New York, 1966.

64. Harvey, W., *Dental Identification and Forensic Odontology,* Henry Kimpton, London, 1976.

65. Keiser-Nielsen, S., *Persons Identification by Means of the Teeth,* John Wright & Sons, Bristol, 1980.

66. Luntz, L. L., Luntz, P., *Handbook for Dental Identification,* J. B. Lippincott, Philadelphia, 1973.

67. Sopher, I. M., *Forensic Dentistry,* Charles C Thomas, Springfield, IL, 1976.

68. Symposium on Forensic Dentistry, *Dent. Clin. N. Am.,* 21(1), 1977.

69. Gladfelter, I. A., Smith, B. E., Evaluation of microdisks for dental identification, *J. Prosthet. Dent.,* 62(3):352, 1989.

70. Rawson, R. D., Nelson, B. A., Koot, A. C., Mass disaster and the dental hygienist: the MGM fire, *Dent. Hyg.,* 57(4):12, 1983.

71. Dahl, J. E., Solheim, T., Computer aided dental identification, *J. Forensic Odontostomatol.,* 3(1):7, 1985.

72. Fellingham, S. A., Kotze, T. J., Nash, J. M, Probabilities of dental characteristics, *J. Forensic Odontostomatol.,* 2(2):45, 1984.

73. Friedman, R. B., Cornwell, K. A., Lorton, L., Dental characteristics of a large military population, *J. Forensic Sci.,* 34(6):1357, 1989.

74. Hashimoto M., Nakamo, Y., Suzuki, K., A coding system for a computer aided dental identification based on the Canobrain Programme, *Ann. Acad. Med. Singapore,* 13(1):20, 1984.

75. Lorton, L., Langley, W. H., Decision making concepts in postmortem identification, *J. Forensic Sci.,* 31(1):190, 1986.

76. Lorton, L., Rethman, M., Friedman, R., The computer assisted postmortem identification (CAPMI) system, *J. Forensic Sci.,* 33(4):977, 1988.

77. Southard, T. E., Baycar, R. S., Walter, R. G., Forensic dentistry: Electronic transmission of computerized dental records, *Mil. Med.,* 150 (Sep.), 492, 1985.

78. Southard, T. E., Pierce, L. J., Application of digitalized Image transmission to forensic dentistry, *Mil. Med.,* 150(8):413, 1986.

79. Burns, K. R., Maples, W. R., Estimation of age from individual adult teeth, *J. Forensic Sci.,* 21(2):343, 1976.

80. Giles, E., Elliott, O., Race identification from cranial measurements, *J. Forensic Sci.,* 7, 147, 1962.

81. Hinkes, M. J., Role of forensic anthropology in mass disaster resolution, *Aviat. Space Environ. Med.,* 60, A60, 1989.

82. Johanson, G., Age determination from human teeth, *Odontol. Revy,* 22(21):126, 1971.

83. Lamendin, H., Baccino, E., Humbert, J. F., Tavernier, J. C., Nossintchouk, R. M., Zerilli, A., A simple technique for age estimation in adult corpses: two criteria dental method, *J. Forensic Sci.,* 37(5):1373, 1992.

84. Maples, W. R., Rice, P. M., Some difficulties in the Gustafson dental are estimations, *J. Forensic Sci.,* 23, 764, 1979.

85. Krogman, W. M., *The Human Skeleton in Forensic Medicine,* Charles C Thomas, Springfield, IL, 1962.

86. Stewart, T. D., *Essentials of Forensic Anthropology,* Charles C Thomas, Springfield, IL, 1979.

87. Morlang, W. M., Wright, L., Lessons from the Big Thompson Canyon, *Gen. Dent.,* 26(5):36, 1978.

88. Ubelaker, D. H., O'Donnell, G., Computer assisted facial reproduction, *J. Forensic Sci.,* 37(1):155, 1992.

89. Averill, D. C., *Manual of Forensic Odontology,* American Society of Forensic Odontology, Burlington, VT, 1991.

90. Bell, G. L., *Mass Disaster Dental Identification Team,* 9730 Third Ave, NE, Suite 204, Seattle, WA, 98115, 1985.

91. Proc. First Natl. Symposium On Dentistry's Role in Mass Disaster Identification, American Dental Association Council on Dental Practice, Chicago, IL, 1988.

92. Griffiths, C. J., Forensic dental training in Australia, *Forensic Sci. Int.,* 36(3-4):279, 1988.

93. Katz, J. O., Cottone, J. A., The present direction of research in forensic dentistry, *J. Forensic Sci.,* 33(6):1319, 1988.

Appendix 9.1: Facial Dissection

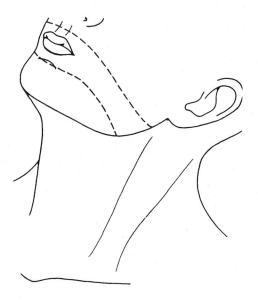

Perioral facial incision.

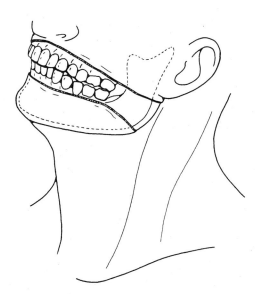

Tissue flap removed showing exposed ramus and alveolar complex.

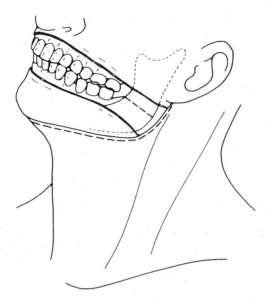

Horizontal ramus bony cut and submental-mylohyoid incision.

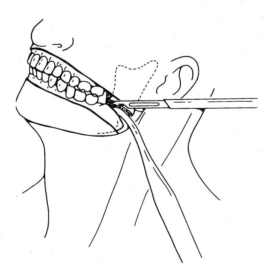

Separate ramus and incise Pterygoid musculature.

APPENDIX 9.2: Equipment, Supplies, and Facilities

Equipment

Up to 50 Casualties

Item	Quantity
50 kVP Endo X-ray unit, portable, self-contained	1
Portable lead screens	4
X-ray badges	9
X-ray film processor, with daylight loader	1
Fiber-optic light	1
Stryker saw (autopsy)	1
Headlamps	2
X-ray view boxes	3
Slide duplicator	1
Extension cords, 50 ft	3
CAPMI computer	1
35-mm camera	1
Polaroid camera	1
Security badges	15
File cabinets, 4-drawer	1

50 to 150 Casualties

Item	Quantity
50 kVP Endo X-ray units, portable 2	
X-ray badges	20
Portable lead screens	8
X-ray film processor, with daylight loader	1
Fiber-optic lights	2
Stryker saw (autopsy)	2
Headlamps	4
X-ray view boxes	6
Slide duplicator	1
Extension cords, 50 ft	5
Microcomputer	1
CAPMI computer	1
35-mm camera	1
Polaroid camera	1
Security badges	25
File cabinets, 4-drawer	1

>150 Casualties

Item	Quantity
50 kVP Endo X-ray units, portable	2
Portable lead screens	8

X-ray badges	20
X-ray film processor, with daylight loader	2
Fiber-optic lights	3
Stryker saw (autopsy)	3
Headlamps	8
X-ray view boxes	10
Slide duplicator	1
Extension cords, 50 ft	6
Microcomputer	1
CAPMI computer	1
35-mm camera	2
Polaroid camera	1
Security badges	35
File cabinets, 4-drawer	2

Supplies — Forensic Dentistry Kit

Up to 50 Casualties

Item	Quantity
35-mm Film, 36 exp	10 rolls
Paper pads	10
Identification forms:	
Postmortem	100
Antemortem	100
Abstract	100
Computer	10
Tags with string or wire	125
Manila envelopes for case records	100
Masking tape	2 rolls
Stapler with staples	2
Felt tip pens (black ink)	12
Large felt tip markers	12
Plastic denture bags	1 box large, 1 box small
Pencils	2 boxes
Clip boards	10
Paper cups	1 box
Work gloves, leather	4 pairs
Scrub suits	20 pairs
Surgical gowns (disposable)	30
Surgical gloves, size 7 1/2 and 8	3 boxes of each
Surgical masks	1 box
Dental X-ray film, periapical	10 boxes
Chemicals for film processing	As required
Polaroid film	5 rolls
Magnifying glass	1
Loupes	2
Clorox	1 gallon
Safety glasses	5 pairs
Fiber-optic light	1

Flashlights	6
Hand saw	1
Straight and curved retractors	1 set
Scalpel handles	4
Scalpel blades (#10, #15, #20)	1 box of each
Large scissors	2
Small scissors	2
Large hemostats	4
Mouth props (large, small)	1 of each
Tongue blades	1 box
Cotton applicators	1 box
Mouth mirrors (front surface)	12
Explorers	12
Periodontal scalers	3
Cutting pliers	1
Straight pliers	1
Straight chisel, single-level	1
Mallet	1
Millimeter rule	3
Spatula, #7 wax	1
Disclosing solution	1
Hydrogen peroxide solution, 1/2 gallon	1
4 × 4 Sponges	10 packages
Toothbrushes	20
Computer terminal paper	1 box
Ribbon for terminal printer	1 roll
Occlusal X-ray film	1 box
Soap (Phisohex)	6 bottles
Towels	10
Scrub brushes	5
Rubber aprons	10
Trash can liners	1 box

50 to 150 Casualties

Item	Quantity
35-mm Film, 36 exp	20 rolls
Paper pads	10
Identification forms:	
Post-mortem	300
Ante-mortem	300
Abstract	300
Computer	300
Tags with string or wire	250
Manila envelopes for case records	300
Masking tape	4 rolls
Stapler with staples	3
Felt tip pens (black ink)	24
Large felt tip markers	12
Plastic denture bags	2 boxes large, 1 box small
Pencils	2 boxes

Clip boards	20
Paper cups	2 boxes
Work gloves, leather	6 pairs
Scrub suits	30 pairs
Surgical gowns (disposable)	50
Surgical gloves, size 7 1/2 and 8	5 boxes of each
Surgical masks	2 boxes
Dental X-ray film, periapical	20 boxes
Chemicals for film processing	As required
Polaroid film	10 boxes
Magnifying glasses	2
Loupes	2
Clorox, gallon	2
Safety glasses	10 pairs
Flashlights	6
Hand saws	2
Straight and curved retractors	2 sets
Scalpel handles	8
Scalpel blades (#10, #15, #20)	2 boxes of each
Large scissors	4
Small scissors	4
Large hemostats	6
Mouth props (large, small)	2 of each
Tongue blades	2 boxes
Cotton applicators	2 boxes
Mouth mirrors (front surface)	24
Explorers	24
Periodontal scalers	6
Cutting pliers	2
Straight pliers	2
Straight chisels, single-level	2
Mallet	2
Millimeter rule	4
Spatula, #7 wax	6
Disclosing solution	1
Hydrogen peroxide solution, gallon	1
4 × 4 Sponges	20 packages
Toothbrushes	20
Computer terminal paper	1 box
Ribbon for terminal printer	1 roll
Occlusal X-ray film	1 box
Soap (Phisohex)	12 bottles
Towels	20
Scrub brushes	12
Rubber aprons	15
Trash can liners	1 box

>150 Casualties

Item	Quantity
35-mm Film/atch, 36 exp	20 rolls

Paper pads	10
Identification forms:	
Post-mortem	500
Ante-mortem	500
Abstract	500
Computer	500
Tags with string or wire	500
Manila envelopes for case records	500
Masking tape	4 rolls
Stapler with staples	4
Felt tip pens (black ink)	36
Large felt tip markers	12
Plastic denture bags	2 boxes small, 3 boxes large
Pencils	2 boxes
Clip boards	20
Paper cups	2 boxes
Work gloves, leather	8 pairs
Scrub suits	30 pairs
Surgical gowns (disposable)	50
Surgical gloves, size 7 1/2 and 8	6 boxes of each
Surgical masks	3 boxes
Dental X-ray film, periapical	20 boxes
Chemicals for film processing	As required
Magnifying glasses	2
Loupes	2
Clorox, gallon	3
Safety glasses	10 pairs
Flashlights	6
Hand saws	3
Straight and curved retractors	3 sets
Scalpel handles	8
Scalpel blades (#10, #15, #20)	3 boxes of each
Large scissors	6
Small scissors	6
Large hemostats	9
Mouth props (large, small)	3 of each
Tongue blades	3 boxes
Cotton applicators	3 boxes
Mouth mirrors (front surface)	36
Explorers	36
Periodontal scalers	6
Cutting pliers	3
Straight pliers	3
Straight chisels, single-level	3
Mallet	3
Millimeter rule	4
Spatula, #7 wax	6
Disclosing solution	1
Hydrogen peroxide solution, gallon	1
4 × 4 Sponges	40 packages

Toothbrushes	20
Occlusal X-ray film	1 box
Soap (Phisohex)	12 bottles
Towels	40
Scrub brushes	24
Rubber aprons	25
Trash can liners	1 box
Polaroid film	20 boxes

Facilities

Up to 50 Casualties

Access to:

Xerox machine
Watts telephone line — 1
Tables or gurney carts
Refrigeration
Office facilities:
    Room for antemortem records
    Room for postmortem records
    Post-mortem exam area
    Computer room

50 to 150 Casualties

Access to:

Xerox machine
WATS telephone lines — 2
Tables or gurney carts
Refrigeration
Office facilities:
    Room for ante-mortem records
    Room for post-mortem records
    Post-mortem exam area
    Computer room

>150 Casualties

Access to:

Xerox machine
Watts telephone lines — 3
Tables or gurney carts
Refrigeration
Office facilities:
    Room for ante-mortem records
    Room for post-mortem records
    Post-mortem exam area
    Computer room

Appendix 9.3: Charting Format

AUTHORIZED DESIGNATIONS AND ABBREVIATIONS

A4-1. Authorized Designations and Abbreviations. Use these approved entries to ensure uniformity:

a. Designation of Teeth. Use the # symbol before each tooth number or before each series of tooth numbers, example: Teeth #5, 7, 8, and 9.

Maxillary, Right Side		Maxillary, Left Side
#1	Third Molars	#16
#2	Second Molars	#15
#3	First Molars	#14
#4	Second Premolars	#13
#5	First Premolars	#12
#6	Canine	#11
#7	Lateral Incisors	#10
#8	Central Incisors	#9

Mandibular, Right Side		Mandibular, Left Side
#32	Third Molars	#17
#31	Second Molars	#18
#30	First Molars	#19
#29	Second Premolars	#20
#28	First Premolars	#21
#27	Canine	#22
#26	Lateral Incisors	#23
#25	Central Incisors	#24

b. Abbreviations for Tooth Surfaces:

M	Mesial
I	Incisal
O	Occlusal
D	Distal
F	Facial (Buccal and Labial)
L	Lingual

c. Combinations. When more than one tooth surface is involved, use a combination of the abbreviation and capital letters.

d. Other Authorized Abbreviations. The following abbreviations are not mandatory. Upper or lower case letters may be used.

DESCRIPTION	ABBREVIATION
abrasion	abr
abscess	abs
abutment	abut(s)
acrylic resin	acr
adjust(ed)(ment)	adj
alveolar	alv
alveolectomy	alvy
amalgam	am
anesthesia(thetic)	anes
anterior	ant
apicoectomy	apico
appliance	appl
appoint(ment)	appt
arch wire	AW
base	B

bitewing(s)	BW
bleeding index	BI
blood pressure	BP
bracket	bkt
broken appointment	BA
calcium hydroxide	CaOH
calculus	cal
cancel(lation)	canc
caries	car
caries prevention treatment acidulated phosphate fluoride	CPTAPF
caries prevention treatment sodium fluoride	CPTNaF
caries prevention treatment stannous fluoride	CPTSnF
cement	cem
centimeter	cm
centric occlusion	CO
centric relation	CR
centric relation occlusion	CRO
cephalometric	ceph
chief complaint	CC
chronic	chr
class	cl
complete	com
composite resin	cmpst
computerized tomography	CT
consult(ation)	cons
crown	crn
cystectomy	cystmy
defective	def
demonstration	demo
denture	dtr
diagnosis	dx
discontinue	dc
drain	dr
dressing	drs
duty not involving flying, alert, or special operational duty	DNIF
each	ea
elastics	el
electric pulp test	EPT
emergency room	ER
endodontic(s)	endo
epinephrine	epi
equilibrate(ation)	equil
eugenol	eug
evaluate(ation)	eval
examination	exam
exposure	exp
extract(ion)	ext
fixed partial denture	FPD
flap curettage	FC
fracture	Fx
free gingival graft (free soft tissue autograft)	FGG
full mouth	FM
general(ized)	gen
gingival(itis)	ging
gingivectomy	gtmy

glass ionomer cement	GIC	post operative treatment	POT
gutta percha	GP	posterior	post
health care instructions	HCI	pound(s)	lb
heavy	hvy	preliminary	prelim
high blood pressure	HBP	premedicate	premed
history	hx	prepared(ation)	prep
history of present illness	HPI	prescription	Rx
hospital	Hosp	Presidential Support Program	PSP
immediate	immed	primary	prim
impacted(ion)	imp	prophylaxis	pro
impression	impr	prosthodontics	pros
incision and drainage	I&D	pulpectomy	pctmy
incomplete	incom	pulpitis	pitis
indirect pulp cap	IPC	pulpotomy	potmy
insert(ion) (ed)	ins	quadrant	Q
intermaxillary fixation	IMF	quarters	qtrs
Intermediate Restorative Material	IRM	range of motion	ROM
intravenous	IV	reappoint(ment)	reappt
laboratory	lab	recement(ed)	recem
lateral cephalograph	lat ceph	red cross volunteer	RCV
left	lt	refer(red)	ref
ligate(ture)	lig	reference	RE
local	loc	rehabilitation	rehab
lower left	LL	reinforced acrylic resin pontic	RAP
lower right	LR	removable partial denture	RPD
maintenance (maintain)	maint	remove(al)	rem
mandible(ular)	man	repair(ed)	rep
maxilla(ry)	max	respiration	resp
medical evaluation board	MEB	restoration	res
medication(s)	med(s)	return to clinic	RTC
millimeter	mm	right	rt
moderate	mdr	root canal treatment	RCT
month(s)	mo(s)	root plane(ing)	rp
mucosal	muc	rubber dam	rd
necrotizing ulcerative gingivitis	NUG	scaling	sc
negative	neg	sedation(ed)	sed
occlusion	occ	slight	slt
operating room	OR	space available	space A
operative	oper	stainless steel crown	SSC
oral hygiene	OH	subjective, objective, assessment, plan	SOAP
oral/maxillofacial surgery	OMFS	supernumerary	supernum
orthodontics	ortho	surgery	surg
panoral radiograph	pano	suture	su
partial	pr	symptoms	sx
past medical history	PMH	temperature	temp
pathology	path	temporary	tem
patient	pt	temporomandibular disorders	TMD
pediatric dentistry	ped dent	temporomandibular joint	TMJ
percussion	perc	transitional	trans
periapical	per	treatment	tx
pericoronitis	pecor	type	T
periodic dental exam program	PDEP	unerupted	uner
periodontics	perio	upper left	UL
periodontitis	pedoni	upper right	UR
personnel reliability program	PRP	varnish	var
pit and fissure sealant	PFS	vital signs	vs
plaque	plq	within normal limits	wnl
polish	pol	x-ray, radiograph	xr
polycarboxylic acid	PCA	zinc oxide	ZnO
porcelain	porc	zinc oxide and eugenol	ZOE
porcelain fused to metal	PFM	zinc phosphate	ZnPhos
post and core	P&C		

INSTRUCTIONS FOR CHARTING MISSING TEETH
AND EXISTING RESTORATIONS
(See Figure A6-1)

A6-1. Edentulous Arch or Mouth. Inscribe two crossing lines, each running from the uppermost aspect of one third molar to the lowermost aspect of the third molar on the opposite side.

A6-2. Individual Missing Teeth. Draw an "X" on the root or roots of each natural tooth that does not appear in the mouth at the time of the examination. Mark unerupted, extracted, or congenitally absent teeth, regardless of whether they have been replaced by fixed or removable partial dentures.

A6-3. Primary Teeth. Identify the relative position of primary teeth with a block letter "D" around the tooth number.

A6-4. Restorations. Draw the restoration in the diagram of the tooth. Show the approximate size, location, and shape. Identify restorative materials as follows:

a. Amalgam Restorations. Outline and block in solidly. Chart proximal restorations in posterior teeth on facial and lingual surfaces only when the restoration extends onto these surfaces.

b. Single Gold Restorations. Outline and inscribe horizontal parallel lines within the outline of the restoration.

c. Nonmetallic (Silicate, Porcelain, Resin, Glass Ionomer Restorations, Artificial Crowns, and Facings). Draw only the outline of the size, location, and shape of the restoration, and each aspect of the crown or facing.

d. Combination Restorations. Outline the area. Show the approximate overall size, location, and shape; partition at junction of materials used. Show each type material used.

e. Post Crown. Outline each nonmetallic material and show restorative metallic materials. Outline approximate size and position of the post or posts.

f. Root Canal Filling. Outline each canal filled and block in solidly.

g. Apicoectomy. Draw a small triangle with the apex away from the crown and place a line at the approximate line of the root amputation.

h. Overdenture Abutment. Draw a horizontal line at the approximate root length. Block in solidly to show root canal filling. If amalgam restores the abutment, show size and location by solidly blocking. Sketch restoration and fill with horizontal lines to show precious metal coping.

i. Dentures. Place a horizontal line between the outline of the teeth and the numerals to designate teeth replaced by complete or removable partial dentures. In the "Remarks" section, describe complete and removable partial dentures. Indicate whether they are maxillary or mandibular, and the type of material/metal. State whether the denture is serviceable or unserviceable, for example, "Rem Pr Dtr Man (Acrylic or gold, or Chrome-Cobalt) serviceable," or "Dtr Com Max Acr, unserviceable."

j. Fixed Partial Dentures. Outline each aspect; include abutments and pontics. Show partition at junction of materials and show each material used. EXCEPTION: Inscribe diagonal parallel lines to show gold. Note defective fixed partial dentures in "Remarks" section, e.g., Defective pontic #10 or defective Crown #11.

k. Remakes. Add any other pertinent information that relates to missing teeth and existing restorations.

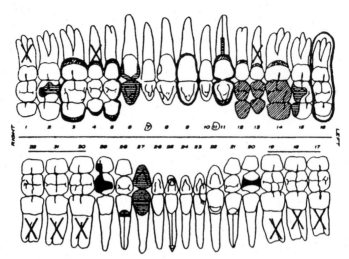

Figure A6-1. Instruction for Charting Missing Teeth and Existing Restorations.

#1 Missing tooth

#2 Combination Restoration, ^m/Gold

#3-5 Ceramo-metal Fixed Partial Denture, Complete Ceramic Coverage

#6 3/4 Gold Crown

#7 Primary Tooth #7 present. If permanent #7 is impacted, circle, as shown for #16

#8 Distal Non-metallic Restoration

#9 Non-metallic Jacket Crown

#11D Retained Primary Cuspid between 10 and 11

#11 Root Canal, Ceramo-metal Crown Complete Ceramic Coverage, Cast Gold Post and Core

#12-14 Ceramo-metal Fixed Partial Denture, Ceramco Facings only

#15 Mesio-Occlusal-Lingual Gold Inlay

#16 Impacted Tooth

#17-19, 30-32 Extracted, Replaced by Removable Partial Denture

#20 Mesio-Occlusal-Distal Amalgam (MOD)

#21 Root Canal and Overdenture with Gold Coping

#22 Facial Non-metallic Restoration

#23 Disto-Incisal Non-metallic Restoration with Pins

#25 Root Canal and Apicoectomy with Lingual Non-metallic Restoration

#27 Complete Gold Crown

#28 Root Canal and Overdenture Abutment with Gold Coping

#29 Distal-Occlusal-Lingual Amalgam Restoration with Pins

INSTRUCTIONS FOR CHARTING DISEASES AND ABNORMALITIES
(See Figure A7-1)

A7-1. Caries. Draw an outline of the carious portion on the diagram of the affected tooth. Show approximate size, location, and shape; block in solidly.

A7-2. Extraction (Removal) Indicated. Draw two parallel vertical lines through all aspects of the involved tooth and roots. When removal is indicated, apply this also to unerupted teeth. When a tooth is retained, draw two parallel lines in the direction of the long axis of the root through the part that is retained.

A7-3. Abscess or Cyst. Outline the approximate size, form, and location of the abscess or cyst.

A7-4. Fistula. Draw a straight line from the involved area. End it in a small circle in a position on the chart that corresponds to the location of the tract orifice in the mouth.

A7-5. Unerupted Tooth. Outline all aspects of the tooth with a single oval.

A7-6. Fractured Tooth. Trace a jagged fracture line in the relative position on the crown or roots.

A7-7. Resorption. Indicate gingival recession with a continuous line drawn across the roots to approximate the extent of involvement. Draw another continuous line at the proper level across the roots of the teeth to indicate the extent of alveolar resorption. Base this finding on clinical and roentgenographic findings.

A7-8. Resorption of Root. Draw an even line that shows the extent of resorption of the root.

A7-9. Defective Restoration. Outline the defective restoration. Include the carious or otherwise defective area and block it in solidly.

A7-10. Inclination of Impacted Teeth. Place an arrow that indicates the direction of the long axis of the tooth in the crown portion of the tooth form.

A7-11. Abnormalities of Occlusion and Remarks. Describe malocclusion and any other pertinent remarks that pertain to diseases and abnormalities found, such as, a history of therapeutic radiation to the oral or perioral structures, etc.

A7-12. Special Entries for Identification. Record under the "Remarks" section, findings such as erosion, abrasion, mottled enamel, hypoplasia, Hutchinson's teeth, presence of supernumerary teeth, abnormal interdental spaces, mucosal pigmentation, leukoplakis, diastema, torus palatinus or mandibularis, embedded foreign bodies, and unusual restorations or appliances.

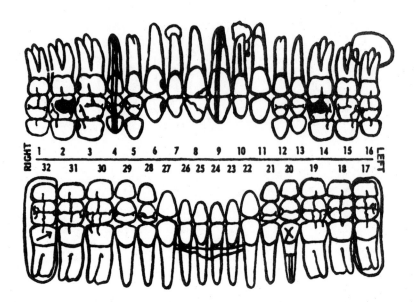

#2 Mesio-Occlusal Caries
#3 Distal Caries
#4 Extraction indicated
#6 Mesial Caries
#7 Abscess Periapical
#8 Fractured Crown
#9 Fractured Root-Extraction Indicated
#10 Abscess and Fistula, underfilled root canal filling
#11 Resorbed Root
#14 Defective Restoration-Outline area of

restoration to be replaced and defective area
#16 Cyst involving #15 and 16
#17 Unerupted Tooth. (If not visdible in oral cavity, an "X" would apppear on corresponding tooth on chart "Missing Teeth and Existing Restorations")
#20 Residual Root requiring removal
#23-26 inclusive. Gingival Crest-Continuous line. Alveolar Crest-Continuous line.
#32 Impacted Tooth with mesial inclination

★ FigureA7-1. Instructions for Charting Diseases and Abnormalities.

INSTRUCTIONS FOR COMPLETING AF Form 1801, POSTMORTEM DENTAL RECORD

(See Figure A15-1)

A15-1. Section I. Postmortem Examination Data. Type or print all entries in ink.

Item 1. Body Number: Enter the identification number or letter assigned by the person exercising legal jurisdiction over disposition of the remains.

Item 2. Age, Race and Sex: If known, self-explanatory. If unknown, enter "Unk."

Item 3. Date: Self-explanatory.

Item 4. Examiners: Enter the initials, surname, abbreviation of rank, service and corps of all examiners. If civilian, enter "AF Civ" in lieu of grade and corps.

Item 5. Place of Examination: Enter base and abbreviation of state in which examination was performed.

A15-2. Section II. Examination Findings, Description/Computer Codes (See Figure A15-1):

a. Type or print all entries in ink.

b. Use CAPMI, Computer Assisted Postmortem Identification, one and/or two letter computer codes provided on AF Form 1801, POSTMORTEM DENTAL RECORD in lieu of Authorized Designations and Abbreviations for the completion of SFs 603, HEALTH RECORD-DENTAL and 603A, HEALTH RECORD-DENTAL-Continuation, set forth in AFR 162-1, attachment 4 and para A4-1(d).

c. Entries Format. On the numbered line provided for each tooth, if known, enter the appropriate CAPMI symbol for tooth condition.

(1) Erupted crowns of teeth without caries or restorations are described as present not restored. See #4.

(2) Erupted crowns of teeth with caries are described by surface and disease. Caries is not charted in Section III. Restorations & Missing Teeth.

(3) Erupted crowns of teeth partially restored by dental materials are described by surface and restorative material. See #3.

(4) Erupted crowns of teeth restored by single unit permanently cemented cast restorations are described by the restoration. See #19.

(5) Erupted crowns of teeth restored by multiple unit permanently cemented fixed partial dentures are described by the type of prosthesis, and the retainer restoration. Missing teeth restored by fixed partial dentures are described by the type prosthesis and tooth condition of extracted or unerupted, as appropriate. See #13-15.

(6) Erupted teeth in which the clinical crown has been fractured from the retained root are described. See #20-22.

(7) Conventional and surgical endodontic root therapy is described subsequent to all notations regarding the tooth crown. See #13.

(8) Teeth restored by a removable partial or complete denture are described by the type prosthesis and the tooth condition. Malpositioned abutment teeth to removable partial dentures are described as rotated. See #28-32.

(9) Missing teeth are described as unerupted or extracted. Retained roots subsequent to extractions are described. See #17.

(10) Unknown tooth condition through postmortem traumatic avulsion from the alveolar process or missing fragments of the alveolar process are described as appropriate. See #6-11, #23-26.

A15-3. Section III. Restorations and Missing Teeth (See Figure A15-1):

a. All entries must be in ink.

b. Charting of restorations and missing teeth is performed IAW AFR 162-1 Attachment 6, INSTRUCTIONS FOR CHARTING MISSING TEETH AND EXISTING RESTORATIONS, A6-1 through A6-4a-k (See Figure A6-1, AFR 162-1).

c. Charting of fractured tooth crowns and retained roots is performed IAW AFR 162-1 Attachment 7, INSTRUCTIONS FOR CHARTING DISEASES AND ABNORMALITIES, A7-2 and A7-6 (See Figure A7-1, AFR 162-1). Charting of caries is not performed.

d. Postmortem avulsion of teeth from the alveolar process of the jaw is charted by drawing a straight vertical line from the uppermost to lowermost part of the tooth in the distal interproximal space of the two most posterior affected teeth and inscribing two crossing diagonal lines between the ends of the opposing vertical lines. See #23-26.

e. A missing fragment of the alveolar process is charted by drawing a straight vertical line from the horizontal line which forms the chart border to the horizontal line separating the maxillary from mandibular tooth numbers in the distal interproximal space of the two most posterior affected teeth and inscribing two crossing diagonal lines between the ends of the opposing vertical lines. See #6-11.

A15-4. Section IV. Remarks (See Figure A15-1):

f. Type or print all entries in ink.

g. Record any pertinent information or findings such as diastema, torus, tooth erosion or abrasion, supernumerary teeth, periapical pathology.

POSTMORTEM DENTAL RECORD

BODY NUMBER: A-89-3 EST. AGE: Unk. RACE: Unk. SEX: Unk. DATE: 30 Jan 89

EXAMINERS: RK GOODE, LtCol USAF DC   PLACE OF EXAMINATION: Andrews AFB, MD

KS HARTMAN, Col USAF DC

DESCRIPTION/COMPUTER CODES

1. X
2. OL - AM, F - AM
3. MODL - AM
4. PN
5. O/O - AM
6. JM
7. JM
8. JM
9. JM
10. JM
11. JM
12. PN
13. FP - CV, RF - AP
14. FP - X
15. FP - CF
16. X
17. X - RT
18. CP
19. CF
20. FX
21. FX
22. FX
23. TA
24. TA
25. TA
26. TA
27. PN
28. DO - GI
29. RP - X
30. RP - X
31. RP - X
32. MO - GI, RO

AF Form 1801 MAY 87

RESTORATIONS & MISSING TEETH

CAPMI SYMBOLS

AM	AMALGAM	CF	CROWN FULL
GI	GOLD INLAY	CP	CROWN PARTIAL
GF	GOLD FOIL	CV	CROWN VENEER
SS	ANY OTHER METAL REST	FP	FIXED PARTIAL
CO	COMPOSITE RESIN	RP	REMOVABLE PARTIAL
JM	JAW FRAGMENT MISSING	CD	COMPLETE DENTURE
TA	TRAUMATIC AVULSION	M	MESIAL
FX	FRACTURED CROWN	D	DISTAL
RT	ROOT TIP	O	OCCLUSAL
PN	PRESENT NOT RESTORED	I	INCISAL
RO	ROTATED	F	FACIAL
RF	ROOT CANAL FILLING	L	LINGUAL
AP	APICOECTOMY	C	CARIES
IR	INTERMEDIATE REST	U	UNERUPTED
CT	CROWN TEMPORARY	X	EXTRACTED

REMARKS: BILATERAL MANDIBULAR TORI

INSTRUCTIONS FOR COMPLETING AF Form 1802, ANTEMORTEM DENTAL RECORD
(See Figure A16-1)

A16-1. Section I. Antemortem Record Examination Data. Type or print all entries in ink:

a. Item 1. Name: Last, First and MI.

b. Item 2. SSN: Enter the Social Security Number of the named individual. Do not use the SSN of the sponsor when examining the record of a family member.

c. Item 3. Rank is self-explanatory. For family members of active duty personnel, enter "FM."

d. Item 4. Sex, Race and Age are self-explanatory.

e. Item 5. X-Ray Type and Date: Enter abbreviations for periapical (PER), bitewing (BW), panographic (PANO) and occlusal (OCC) with date, if known.

f. Item 6. Examiners: Enter the initials, surname, abbreviation of grade, service and corps of all examiners. If civilian, enter "AF Civ" in lieu of grade and corps.

g. Item 7. Date Reconstructed is self-explanatory.

h. Item 8. Records Supplied By: Enter place and abbreviation of state in which antemortem record examination was performed.

A16-2. Section II. Restorations and Missing Teeth (See Figure A16-1):

a. All entries must be in ink.

b. Charting of restorations and missing teeth is performed according to attachment 6, para A6-1 through A6-4a-k (see figure A6-1).

c. Charting of fractured tooth crowns and retained roots is performed according to attachment 7, para A7-2 and A7-6 (see figure A7-1). Charting of caries is not performed.

d. In the event that sufficient antemortem information to determine the tooth condition is missing, such cases are charted by drawing a straight vertical line from the horizontal line which forms the chart border to the horizontal line separating the maxillary from mandibular tooth numbers in the distal interproximal space of the two most posterior affected teeth and inscribing two crossing diagonal lines between the ends of the opposing vertical lines.

A16-3. Section III. Examination Findings, Description/Computer Codes (See Figure A16-1):

a. Type or print all entries in ink.

b. Use CAPMI, Computer Assisted Postmortem Identification, one and/or two letter computer codes provided on AF Form 1802, ANTEMORTEM DENTAL RECORD in lieu of Authorized Designations and Abbreviations for the completion of SFs 603, HEALTH RECORD-DENTAL and 603A, HEALTH RECORD-DENTAL-Continuation, set forth in attachment 4.

c. Entries Format. On the numbered line provided for each tooth, if known, enter the appropriate CAPMI symbol for tooth condition.

(1) Erupted crowns of teeth without caries or restoration are described as present not restored. See #4.

(2) Erupted crowns of teeth with caries are described by surface and disease. Caries is not charted in Section II. Restorations & Missing Teeth. See #18.

(3) Erupted crowns of teeth partially restored by dental materials are described by surface and restorative material. See #19.

(4) Erupted crowns of teeth restored by single unit permanently cemented cast restorations are described by the restoration. See #9.

(5) Erupted crowns of teeth restored by multiple unit permanently cemented fixed partial dentures are described by the type of prosthesis, and the retainer restoration. Missing teeth restored by fixed partial dentures are described by the type prosthesis and tooth condition of extracted or unerupted, as appropriate. See #13-15.

(6) Erupted teeth in which the clinical crown has been fractured from the retained root are described.

(7) Conventional and surgical endodontic root therapy is described subsequent to all notations regarding the tooth crown. See #13.

(8) Teeth restored by a removable partial or complete denture are described by the type prosthesis and the tooth condition. Malpositioned abutment teeth to removable partial dentures are described as rotated. See #29-31 and #32.

(9) Missing teeth are described as unerupted or extracted. Retained roots subsequent to extractions are described. See #16 and 17.

(10) Unknown tooth conditions are described as jaw fragment missing.

A16-4. Section IV. Remarks (See Figure A16-1):

a. Type or print all entries in ink.

b. Record any additional pertinent information or findings such as diastema, torus, tooth erosion or abrasion, supernumerary teeth, periapical pathology.

ANTEMORTEM DENTAL RECORD

NAME: SMITH, JOHN C.   SSN: 123-45-6789   RANK: MAJ. USAF

SEX: M   RACE: C   AGE: 38   X-RAY TYPE & DATE: PA/85, BW/87

EXAMINERS: RK GOODE, LtCol USAF DC   DATE RECONSTRUCTED: 30 JAN 89

           KS HARTMAN, Col USAF DC   RECORD SUPPLIED BY: Andrews AFB, MD

RESTORATIONS & MISSING TEETH

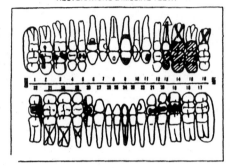

DESCRIPTION/COMPUTER CODES

1. _U_
2. _OL - AM, F - AM_
3. _MO - AM, DO - AM_
4. _PN_
5. _O/O - AM_
6. _F - GF_
7. _M - CO_
8. _L - IR, RF_
9. _CV_
10. _MI - CO_
11. _DL - AM_
12. _PN_
13. _FP - CV, RF - AP_
14. _FP - X_
15. _FP - CF_
16. _X_
17. _U_
18. _MODL - C_
19. _MOD - AM_
20. _MO - AM_
21. _DO - AM_
22. _ML - CO_
23. _PN_
24. _CT - RF_
25. _PN_
26. _PN_
27. _PN_
28. _DO - GI_
29. _RP - X_
30. _RP - X_
31. _RP - X_
32. _MO - GI, RO_

CAPMI SYMBOLS

AM	AMALGAM	CF	CROWN FULL
GI	GOLD INLAY	CP	CROWN PARTIAL
GF	GOLD FOIL	CV	CROWN VENEER
SS	ANY OTHER METAL REST	FP	FIXED PARTIAL
CO	COMPOSITE RESIN	RP	REMOVABLE PARTIAL
JM	JAW FRAGMENT MISSING	CD	COMPLETE DENTURE
TA	TRAUMATIC AVULSION	M	MESIAL
FX	FRACTURED CROWN	D	DISTAL
RT	ROOT TIP	O	OCCLUSAL
PN	PRESENT NOT RESTORED	I	INCISAL
RO	ROTATED	F	FACIAL
RF	ROOT CANAL FILLING	L	LINGUAL
AP	APICOECTOMY	C	CARIES
IR	INTERMEDIATE REST	U	UNERUPTED
CT	CROWN TEMPORARY	X	EXTRACTED

REMARKS: BILATERAL MANDIBULAR TORI

AP Form 1002, MAY 87

INSTRUCTIONS FOR COMPLETING AF Form 1803, DENTAL IDENTIFICATION
SUMMARY REPORT
(See Figure A17-1)

A17-1. Section I. Antemortem and Postmortem Data. Type or print all entries in ink:

Item 1. Name of Deceased: Enter the deceased name as recorded on AF Form 1802, ANTEMORTEM DENTAL RECORD.

Item 2. Body Number: Enter the identification number or letter assigned to the remains as recorded on AF Form 1801, POSTMORTEM DENTAL RECORD.

Item 3. Rank, Age, Race and Sex: If known, self-explanatory. If unknown, enter "Unk."

Item 4. SSN: Enter as recorded on AF Form 1802, ANTEMORTEM DENTAL RECORD.

Item 5. Examiners: Enter the initials, surname, abbreviation of rank, service and corps of all examiners. If civilian, enter "Civ" in lieu of rank and corps.

Item 6 Date: Self-explanatory.

Item 7. Place: Enter place and abbreviation of state in which summary report was prepared.

A17-2. Section II. Comparison of Antemortem and Postmortem Records (See Figure A17-1):

a. Type or print all entries in ink.

b. Entry Format.

(1) On the numbered line provided for each tooth, enter the appropriate CAPMI symbol for tooth condition found to be concordant based on review of antemortem and postmortem dental records.

(2) On the numbered line provided for each tooth, enter a dash symbol (-) when, based on review of antemortem and postmortem dental records, no concordant points were observed.

A17-3. Section III. Remarks (See Figure A17-1):

a. Type or print all entries in ink.

b. Record any concordant pertinent information observed in the comparison of antemortem and postmortem dental records. If none, so state.

A17-4. Section IV. Findings (See Figure A17-1):

a. Indicate the classification determined from comparison of antemortem and postmortem dental records and radiographs by inscribing, in ink, a circle around either: positive identification, consistent with or unidentified.

b. Suggested criteria for classification:

(1) positive identification: absolute certainty that there is no other possible individual who these remains could be identified as, based on comparison of antemortem and postmortem dental records and radiographs. There can be no unresolved contradictory dental findings.

(2) consistent with: based on comparison of antemortem and postmortem dental records, reasonable certainty exists that the postmortem remains are the individual named. There can be no unresolved contradictory dental findings.

(3) unidentified: there are insufficient or contradictory findings in comparison of antemortem and postmortem dental records to justify identification.

A17-5. Signature (See Figure A17-1):

a. All entries must be handwritten in ink.

b. No AF Form 1803, DENTAL IDENTIFICATION SUMMARY REPORT shall be valid without the confirmatory signature of the Dental Team Leader.

DENTAL IDENTIFICATION
SUMMARY REPORT

NAME OF DECEASED: SMITH, JOHN C.   BODY NUMBER: A-89-3

RANK: MAJ   SEX: M   RACE: C   AGE: 38   SSN: 123-45-6789

EXAMINERS: RK GOODE, LtCol USAF DC   DATE: 30Jan89   PLACE: Andrews AFB, MD
           KS HARTMAN, Col USAF DC

COMPARISON OF ANTEMORTEM AND POSTMORTEM DENTAL RECORDS AND RADIOGRAPHS REVEAL CONCORDANCE ON

TEETH NUMBER (DESCRIBE FEATURE):

#		#		#		#	
1	—	9	—	17	—	25	—
2	OL-AM, F-AM	10	—	18	—	26	—
3	—	11	—	19	—	27	PN
4	PN	12	PN	20	—	28	DO-GI
5	O/O-AM	13	FP-CV, RF-AP	21	—	29	RP-X
6	—	14	FP-X	22	—	30	RP-X
7	—	15	FP-CF	23	—	31	RP-X
8	—	16	X	24	—	32	MO-GI, RO

REMARKS: BILATERAL MANDIBULAR TORI NOTED. NO UNRESOLVED, CONTRADICTORY
FINDINGS. TEETH 3,18,19 TREATED BY CIVILIAN DENTIST 1988, TEETH
1,17 EXTRACTED WHILE TDY ICELAND 1988; SOURCE - NEXT OF KIN

FINDINGS (CIRCLE ONE): (POSITIVE IDENTIFICATION)   CONSISTENT WITH   UNIDENTIFIED

SIGNATURE OF EXAMINERS: _____   _____

FINDINGS CONFIRMED BY: _____   (DENTAL TEAM LEADER)

AF Form 1803, MAY 87

Mass Disaster Experiences

10

PAUL G. STIMSON
CURTIS A. MERTZ

In this chapter, the authors will share their experiences in mass disasters and the evaluations of many aircraft disaster reports. We hope in this manner to be of help in this most difficult of situations. This book already has an excellent chapter on the organization of the disaster team (see Chapter 9). This chapter is to offer help in those areas not covered in the disaster team organizational material.

A great deal of time and effort is needed to develop a procedure manual unique to each town, city, location, or state. This manual will list all the names, telephone numbers, addresses, and social security numbers (for identification and pay purposes) of the key individuals who will be called in for duty in the emergency. Each individual may also be given their own unique identification number that will be compared with a master list to prevent unauthorized individuals from entering the scene or the morgue. Each key person should have a copy of this list and it should be updated as necessary. How each of the trained individuals is going to cover his or her individual business or practice and for how long should be considered. If the operation is going to take three weeks to completion, can the chief forensic dentist take that much time from his or her office? Methods to maintain their regular position or maintain their practice must be covered during their emergency leave period.

One agreement that must be listed in the operations manual, more than once, is the requirement of absolute confidentiality. No information is to be given or shared with anyone except the immediate supervisor of the section. Nothing is to be shared or talked about concerning the operation with anyone outside their section. This should be covered in a paragraph in the initial paperwork required to be a member of the team. Violations of this agreement should lead to immediate dismissal of the individual, no matter their position, to prevent sabotage of the entire operation.

Each member of the team will be subject to many kinds of pressure, both political and nonpolitical and from the news media. The chain of command must be established in every accident scenario. This individual must have the authority to hire and set realistic rates of pay and delegate the necessary procedures. As far as possible, every segment of the mass accident should be preplanned. Each plan will be changed due to unforseen situations, but without a plan chaos exists. This is especially important when trying to estimate the numbers of forensic pathologists, anthropologists, and dentists who are trained and available. Multiple listings are necessary since some may not be available at the time of the accident, or probably cannot spend much time on the scene or in the morgue. The hourly pay rates should be agreed on prior to any disaster, so each individual can be paid according to experience and training.

Without fully discussed plans and agreements and mock testing, misunderstandings will occur and the problems will compound very quickly. When working with inexperienced or poorly trained people mistakes will occur. Untrained and well-intentioned people do their utmost, but due to the stress of the situation they often cause an increase in time and costs. Unfortunately, they also cause some unintentional poor publicity for the entire team. At least twice a year the key people in the plan should meet and discuss any new ideas or changes to the plan. Mock exercises should be planned and scheduled regularly. This should be a part of the coroner's or medical examiner's object for training.

At the time of a mass disaster, the secretarial staff of the office should be instructed to screen every telephone call directed to the coroner, medical examiner, or individual in charge, to prevent wasting their valuable time and talents. The instructions for this screening should be part of the overall plan. A period of time for each of the screeners should be set aside for them to explain the nature of the call, and after receiving an answer, they usually can return the call. This allows the in-charge individual to stay off the phone, unless absolutely necessary. Lists of necessary contact individuals who can talk to the individual in charge should be provided. Every call should be handled in a courteous, concerned manner. This may be difficult for a tired individual under considerable stress and duress. Extra rest time should be provided to the initial phone contact individuals. People will use false names and other mechanisms to get early "scoops" on accident information. Know who you are talking with, and be prepared to refer them to someone higher in the command chain for information release. Depending on the resources of your state, the governor can declare the scene a disaster area. After this occurs, the office of the governor can contact the president of the United States requesting assistance. The president can then authorize the Federal Emergency Management Association (FEMA) to take over the disaster situation. Once this occurs the operation is under the FEMA team and local and other state individuals are used as the FEMA team leader sees fit. The other aspects of the resources of the federal government can be used by the FEMA team as necessary. The FEMA plan, once authorized, supersedes the state, regional, or local plans when implemented.

Some thought must be given to the identification badges to be worn on site each day. A plan must exist to change them daily to preserve the confidentiality of the operation. Each section should have proper identification; for example, search, rescue, and body recovery teams. There is no reason for them to be in the morgue situation and their identification badge would prevent them from passing into this area. The morgue area is congested enough without other team members being on the scene. The records and personal effects areas are very critical and the identification process must be secure.

Trained local people should negotiate convenient motel and hotel reservations with preagreed rates, to house out-of-town specialists. Rooms are going to be at a premium when there is a big influx of reporters to the scene. Arrangements must be made in advance to insure adequate housing of the members of the team. Arrangements should be made with restaurants for private dining for the team members to prevent the news media from bothering them with questions during their meal periods. The plan should include having a uniformed officer along with the other members of the team when having their meal, to persuade the intruder that this is neither the time nor place for an interview.

The individual in charge of the overall planning for a mass disaster should have an accountant (a Certified Public Accountant is preferred) as a member of the administrative team. One reason the military does very well in a disaster scenario is that everything used, ordered, brought to the scene, etc. is cataloged and recorded. After the completion of the disaster scene, the materials and expenses can be accounted for almost to the penny. The names, rank, and pay rate of every individual can also be easily substantiated. During a victim recovery and identification process any other agency will have the same responsibility. The total recovery will cost many thousands of dollars, and no insurance carrier or other company which may be partially or fully responsible is willing to recompense without substantiated records for the expenses and monies that were spent.

A forensic anthropologist and/or a forensic archeologist should also be on the team. They are most valuable initially to help grid the accident area with reference stakes and points for the proper recovery of aircraft and human parts. The staked grids are invaluable in the recovery and identification of the aircraft, truck, or train parts. They are also valuable in the location of the passengers, crew, or other unfortunate bystanders in the accident. The professionals now use a theodolite laser plotting technique for gridding and recovery of the impact or accident area.

These suggestions are not presented in any particular order; so many things are going on simultaneously at the scene and at the local medical examiner's office or the office of the coroner that these are planning suggestions only. Arrangements should be made with the administrator of each hospital in the area to know how many emergency room patients they are capable of handling. It is also imperative that the hospitals develop major accident policies which define who is to be in charge of the admission of patients in a given emergency and who is authorized to accept or reject patients. At the scene, as each ambulance or other means of conveyance to the emergency rooms is filled, the unit number or license plate should be recorded. The name (if known) or grid number of the recovery area should also be recorded. The body recovery vehicles and their contents must be similarly recorded. The on-site supervisor in charge of triage and the dispatch of injured individuals should have some type of communication with the hospitals. In this way no single hospital will be overloaded with patients and to turn them away due to lack of space. A recovery manual for both injured and dead should be a part of the procedures found in the Mass Accident Manual for each county, city, or region. Exercises should be staged to test the various scenarios portrayed in the manual. Up-to-date notes should be kept of each exercise and the manual revised as necessary.

The massive accident may be in a location where there is extreme difficulty getting the emergency vehicles close enough for utilization. Each disaster plan should include how problems in topography, lake size, oceans, or whatever the obstacle, is to be solved. The well-trained emergency crews need to be on the scene as rapidly as possible. Severe trauma, unless rapidly treated, will cause undue pain and suffering. The maximal survival of victims is highest within the first 24 to 36 hours after the accident, depending on their treatment. Survival will be less in extremes of temperatures. The plan for any given area should be that the search teams will try to find most of the living victims on the first search attempt. Depending on the type of accident that has occurred, other living victims are rarely discovered on later searches. Live victims are possible, as the individuals may have been unconscious during the first search. After at least two searches of the scene, the recovery then should switch to that of body recovery. Usually this is a difficult transition for the search members as they are extremely motivated for live victim recovery. Is there enough first aid and other equipment on hand in the locality for the victims at the scene? Where will we get it? When these materials are "borrowed" from hospital supply businesses in the area or hospital emergency rooms, receipts must be signed. The plan should authorize who is to request and sign for this material to prevent unnecessary duplication and theft of materials. Even in a time of local crisis, there are those who would try to turn the situation into a profit.

The mass disaster plan should give details of who is the ultimate authority in the location of the disaster and the proposed chain of command. It can be a medical examiner's office or a coroner. In states with a state medical examiner, the plan is split into regions. Many states have a coroner system that is either an elected or appointed office. Some states require that the coroner be a physician, but in most states the individuals can have almost any type of background. Because of the political nature of the coroner's office and the frequent changes that ensue, there may not be anyone in the office that has the skills, training, or experience to help if this is the office's first disaster. The office should have a well-designed disaster plan. The plan should have a training program and the possibility for "mock disaster" drills in it, so logistical problems that will be encountered can be solved. One problem in politically appointed situations, such as coroners' offices, is that the plan may be out of date or there is no one who has had first-hand experience with it.

The manual must list requirements for the necessary materials for mass disasters covered in Chapter 9. We suggest carefully going over this listing and finding a source for the materials and a place to store the necessary supplies. Lists should also be prepared summarizing what each team member is required to bring with them for their needs. This may include warm clothing, raincoats, rainproof footwear, and a spare flashlight. Roster sheets, time cards, shorthand pads, and dual receipt books (without carbon paper) are necessary. The usual office supplies must be available. Find a source for the usual office machines (typewriters, copy machines, adding machines and computers and a stand-alone fax machine) and keep the contact telephone numbers and individuals supplying them up to date. The reason for a stand-alone fax machine is this frees up one telephone line for incoming written and printed material. Preliminary dental records can be obtained in this way; tattoo descriptions and many other types of records can be obtained while waiting for the original or better copies to arrive. It is imperative that the individuals in charge of the operation are furnished a private unlisted telephone line. Using this line, the charge individual can then communicate with federal and state agencies, the state governor, or perhaps the president of the United States. Who the unlisted line is shared with and the security of this line should be carefully thought out and written in the communications section of the manual. Cellular telephone use should be kept to a minimum as these communications can be easily monitored and copied. Two-way radio communications are afflicted with the same problem — unauthorized monitoring. Communication with the outside world is critical. These lines are for the business of saving lives, clearing the scene, and recovery and identification of the deceased. If public phones are furnished for use by the news media, they must be in a location away from the principal work area. It may seem that this is "overkill" on our part, but the entire operation for identification rests on the trust between the family unit and the individual in charge of the operation. Thoughts about death and dying are gruesome enough, but when it is a loved one the entire picture for the family changes.

One or two scheduled news briefings should be given daily by a selected spokesperson. Only the spokesperson is to talk with the news media. This policy prevents news leaks and the possibility that some identifications may be given that later prove to have been provisional or unconfirmed. Families take a dim view of being told that there was a mistake made and it is not their loved one that has been identified. An agreement must be made with the local or regional telephone system to insure that the lines to the headquarters area are private and are monitored for intrusions. Discuss with the phone company methods for changing the telephone numbers if intrusions are detected. If the story is big enough for world news coverage there will be intrusions into the communications net to obtain information for the news media. This is not to imply the news services will do this, but for a price there are unscrupulous individuals who try to monitor fast-breaking news. Suffice to say that the phone lines are critical and need security and protection, and the manual should request as many phone lines as the planners think are sufficient and then add another four or five private lines. Recall the O. J. Simpson trial and the news media coverage. This is a necessary service, but the needs of the search, rescue, and identification operation are more critical than sharing every detail of it with the world as the operation unfolds.

When planning the manual, due consideration must be given for the location of a temporary morgue. The local high school gymnasium should *not* be considered; unless the floor is completely covered with material impervious to liquids, the floor will be ruined. How much will it cost to replace this beautiful hardwood floor? When the floor is covered, the portable gurneys cannot roll around as the material or plastic will bunch up and jam the wheels. When planning for temporary cold-storage truck trailers to store body bags awaiting autopsy and identification procedures, make sure that they have a metal floor as well as sides to prevent odor problems after the operation. Tarpaulins should be placed over the truck trailers to cover the name of the company that furnished them. The medical examiner or coroner should thank the company and be prepared to pay for the rental charges for the trailers upon completion of the operation. This is much better than having the name of the company on nationwide television stating it is "a body storage area." This is not good public relations. If the body recovery is done in subfreezing winter weather, a need exists to keep the remains from being solidly frozen and unmanageable. Assign an individual to stay with each locked trailer. Only this individual is allowed to release or gain access to body bags for their unit. This individual is responsible for the tally of the body bags in their trailer location. When a body bag is to traverse the identification process, an individual should stay with the bag until examinations are completed to prevent a mix-up of bags in the process.

Where and how are the personal effects of the body being taken care of? Locked files must be provided for records, both ante- and postmortem. Locked files must be provided for personal effects recovered with the remains or removed from the remains. These are sometimes helpful in suggesting a set of records to compare with an unknown body. An area must be provided for the computer that logs records and body tracking. Another computer may be used for the comparison of ante- and postmortem dental information. Space for the ante-mortem dental team for computer input must be made available. This is usually one of the more difficult areas and requires very experienced dental practitioners. The reason for this is that dentists use a variety of recording schemes and their own shorthand notes. Using the most recent bite wing films and the written record can help in this area. All of the records must be converted into one standardized type if computer comparisons are to be made. The computer cannot compare three or four different types of layouts of records. The ante-mortem and post-mortem comparison records must be standardized. What type of record does the local dental identification team prefer? The standard military mortuary antemortem and postmortem forms should be considered for use. Consideration can be given to stamping a large letter "M" or "F" to differentiate males and females to ease record sorting and hasten comparisons.

If body recovery is done during wet weather, in the rain or with snow on the ground, the clothes recovered with the body must be dried before being placed in a storage bag. If placed in a bag wet and soiled with body fluids or blood, the clothing becomes an infectious hazard and an odor producer as the fluids and tissue fragments decompose. The manual should cover this possibility and obtain an electrical clothing dryer and the necessary power to operate it. After the operation, depending on the use of the dryer, it may have to be salvaged. Autopsy tables, when temporary, do not require water. The lack of water will limit the amount of the examination that the pathologist can do. Plans must include the opportunity for the autopsy team members to wash their hands and instruments. The dental identification area also needs a source of water for their examinations. Radiographs can be taken on the site and developed somewhere else. Problems occur with this approach, however. If the radiographs are improperly exposed or the angulation is not correct when the finished film is viewed, the body must now be brought back to the area and radiographs retaken. This is one advantage of using film that can be developed on the site without a darkroom. All that is necessary is a small amount of water to wash the finished film. One of us (PGS) prefers to use larger, occlusal-type radiographic film, thus the maxilla and mandible can be radiographed on a single film. This makes the film a sort of bite wing with roots. This works very well in skelatinized material and can be used in other recovery situations. One problem that will plague the dental examiners is that of many small periapical films without any method of identification on them. The larger occlusal films are big enough that necessary body identification numbers or other codes can be written on them without infringing on critical diagnostic areas. Be sure that the plans include proper radiation shielding for the individuals taking the films and the bystanders and other workers in the area. An antemortem and postmortem room for radiographic comparisons of dental and other body films should be in the plan.

Possible emergency morgue plans must be listed and reviewed as new locations are found or old buildings are no longer available. The list must describe in detail the type of facility, the size, floor plans, type of floor in various areas, the ease of access, and security from intruders, video cameras, and photography. Ambulances and body cars should load and unload out of public view and shielded from the prying eyes of the news media. Some plans call for a large tent to be erected at the loading site, and the ambulance backed into the tent for privacy and security. The location of the temporary morgue must be secure and have adequate parking around it. Have there been any plans for area surveillance and perimeter security? One group that will be helpful is the local funeral directors' association. They are aware of the problems that will be faced and are usually very willing to give some assistance. Discuss with the directors the possibility of contracting with them to have embalming of victims or portions of victims done at locations away from the temporary morgue. To do these procedures on the site may violate OSHA regulations and cause exposure of the other workers in the location to potentially hazardous chemicals. Plans should include this procedure, along with whom to contact and where.

Are adequate sample tubes on site for alcohol, drug, and medication samples? The federal regulations require that aircraft crew, train crew, or interstate truck drivers be autopsied and tested, should this be that type of accident. Autopsies on the remainder of the passengers are at the discretion of the local authority. The Department of Transportation (DOT) requests this material for their own testing, plus the testing that local medical examiner or coroner may require. How many autopsies and how much testing is going to be done on the passengers? If two 747s collide this could be upwards of 600 or more bodies. How critical is it to know the levels of various toxological materials in each body? DOT is interested in the crew only, usually. The security of this material needs to be addressed in the overall plan. Who will receive and process these reports? This information is very sensitive and confidential and must be treated as such.

Embarrassment and untoward negative publicity can be prevented with extra caution and preplanning. Understanding that not all individuals at an accident site are honest is imperative. One critical team to be selected is the personal effects team. Another critical team is the one that will have the task of securing the area from all persons except those authorized to be on the scene. The personal effects team members should have the most background scrutiny of any of the teams that will be assembled. Imagine for a moment that someone in a commercial aircraft crash is a drug courier with $1 million in small unmarked bills. Unfortunately, this is not an unlikely scenario in America today. Another passenger may be wearing very valuable jewelry, etc. Anyone caught stealing anything, regardless of how large or small, should be prosecuted to the full extent of the law. A good source of reliable individuals can come from the local funeral directors with some of their part-time help. Another good source are retired school teachers who are used to keeping very detailed records and have dealt with people most of their teaching life. They must be paid for this service, as they will prevent all sorts of embarrassment and unneeded problems through their efforts. If this is a common carrier accident (bus, plane, train, etc.) the insurance carrier will be willing to pay reasonable fees for all involved in the recovery and identification procedure. Note the choice of the word *reasonable*. Insurance carriers are not willing to pay the chief forensic officer more than their chief executive officer earns in a year, for any accident. These management-type problems have vexed disasters in the past and have made some companies very suspicious of any attempt at payment. With proper planning, this should not be a problem.

The reasons for a spokesperson to handle news conferences are obvious. Let us illustrate this with a true incident. At a major aircraft accident an unusual problem developed. A male passenger was very inebriated and was seated in the first row of the first-class section near the cockpit. The accident occurred during takeoff with a fire breaking out after impact. Unfortunately, no one survived the crash. Almost every individual on the plane was burned beyond recognition. One male individual who was dressed in a white shirt and blue pants was thrown forward through the windshield of the plane. When the body count was done there was one missing individual. The next day an inspection was done of the area where the plane slid forward into an unmowed area. Using only circumstantial evidence, the found body in the white shirt and blue pants was presumed to be one of the pilots and his body was scheduled to be released early the morning of the second day. When the blood alcohol levels were completed on his body it was determined that the individual was over the level considered to be alcohol incapacitated (dead drunk). The release of the body was delayed and further identification measures were instigated. It was later proved that he was the passenger from the first-class section. Imagine what a problem in public relations this would have been for the airline and the disaster team working the accident if the presumed identification had been labeled as a "drunk pilot"! Why a presumed identification was going to be used for body identification is another portion of the story we will not talk about. Using a passenger manifest for identification also presents problems as people who are drug runners or money couriers travel under assumed names.

Planning should include the type of body tags that are to be used in the disaster. Make it a written policy that tags will be placed on extremities or torsos. Should only the head or skull remain, place the tag in an inconspicuous place. Photographs will be taken from great distances by photographers hoping to sell them to news services. The area should be secure from view from tall buildings or hills, etc. nearby. This is another reason for tags in proper places to prevent another news release problem. The public is sensitized to the accident and everything should be done to reduce the notoriety and trauma of the procedures. Some very good tags are now available. This tag must remain readable and intact through the worst case scenario imaginable. Everyone who is going to be in contact with bodies, body parts, clothing, or personal effects must wear rubber or similar gloves. Adequate protective clothing and an area in which to change and clean up before ending a the work day must be provided. Supplies and equipment needed during the recovery and identification processes must be scheduled to arrive when practical. Each purchase order should have a code such as A, B, C, etc. written in front of the usual purchase order number. The letter code will identify and specify delivery routing. This helps to prevent confusion when supplies are being delivered to one specific location. It also prevents dishonesty and theft. Thought should be given to having a reputable jeweler describe the type and details of the recovered materials that should then be tagged and placed in the personal effects files. Anything that may be carried with a passenger or worn should be described. Look for money belts, passports (it could be stolen), cross dressing by transvestites, unusual lifts in shoes, breast prosthesis indicating mastectomy surgery, etc. Keep an open mind and catalog all recovered materials and where they was recovered using the grid system. Credit cards, money, jewelry, and other valuables must be tagged, cataloged, and stored under security provisions away from the body. Never keep them in the body bag.

As the pressure of the accident begins to diminish slightly, the accident identification team leader should meet with the other key people under his or her command. This should be a closed meeting as there is a need to discuss the good and bad things that are occurring and the group thinking of the best way to correct the problems. Notes should be kept so that problems encountered can be prevented should another accident of this type occur.

The National Foundation of Mortuary Care has a portable morgue that can be requested. It can be quickly flown to almost any area of the U.S. It has been used in various field exercises for training by many teams and it is well stocked and designed. Your medical examiner or coroner can request assistance from this group and the use of this portable morgue.

Individuals working at the scene or at the morgue should be rotated within six to eight hours. The stress of the situation leads to mistakes made in good faith by individuals who are physically and emotionally exhausted. Mistakes then foster more mistakes and a difficult situation becomes almost impossible. Most group leaders and the individual in charge want to accomplish the identification procedure in the shortest time possible. This is admirable and a goal to shoot for. When mistakes happen this goal becomes very difficult to meet and the procedure becomes very complex. In spite of the pressures, the recovery situation and the morgue environment should be shut down after ten hours of operation if well-trained relief crews are not readily available.

One problem that the disaster director will have is that of volunteers. Individuals from literally all over the world as well as the U.S. will call to volunteer. Some of them even travel to the scene and will present themselves, ready to go to work. The director and many group leaders may not know these individuals or their background. A preplanned list of those that are to be called for the disaster will be used. Consideration of "outsiders" is possible only after a thorough interview on the telephone and verification of their skills, ability, and training. References given must be contacted for personal verfication of work experience, collegiality, and ability to get along with their co-workers. Some invited specialists can probably provide names of individuals who can be trusted and have skills necessary for the resolution of the disaster or a special problem.

After each disaster is completed there should be a postdisaster meeting with the objective to write a report of the efforts of the entire team. This report will serve to help the coroner or medical examiner obtain the necessary funding from either government, insurance, or other funding sources to pay for the time, effort, and supplies used in the disaster. It will also help others planning for similar experiences to avoid some pitfalls and use the strengths discovered in the calamity.

Litigation, unfortunately, is also part of each of these types of investigations. Inexperience and poor planning lend themselves to problems with family units and attorneys. Recently, after an aircraft crash, maxillas and mandibles were removed from viewable bodies (bodies that have almost no injury to the facial area and can have an open casket funeral). This is one way to ensure a positive dental identification, but it created many legal problems for the identification team. Other means for identification should be pursued in these types of cases and dental identification left for the final method, assuming all other methods for positive identification fail. Preplanning and organization would have prevented this unfortunate problem. Some body parts that were previously not identified can now be placed together with the same victim through the use of DNA testing. This testing is expensive, but the technology exists for this type of examination.

One final comment. Stress, both physical and mental, are inherent in a disaster situation. Team leaders and others must be aware of changes in attitude or efficiency of individuals. This is a situation where things that are very disconcerting begin to build in the psyche of the individuals involved. Psychologists and psychiatrists should be available to help individuals who become mentally exhausted or confused. Do not relieve the individuals and merely send them home for a rest. These individuals should be relieved of duty and taken to trained professionals for help. The entire team will need help regarding their mental health after the operation is completed. Situations like a disaster are very trying on the individual's psyche. Each individual carries away from the event his or her own particular set of memories and problems. Postevent counseling is critical for all individuals involved and must be planned as a part of the operation.

It is our hope this short collection of potential problems and information on how to overcome them has been helpful and has aided in planning efforts.

Appendix 10.1

"Forensic Nuggets"

Forensic skeletal material exposed to the elements for several months, depending on the latitude and climatic conditions, can have a moderate amount of soft tissues remaining. The material is in some state of decomposition. If the taking of dental radiographs is necessary, some techniques can be used. The mandible can be disarticulated from the skull. The maxilla can be detached from the base of the skull with the use of a Stryker® saw, a metal saw, or a set of large pruning shears. Dr. Maples and other anthropologists prefer that the maxilla not be detached from the skull. After obtaining permission from the medical examiner or coroner, the skull can be defleshed. This is not a pleasant task as the skull must be boiled and the decomposing tissues subsequently stripped off. The odors produced from the boiling procedure are penetrating, obnoxious, and if not done in a proper environment can cause the individual doing the procedure multiple problems. Complaints to law enforcement officials will be investigated and the procedure could possibly be stopped if the odors are extremely disturbing to a neighborhood or city area. The best action in this type of situation is to utilize the services of a forensic anthropologist, and then study the material after the skull has been properly cleaned and defleshed.

If necessary, the mandible can be taken into a dental office for radiographs if it is tightly and securely bound in Saran Wrap® or some similar material. If the maxilla has been removed from the base of the skull, it can be treated similarly. Should this technique be chosen, be extremely careful to avoid puncturing the wrapping on the specimens. The noxious gases produced by decomposition, principally putrescine and cadaverine, will adhere to any fabrics in the dental office environment. This means that fabric-covered chairs, couches, drapes, rugs, etc. will all have the odor of decomposition in them. All attempts to mask the odor will fail. The materials exposed must be replaced. This means that the trade-off for a set of dental radiographs could become quite expensive. The plastic-wrapped materials work well for odor control. The specimens can be soaked in 10% neutral buffered formalin to help to contain the odor, but this procedure will take time. The specimens should be checked daily and the solutions changed to insure proper fixation. Should maggots be present, they are sometimes difficult to remove and present fixation problems. What we are describing is not a very pleasant situation, but one that the forensic dentist must contend with and find a solution for in their own situation.

A better course of action is to take radiographs in a morgue or a funeral home preparation room. If a portable dental radiograph machine can be obtained, it can be used in either of these locations. Using a portable dental radiographic machine is also possible, under some type of cover, in the field. A recently improved dental radiographic film that can be developed on the site with very little additional material is ideal for use in this type of situation. The name of the film is Phil-X 30© (American Diversified Dental Systems (1-800-637-2337)). This film is an instant-developing X-ray film packet that has a packet of both developer and fixer with it. This allows development of the film in full daylight. A special crystal temperature-reading strip is included to control development of the film at the particular room or environmental temperature. The only thing necessary is a sink with some running water for final chemical removal. Caution is necessary to place the identification point in the proper orientation. The film contains no lead foil so it can be exposed from either side of the holder. Therefore, it can be reversed. Other uses of this film are for dental examination by various State Dental Examining Boards, or endodontic examinations. The manufacturer includes a metric grid that can be placed over the film for accurate positioning of the length of endodontic files and filling material.

After all "usual" methods of identification have been completed, the agency in question may still be faced with an unidentified body. All the usual tests have been done, radiographs taken, and no clues are present to suggest help for the identification. DNA tests can be done; however, they are expensive. These tests, like dental identifications, also require an individual or family to compare the unknown sample to. The next individual to turn to is the forensic anthropologist. The body can be shipped to the anthropologist in a sealed container. One method to ship only a partially fleshed skull is to wrap it entirely airtight in a plastic wrap (Saran Wrap® or similar material). Using a large can that popcorn is purchased in, the airtight wrapped skull is placed in styrofoam pellets (or popcorn) for shipping protection. Wrap the mandible separately and pack it in the same can. Use plenty of packing material so no rattle of the specimens can be detected. The metal can may be shipped via parcel post. They will accept the can if at least two sheets of plastic film is placed over the opening of the can. Put the lid on the can carefully to ensure that it is airtight, and seal the can top with fiberglass tape. Place a biomedical materials tag on the outside of the can. Include a return address and phone number (should the can be damaged and the contents exposed) and send it "return receipt requested". Be sure to advise the laboratory or anthropologist that a specimen is coming and to acknowledge the arrival of the specimen. One of the authors (CAM) has shipped many specimens in this manner with no problems or damage.

Be prepared to invest time; the preparation and cleaning of the skeleton takes considerable time. In doing the cleaning procedure, artificial joints, such as hips, may be discovered. These may have been overlooked in the original workup of the case if whole-body radiographs were not done. Should an artificial joint be discovered, the need for a competent orthopedic surgeon becomes necessary. Most of the time the surgeon can suggest the manufacturer of the joint implant and can understand and interpret the marking on the implant that may be of help. Often, lot numbers and individual prosthesis identification numbers are not present. Right now, most replacement parts for knee, femur, hip, shoulder, elbow, and other parts are not marked. The present method of marking makes the finished product subject to possible corrosion and fracture at the site of the marking. This is why they are not presently marked. Check with the hospitals in the area and you might be lucky enough to find a suggestion of the unknown individual. A good reference about orthopedic implants and their use is *Campbell's Operative Orthopaedics*, (Volume 2, 8th edition, edited by A. H. Crenshaw. and published by C. V. Mosby, St. Louis, 1992). There is at present no pressure on the manufacturers to mark and number their appliances. With the pressures of medical and forensic matters, such as identification and malpractice, they might begin to do this in the future.

The authors have attempted to discover if there are any lists of markings on replacement lenses inserted after cataract surgery. To date we have been unable to find any information about this area of possible identification that will be present in the older age group in this country. One problem that occurs after cataract surgery is dryness of the eyes. A small plastic tube is inserted in the lacrimal canal in many individuals postsurgery to ensure that the lacrimal duct remains patent. The tube ensures an adequate amount of natural lubrication (tears) to the eye. Should this small tube be found during a forensic examination, it might suggest that cataract surgery or other similar eye surgery had been done. In partially skelatinized remains, the eye area should be checked very carefully if the skeletal remains suggest an older individual.

We have mentioned in other sections of this text the necessity of not sharing any information with the news media. The only individual who was always correctly quoted was the father of the atomic submarine, the late Hyman Rickover. Early in the development of this new technological marvel he was once misquoted. This almost caused the project to be canceled. He sued a major newspaper reporting service and was awarded a large sum of money. The news media respected him after this incident and he was given copy to correct before publication. The moral to this short story is that we, as forensic and law enforcement individuals, do not have this type of understanding. The only way to protect ourselves and the investigation is to refer the inquiring reporter to the individual in charge. We have experienced situations in the past where a well-intentioned member of a dental team gave statements to the television media. Some material mentioned was not deemed appropriate for public dissemination at that time as the next of kin had not yet been notified and the accident investigation was continuing. This caused a dental identification team to be replaced by other more trusted individuals. Never discuss the details of your efforts with anyone except other members of your team. If this is a mass disaster, the National Transportation Safety Board will usually hold one or two press conferences each day for the benefit of the media. To sell or receive a gift for the "inside" release of information, photographs, or other material is a breach of the operating rules of the medical examiner, coroner, or other official agency for which you are working. Recently in the Value Jet crash in Florida, the news media reported that a truck driver kept some aircraft pieces he was hauling for "a souvenir." He now faces federal charges for impeding the investigation.

Some identification groups with little experience are proposing that all remains should be photographed as part of the original identification process. Photographs are essential and are necessary to document injuries and other information. Be cautious of who is chosen to develop photographic material. It is pleasing to get things developed and printed in less than two hours, but some unscrupulous individuals in the processing area may sell copies of your material to the media. If the story is worldwide or national news, the media will stop at nothing to obtain material. No photographs should be taken during the identification process unless authorized by the chief of the operation. In larger operations a photographer is part of the team and will furnish the proper photographs. The person requested to take photographs must make sure that the film is personally handed to a qualified and identified person and a receipt issued for the film or any other materials to show that an authorized individual has taken possession of it. An unspoken truth in a major accident is that there will be many lawsuits filed and the material that the team is helping to gather and process will be part of the proceedings. More important than that, however, is the impact in the total picture of the identification process.

Survival Techniques in Another World — The Courtroom

11

PAUL G. STIMSON
CURTIS A. MERTZ

The playing field of the courtroom is quite different from the environment of the dental or other forensic office. Expert witnesses present their opinions as evidence in a judicial forum in which the rules and procedures have been created by lawyers and judges.

A Forensic Dental Consultant or other type of Forensic or Law Enforcement Consultant may be asked for suggestions in the preparation of depositions and court exhibits. A Forensic Odontologist will be of special value in a case of bite mark evidence. In this book, Chapter 6 specifically covers bite mark photography and analysis techniques, and many other references that will be of help appear in the Appendixes. The following are a few often-overlooked suggestions listed in no particular order:

We prefer to use ASA 100 speed film for color negatives. The colors may be easier to balance. The enlargements will be sharp and crisp. The film processor can enlarge the negatives into larger exhibits. Both Kodak® and AGFA® film have served the authors well. When processing color negative film in any forensic case, have the initial prints made in the 4 × 6 in. size. Their cost is negligible and the attorney will find it easy to select the best negatives to enlarge as 8 × 10 prints or larger exhibits to introduce for depositions or in court.

Slow speed (Kodachrome® ASA 64) color slide film is often the easiest to use. It will retain its color stability over a long period. Some prefer to use Ektachrome® ASA 100 film that will give the color slide a slight blue tint counterbalanced by the red in the projection lamp. This gives a projected image that is very close to what was in the original. Keep in mind that the higher the speed of the film, the larger the grain size of the emulsion, and when attempting to create big enlargements (five times life size) the finished product will have a fuzzy appearance. When conditions warrant, high-speed film should be used. If the light is very poor, or the situation prevents the use of a strobe flash, or for surveillance work, etc., then higher ASA films can be used. Always carry a roll or two of very high speed film (ASA 800 or 1000) with the photographic equipment. This is used should the electronic flash unit stop working. Satisfactory photographs can be obtained with ambient light using a through-the-lens camera with a built-in light metering system and ultra-high-speed film. Only occasionally will it be preferred to want or need to use projected slides in a courtroom. Try to avoid using a slide projector due to poor lighting conditions in the courtroom. Having the screen situated where the jury can see the projected material well is sometimes difficult. Because of the poor control of the lighting in the courtroom slides will be difficult to see and the subtle colors will be lost in the bright room. If slides must be used, use a lenticular screen and a powerful projector. Carry a spare bulb and do a test prior to testimony. Check out the courtroom situation and decide which visual technique is best to use to illustrate the case. Photographic exemplars can be taken into the jury room for further study and reference, should this be necessary.

When doing depositions, use enlarged color photographs whenever possible. Most jurors remember more of what they see, in preference to what they hear. Make every point in the exhibit readily understandable. Never use a photographic exhibit that is smaller than 8 × 10 in. Color photographic copier enlargements of 8 × 10 in. or larger turn out very well, are reasonable in price, and quick to copy when an emergency or the need for fast results is necessary.

Never use any exhibit that looks unprofessional or is in poor taste. Since nothing is known about the jury and their hidden feelings or prejudices, things in poor taste could be offensive to one or more of them. This could jeopardize and diminish the consultant's effectiveness in the trial. Explain all of the parts of a technical exhibit in a simple, understandable manner. Make sure that the entire jury will be able to, and does, follow the explanation. Do not use words that may not be in the vocabulary of an average juror. Using words beyond the comprehension of the average individual immediately makes him or her feel inferior, it causes the attention to wander, and stifles comprehension. Maxillary and mandibular dentures are "plates" or "false teeth".

Labels for the photographic exhibits are very critical and important. Using an 8 × 10 in. enlargement, make a color copy on a copy machine. Place the color copy in a typewriter and insert the word labels. This is an inexpensive way to create a mock-up of the exhibits. This will also allow a discussion of the exhibits with the attorney and indicates how effective they are or will be. It allows an opportunity to change them if necessary. Your attorney should have some indication of what the judge will allow in the courtroom in the way of photographs. How much is considered inflammatory and offensive to the jury? This varies with the background and experience of each judge.

What type of labels will the judge allow? Some insist that the label be off to the side with a line drawn to the area so "nothing important is concealed."

When initially discussing the case with the attorney try to give a rough estimate in dollars of what the minimal exhibits and exemplars will cost. Try to be as realistic as possible in this estimate. If it is felt that more extensive or expensive exhibits are necessary, now is the time to justify them. If the attorney feels that his or her case is sufficient in other areas to be properly presented, it may require the use of minimal materials. The attorney — like a quarterback on a football team — calls the plays and runs the team.

Requesting a retainer before beginning work on a case for an attorney is customary. The dollar amount of the retainer is the consultant's choice. Discuss the retainer amount with other experts doing similar work and with a personal attorney. A retainer of $500 to $1000 dollars would not be unreasonable.

If no retainer is forthcoming, no opinions or other information should be given to the attorney. We have asked our bank to flag the check given by the attorney. Should it fail to clear, they notify us immediately. We prefer the retainer check to be included with the case materials we have been given to review. This may sound a little mercenary, but to not be compensated for a tremendous amount of effort, photography, research, etc. is very disappointing. There are good attorneys, dentists, physicians, forensic scientists, etc., however, a bad experience places one on guard. The few individuals who do not meet their financial obligations make these recommendations necessary. Usually there are no problems. Keep in mind that the attorney hired you, not the client. Speaking from experience, one case will bring these suggestions to your attention very quickly when there is a failure to be compensated. "Once burned, once learned"!

When the retainer is almost depleted and more work on the case is necessary to complete it, communicate this fact with the attorney. Give the attorney a reasonable estimate of what is needed in time or other expenses. If the time lag is more than two weeks between your request and a check arriving, call the attorney to explore the delay.

It is unethical to accept a case where the agreement is that payment is based on a contingency fee as a percentage of the recovery. This is ethical for an attorney, but it is not for professional individuals. Proving that an expert witness is giving honest opinions in this situation would be difficult. You will be asked about the financial arrangements made with the attorney in either a deposition or the courtroom. This is standard procedure, and how to answer this question must be discussed with your attorney. This is an attempt to point out to the jury that you are a "hired expert." It is a standard attorney ploy, but obviously they are working on a fee arrangement also. Answer the question honestly (recall being under an oath, probably) and do not try to spar or play word games with the opposing attorney. It is their arena and they are in charge at that moment in time. Be courteous and do not lose your temper or become rattled. The jury senses the expert witness is uncomfortable on the stand, and they understand and respect that.

When you have gained a reputation as an honest forensic dentist or scientist, be wary of the unscrupulous attorney who may name you as the plaintiff's expert witness. This attorney has never discussed any part of the case with you. What is hoped is that the case will have a quick settlement because of your name and reputation. If this occurs, consult your personal attorney about guidance for a formal complaint to the State Legal Bar Association.

Should there be a complaint about late, delayed, or lack of payment of fees, again contact your personal attorney. In some states the Association Legal Bar will be of some assistance. A personal attorney can make direct or indirect suggestions of the best method of approach. We recommend the use of some type of expert witness agreement such as the one at the end of Chapter 12 on dealing with attorneys. This becomes a contract when properly endorsed and signed, and now there is a breech of contract issue. This issue is easier to deal with and prove. Consult your personal attorney for details.

We would like to make a suggestion of how best to organize the materials in a given case for quick reference: use hanging files and use the same color for each case. Label the manila file folders to fit inside the hanging files. The first file can be the initial contact, financial arrangements, and agreement. Keep copies of all necessary expenses, statements sent, monies received, etc. in this file.

In the second hanging file is the actual case material. Notes on requests for radiographs, more information, etc. is filed here. All telephone notes (date, time, and information discussed) are also kept here.

A third file folder could hold all of the information concerning client interviews, patient examinations, notes on oral examinations, etc. When you are going to examine a patient, instruct them to bring receipts for all treatments rendered. They should also bring all letters, notes, or other communications from others who have examined or treated them. Find out if there are unpaid balances due in the accounts receivable records. At this time take any photographs or other necessary clinical information. If the radiographs are not adequate, or are poor copies, they may be repeated at this time. If a dentist or physician is doing a clinical examination, now is the time to complete a thorough examination with proper charting of everything necessary. As a dentist, this should include a complete periodontal examination with depth probing and charting, if teeth are present. The dentist or physician may be examining a patient to verify injuries claimed in an accident. They may be examining a patient in a standard of care case (malpractice). Should an opinion be reached that the treatment rendered or the diagnoses given are beneath the standard of care, communicate this to the attorney of record only. Arrange an appointment to meet with the patient (client) and the attorney to explain the findings and the reasons for the opinion reached. Prepare a report and return all case materials.

If the case is going to continue, prepare another file folder. This is the "things to do" file. Communicate to the attorney what has been completed and what further steps in the case are necessary. As further tests, etc. are completed they remain in this file, or are moved to the appropriate file.

The next file contains the reports to the attorney. Discuss what is expected in the preliminary report. This file will probably have notes of telephone calls about the report. Some states consider anything written must be shared with both sides of the case. Check the "work product" statutes with the attorney to prevent problems. Ask what materials may be kept under the attorney-client rules to prevent them from being subject to a discovery hearing by the opposition. Many attorneys do not want anything subject to discovery until after depositions have been taken. Find out when the final report is due to allow sufficient time for preparation.

The next file is the exhibit file. Get permission and general agreement on what types of exhibits will be necessary. Make preliminary sketches or designs of what has been agreed to in the manner of illustrations or labeled photographs. Be attentive to the needs of the attorney and try to provide what is requested. Set up a time schedule in the case and try to maintain it. Keep counsel appraised of your progress and arrange meetings for mutual educational purposes.

If you have testified in previous trials or depositions in similar cases, get them out and review them. In some jurisdictions it is necessary that material be shared with the opposing attorneys. Therefore, some attorneys suggest that when the case is finished, dispose of all records concerning the case. Opinions given a few years ago will change as techniques and materials change. Be prepared to defend why your opinion has changed. Be prepared that some attorneys will try to twist statements and misquote your previous testimony. Ask to be shown the portion of the record where they are quoting your statements.

The next file is for the opposing experts' depositions. When this material becomes available it should be reviewed and notes made. Read it carefully and discuss it with counsel. The notes made are important in preparation for questions for further depositions or trial. Consider placing in this file any material that may help in education of the jury or your attorney to illustrate complex dental, medical, or forensic problems.

The last file is for published articles, books chapters, drug product enclosures, etc. Never place your original material in this file. Make two copies of the original material and place them in this file. From your original materials there should be a series of questions for consideration in the examination of the other experts in the case. A modified copy of that series of questions should be in this file. Make contact and arrangements with medical, dental, or association libraries to obtain the latest information on the areas of concern.

Our last piece of advice: if at this juncture, after all the effort you have put into the case, you do not feel properly qualified or convinced of the issues, now is the time to withdraw. All of the information developed can be shared with your attorney. It is privileged information and none of it can be divulged to anyone else without the original attorney's written permission.

On the day of the deposition or trial, allow yourself enough time so you arrive refreshed—even a day earlier if needed.. The attorney should meet with you before the deposition or taking the stand. To be a credible expert witness is going to require the use of your total being and a clear mind. A tired witness is a careless witness. Unless you are blessed with tremendous stamina, do not schedule more than one deposition per day.

Civil and Criminal Case Involvement — Dealing With Attorneys

12

PAUL G. STIMSON
CURTIS A. MERTZ

Dentistry is often involved in both civil and criminal cases. In this chapter the authors, drawing on years of experience, hope to give some helpful tips and guidelines to assist in the decision or evaluation of cases. Remember that unless you are a party to the action (having been named in a lawsuit or subpoenaed) you do not have to be involved in any case. Should you be forced by court action to enter a legal action, you obviously will be a hostile witness. Most attorneys, unless there is no other option, prefer to work with other than hostile witnesses. When an inquiry comes requesting assistance in any case from an attorney, law enforcement agencies, district attorneys, public defenders, etc. you must determine what type of case it is. What particular skill, technique, experience, or educational knowledge do you possess that will help in the matter at hand? What dental, medical, or other situations are they asking your assistance in? What are they trying to prove or disprove? Before you get too involved, you should pause and consider your own situation. If this is a local case, or one that will be emphasized in the media, will this harm your reputation and practice or business? If you are in a profession, will this involvement cause any problems with your patients? If this is your first time, are you ready for the rigors of a deposition or courtroom appearance? Will this individual allow only an opinion in the case with no further obligation? Do you have the training and expertise to properly critique what was done, or should have been done, in this case? Do you consider that the procedure or treatment rendered is beneath the standard of care?

An often-quoted maxim is "scientists seek the truth — attorneys seek an answer." As the problems in litigation become more complex and difficult to understand by the average juror, the use of expert witnesses is increasing. When you are qualified and experienced in the forensic sciences or any related field for any length of time, you may be used in the capacity of an expert witness. If the particular job or skill you possess is a critical one that is in the limelight of cases being prosecuted, your skills and knowledge will be in great demand. Deoxyribonucleotide (DNA) technology cases were being tried in the courts and little was understood by the average person about them or their use. After the exposure on national television as a portion of the evidence in the O. J. Simpson trial, DNA technology was brought to world attention. Many individuals now have a rudimentary understanding and some expectations about scientific evidence. The movies or television often portray the forensic expert as a "shining knight on a white horse" with all the correct answers.

Many forensic members will recall Jack Klugman, the actor who portrayed "Quincy" on a television drama of the same name. At an American Academy of Forensic Sciences meeting in Los Angeles Klugman thanked the Academy for giving him a great role to play. He also stated that the field of forensics was almost unknown to him before the role and that he was now deeply immersed in it. He said he "was sorry that we have to add to the actual facts of the case to make the shows interesting and exciting." The teledrama was based on actual cases, embellished to keep the interest and excitement at a high pitch until the final scene, where forensic science would triumph. The public expects that you, as a forensic expert, have this "magic formula" and every case is perfect and easy to solve. Nothing could be further from the truth. Always present the evidence and conclusions based on facts. Do not deviate from this basic set of truths, nor allow your attorney to misapply them to "make a better case." You are the only one with a total grasp of the particular piece of evidence; you have studied it and know the significance, or lack of significance of it. Should you be guilty of anything less that the truth, this is considered *unethical* behavior and possibly perjury. The possibility of tampering with the evidence by Officer Furman in the O. J. Simpson case was one factor that might have convinced the jury to mistrust the forensic evidence.

Dentists, physicians, and other health care providers talk about the standard of care. When it is below the expected or what is considered the usual standard or degree of care as outlined in the literature and taught in professional schools, attorneys term this "malpractice." They lodge civil suits against physicians, dentists, and other health care practitioners to a greater degree now than in the past. Not all of them are malpractice. Many are overcharging situations, treatment misunderstandings, etc. At least one in ten professional people today have had some action contemplated against them. You cannot just give an opinion and consider that your involvement is complete, unless this is all that you have agreed to do in the situation. You will be expected ultimately to write a report, become very familiar with the current literature in the particular area of concern, and ultimately give a deposition or testify in a trial. These activities all take time. You must know how much your office overhead is to decide how much of a fee per hour to charge. In our experience, getting a retainer of at least two hours of your agreed-upon fee is one way to prevent any misunderstandings about the case. This is done before you do any analysis or effort on the case. Keep track of the time involved with the case. The easiest way to keep time is in six-minute fractions, making it tenths of an hour. When you have almost exhausted the retainer fee time, or have studied the situation sufficiently to make some decisions and recommendations, call the attorney or agency with whom you are involved. It is your task to quickly educate them in the area you are considered to be an expert. Then outline the strong and weak points of the situation studied.

The entire case and your opinions are confidential. Should anyone ask you about the situation in any way they must be referred to the individual or agency that has hired you. Even if they are law enforcement individuals, you cannot divulge any information without permission. In medicine and dentistry we have the doctor-patient privilege. This situation is the attorney-client privilege. You are not a client, but as a member of the "team" you are under a confidentiality requirement. Some situations, if not pursued by the attorney and client, could be very harmful to the individual against whom the proposed action was contemplated. You could, with a few ill-chosen words, find yourself involved in an ethics situation. Make it a rule to discuss the case you are working on with the attorney of record only. Occasionally the attorney who has asked for your opinion has only a vague idea that there may be a cause of action. Frequently, an attorney will seek recommendations in a case due to extreme pressure from one or more members of a family. Many reviewed cases never get past the initial analysis stage. A well-known malpractice attorney has stated that the ratio is about 1 in 10 to 15 cases reviewed. Often after the review they take a series of depositions and then arbitration between the two groups of attorneys leads to a financial settlement. This is another reason for the confidentiality issue.

Each state has rules of professional conduct or a code of professional responsibility that govern the actions and ethical obligations of attorneys (Moenssens, A. A. et al. *Scientific Evidence in Civil and Criminal Cases,* Foundation Press, Westbury, New York, fourth ed., 1995, p. 92). In Section 1.25 of this text, the authors explain the ethical consideration of both the attorney and the expert witness. They explain that it is professional misconduct for an attorney to knowingly use an expert discovered to be a fraud. They also admonish attorneys about fabricating evidence or helping a witness to testify falsely. Attorneys must not promise a fee contingent on the outcome of the case, nor share fees with the expert (p.93). In Section 1.26 of the text they state that courts are developing rules and laws against expert witnesses who are negligent in their professional behavior. Codes of conduct for physicians, dentists, attorneys, and other forensic and forensically related groups exist. An example is the American Board of Forensic Odontology's Bylaws Code of Ethics and Conduct. In the language of the street, "if you are going to walk the walk and talk the talk of an expert witness, it must be professional, ethical, truthful and nonbiased." It is a sad comment that they burden the ethics committees of many of our professional organizations with cases in which they forgot this simple statement.

One area that constantly generates problems is that of fees. How much is an adequate fee to charge? If you are in private industry or practice, the case and the efforts put in it will take away from your productive and private time. The crucial point is that time must be devoted to these efforts. What do you earn per hour at whatever you do? How much is your overhead and expenses to earn that amount? If you do not charge enough to cover your overhead, you are losing money by being involved in the case. How much to charge was a recent lively debate covering approximately six weeks on the Harvard Internet. The interchange produced some things that are appropriate. Charge whatever you feel is adequate and you can obtain. The charges stated ranged from $65 per hour for a beginner to $1000 for a neurosurgeon. Try to explore what the fees for similar work are in your area. Always make sure that they cover your other fees, travel expenses and other incidentals (photography costs, artwork, etc.). This can be covered in an employment agreement such as the one found at the end of this chapter. This agreement is one for *general guidance*, and is nothing more than a mere suggestion for your use (work agreement). Some are concerned with the statement that an individual is worth what they charge. As an individual gains a reputation from an outstanding job, his or her name is networked to other attorneys. Attorneys also, in this electronic age, have the means to find who the experts(s) are in cases similar to the one in which they are involved. Advertising your services in some journals circulated to attorney groups is permissible. They will ask you the question, "Do you advertise?" Advertising in this country is big business. If you can justify your answer, feel free to advertise. Pick a strategy that works for you and follow it.

We strongly recommend that you seek the aid of competent counsel to develop your own expert witnesses' agreement. This document should prevent any misunderstandings between the two parties, and helps in obtaining any tardy payments due. If the agreement is not accepted by the attorney to whom it is directed, a tremendous saving of time and effort will be realized. It is useful in fee collection situations. The document prevents misunderstandings between parties when used. Whoever is opposing you and your attorney(s) will be as well, or perhaps even better, prepared than you are. An attorney is hiring you as the expert and will expect you to act like one. These are not things that one can procrastinate on, and then in a day or two quickly fill in the blanks and be ready to go. If one area of forensic, medical, or dental science is all that an individual does, then the library and reprint material must be organized and easily available. For most individuals, a library and literature search concerning the question must be done. This will take time and effort. The attorney and client cannot be charged for your effort to become current and more knowledgeable in the area in question.

To be an expert witness you should create a *curriculum vitae* (CV) or a professional resume to send to interested parties. This document is one of many that will be shared with both sets of attorneys. You should be candid, honest, and have this document represent you in a straightforward manner. It should reflect your education, training, and experience. The document will be used to assess and assail you by opposing counsel. Keep it to the point and limit placement of items in it to those that are easy to prove and show. Some individuals like to put every lecture or seminar they have ever attended in their documents. We caution you about doing this, as this may lead to a line of questions by an attorney that may be frustrating or embarrassing, attempting to disprove or discredit your credentials to a court or judge. The more information you have, the broader the area from which questions can be asked. Do not be surprised if the attorney asks you for a listing of cases of involvement, a biographical sketch, and your CV. When you work for and with attorneys, leading and penetrating questions are their stock and trade. They are well trained in the process of asking questions to find weak or questionable areas. Even if these areas are not in your documents they may still ask you about them. A good firm of attorneys has a group of excellent and well-trained investigators who can find out amazing facts about individuals and share them with the firm. If you have anything in your past that could be possibly harmful to your use as an expert witness, you should share it with the attorney contacting you, prior to any agreement. What kind of things are we talking about? Have you ever filed for bankruptcy? Have you been involved in messy divorce or breakup of a partnership? Have you been a party in a malpractice suit? Have you had a chemical dependency problem in the past? Anything that has involved a court or legal procedure, either federal or state, is a matter of public record and can be obtained and used by competent counsel. Attorneys loathe being caught off guard and when they are, and if it concerns you, the attorney-expert witness relationship just may have become adversarial.

If the attorney who asks you to review the case is hesitant about sending a retainer (of at least two hours fee charge) you should be hesitant about taking the case. Our common practice is to put off an answer to the calling party until we can check the calendar to see if we have enough time to be involved. During a 24-hour or more delay, a credit check should be done on the individual attorney or firm. If you feel that this is going to be a very involved and prolonged case, you might also get a Dun and Bradstreet rating on the firm. If you have your own attorney, he or she can also supply helpful information on the individual or firm concerned. The attorney who calls you for service has obviously done some checking on you. You should also evaluate him. If the individual or firm has a poor credit history, you might submit an estimate and ask for what you think the fee time will cost in advance. One excuse for nonpayment by attorneys is that the client has exhausted his funds. This is unfortunate, but the client did not hire you, the attorney did.

When working with attorneys, stay in contact with them. We prefer that the case be discussed in person or on the telephone. Certain states and jurisdictions have regulations that we must make anything written available to both sides. Consequently, written communications must be shared, even if they are preliminary. Other states have rules about what they term "work products", which are reports that are in the process of being developed. They can share the finished product, but the work product is a privileged document. When communicating with the attorney, talk about the strong and weak points of the action. Do not allow the attorney to sway your judgment concerning the case. Be aware that the only one who is sworn to tell the truth and can suffer problems with perjury is the expert witness when testifying under an oath. This applies to a court of law or in a deposition. No one else in the courtroom or at a deposition is under that obligation. Because of this, remain the true scientist and "tell it like it is." Your attorney can skillfully have you emphasize the areas that she or he wants, but the expert for the other side will have the opposing attorney ready to underscore the weak points or problem areas in the case.

If you have never been part of or exposed to an actual court trial, ask your attorney to review the court docket to alert you to a trial that will have expert witness testimony in it. It will be an educational experience for you to spend time in the audience and observe a trial. Pay close attention to the mannerisms of the expert and use of the exhibits he or she is using. Watch the jurors and try to predict which exhibit was most beneficial to them. Trial exhibits must be carefully planned and used. They take time, thought, planning, and acceptance by counsel who will guide the expert witness in their use. When used in court or depositions, exhibits must remain with the case and become part of the record. Having them returned is possible, but the interval may be many years. Photographic exhibits and drawings must be discussed with your attorney. The method of use and labeling varies from jurisdiction to jurisdiction. Exhibits must be professionally done and reflect the quality of your presentation. First-class exhibits are expensive and must be approved by the firm or attorney in the case. Without prior approval, the exhibits that an expert witness provides for use may be at his or her expense. The individual who has hired you as an expert witness has the final say in what will be taken into court or to a deposition to present his side of the case. If you feel that lack of the exhibits will not allow you to fully describe your area of expertise you should further educate the attorney as to why they are necessary. Your first effort is to educate the attorney about your area of expertise, the second job is to make it understandable to a lay jury. Talk to the jury, not down to the jury. Use simple language that is possible for a high school graduate to understand.

When asked a question in trial or in a deposition, allow the examiner to complete the question. Take a short pause before answering the question. Make sure that you understand the question. If you do not understand completely, ask for the question to be repeated or perhaps rephrased. The short pause will give your attorney time to object should he or she wish. Never anticipate what the question will be and begin to answer prior to the examiner finishing it. By anticipating a question, an attorney may trap an expert in an area that was not what the question was about. This occurred because the question was not fully asked and because the expert anticipated the question and rushed an answer. The attorney only partially asked the question, but there was a rushed answer. If you know, answer the question. If you do not know the answer, say "I do not know." When an expert witness begins to guess, or feels that he or she knows related material and can fabricate an answer, that expert is in trouble.

We recommend that when you are asked to give a deposition, do it in a location away from your office or place of employment. This puts the expert in a strange environment and makes him more attentive to the examination and examiner. In a comfortable place, such as an office, it is possible for an individual to say things that they may later regret. Statements such as, "When he first came in the office he was terribly dressed and smelled," may come back to give you trouble. In a strange environment the statement might be, "When first seen in the office the individual was unkempt in both clothing and personal hygiene." This does not seem like a great difference, but attorneys use words, while most people use concepts and larger ideas.

You should raise an index of suspicion when you receive a telephone call asking about a case on which you happen to be working. Always refer the calling individual to the attorney of record that employed you. If the case is big enough, or there might be a large settlement, investigators will use most any trick in their repertoire to gain information. If in doubt, ask for a written request from the individual calling for information. Clear any communication with the attorney of record before giving out any information. If you are involved in a very unusual case do not discuss it with anyone except the attorney of record or his approved individuals. Remember that the individual to whom you are speaking is usually poorly equipped in the beginning to understand the technical aspects of your area of expertise. It is then very easy to be misquoted. It is possible that this misinformation may cause you enough embarrassment that you must withdraw from the case. The best thing to say is, "I am involved in the case you are interested in, but I am not free to discuss any aspects of the circumstances at this time."

When you become involved in any portion of the forensic field, we have some practical suggestions for your consideration. You will need a fireproof filing cabinet large enough to secure case records, exhibits, and other materials for each case. The cabinet or safe must have a combination lock or another means to secure it and the contents. An alarm system should further protect the area where the cabinet or safe is located. In criminal cases, having the prosecutor maintain the evidence is a better policy. Should it be lost or misplaced it becomes his or her problem and not yours. In the business of being an expert in any given field you must contend with the chain of evidence. Anything that you receive or give to anyone else must have a signed and dated receipt. You must have a paper trail and some type of journal logged with proper entries to show the how, what, when, and where of the information or material transfer. One adage in the forensic field is "If it wasn't written, it probably was not done!" A break in the paper trail means that a critical piece of evidence can, if opposed by an experienced attorney, be withheld from the case. Another concern is that of proper maintenance of evidence for months or even years. In criminal cases the file may be open forever, such as on capital murder cases, for example. Plan how, where, and what you are going to have to maintain in records, exemplars, and other types of evidence. Be very careful in sharing case photographs and other materials. They may show up in a situation you might not want or have any control over. In criminal cases the ultimate end of the case is the Supreme Court, so the case is technically active until the criminal is deceased.

The last thing we will talk about is the extent to which you should share the type of forensic work you are doing with your office personnel, fellow investigators, family, and friends. If you are a dentist or physician let everyone in the office know that they can discuss nothing pertaining to any forensic case outside the office environment. This is the rule for patients and patient records as well. It is a good policy to limit your discussions in the office only to matters your staff can assist you with in the case. This is not really an "office" case, but is your case as an expert with their limited assistance. The admonition of not sharing confidential information outside the office confines should be in the employees' manual of every office. If you share the material with a husband, wife, or family be extremely careful. The better plan is to share only vague portions of the case so they have a general understanding of what you are doing. As we mentioned previously, investigators will go to great lengths to obtain material to use against you. A teenager talking to a very friendly person can be tricked into revealing facts that can be potentially very damaging to you or the case. An ex-police officer with 30 or more years experience can gain information from many sources in a very smooth, friendly manner. The best policy is to discuss the case with those you work with, love, and trust *after* it is completed.

APPENDIX A:
Bite Mark Citations

PREPARED BY: HASKELL M. PITLUCK
Tom Krauss Memorial Bite Mark Breakfast
February 23, 1996, Nashville, Tennessee

1. *Doyle v. State*, 159 Texas, C.R.310, 263 S.W.2d 779 (Jan. 20, 1954).

2. *People v. Johnson*, 8 Ill. App.3d 457, 289 N.E.2d 722 (Nov. 16, 1972).

3. *Patterson v. State*, 509 S.W.2d 857 (Tex. Crim. 1974) (Mar. 13, 1974).

4. *People v. Allah*, 84 Misc.2d 500, 376 N.Y.S. 2d 399 (Nov. 20, 1975).

5. *People v. Marx*, 54 Cal. App.3d 100, 126 Cal. Rptr. 350 (Dec. 29, 1975).

6. *People v. Johnson*, 37 Ill. App.3d 328, 345 N.E.2d 531 (Apr. 7, 1976).

7. *People v. Milone*, 43 Ill. App.3d 385, 356 N.E.2d 1350 (Nov. l2, 1976).

8. *Niehus v. State*, 265 Ind. 655, 359 N.E.2d 513 (Jan. 25, 1977).

9. *State v. Routh*, 30 Or. App. 901, 568 P.2d 704 (Sep. 12, 1977).

10. *People v. Watson*, 75 Cal. App.3d 384, 142 Cal. Rptr. 134 (Nov. 28, 1977).

11. *State v. Kendrick*, 31 Or. App. 1195, 572 P.2d 354 (Dec. 12, 1977).

12. *People v. Slone*, 76 Cal. App.3d 611, 143 Cal. Rptr. 61 (Jan. 6, 1978).

13. *State v. Howe*, 136 Vt. 53, 386 A2d 1125 (Mar. 15, 1978).

14. *State v. Garrison*, 120 Ariz. 255, 585 P.2d 563 (Sept. 20, 1978).

15. *State v. Bridges*, 123 Ariz. 452, 600 P.2d 756 (Aug. 2, 1979).

16. *U.S. v. Martin*, 9 M. J. 731 (NCMR 1979) (Aug. 7, 1979).

17. *State v. Jones*, 273 S.C. 723, 259 S.E. 2d 120 (Oct. 11, 1979).

18. *Deutscher v. State*, 95 Nov. 669, 601 P.2d 407 (Oct. 18, 1979).

19. *State v. Peoples*, 227 Kan. 127, 60S P.2d 135 (Jan. 19, 1980).

20. *State v. Sager*, 600 S.W.2d 541 (Mo. App.) (May 5, 1980).

21. *Peole v. Middleton*, 428 N.Y.S. 2d 688, 76 A.D.2d 762 (June 10, 1980).

22. *State v. Kleypas*, 602 S.W.2d 863 (Mo. App.) (July 10, 1980).

23. *Exparte Sue Dolvin*, 391 So.2d 677 (Alabama Sup. Ct.) (Sep. 12, 1980).

24. *State v. Temple*, 302 NC.I., 273 S.E.2d 273 (Jan. 6, 1981).

25. *People v. Smith*, 443 N.Y.S.2d 551, 110 Misc.2d 118 (July 24, 1981).

26. *State v. Geer*, 624 S.W.2d 143 (Mo. App,) (Sept. 22, 1981).

27. *People v. Middleton*, 54 N.Y.2d 42, 429 N. E.2d 100 (Oct. 27, 1981).

28. *Aguilar v. State*, 98 Nev. 18, 639 P.2d 533 (Jan. 28, 1982).

29. *Kennedy v. State*, 640 p.2d 971 (Oklahoma) (Feb. 3, 1982).

30. *State v. Turner*, 633 S.W.2d 421 (Mo. App.) (Mar. 2, 1982).

31. *U.S. v. Martin*, 13 M.J. 66 (CMA 1982) (Apr. 19, 1982).

32. *State v. Green*, 305 N.C. 463, 290 S.E.2d 625 (May 4, 1982).

33. *Bludsworth v. State*, 98 Nev. 289, 646 P,2d 558 (June 18, 1982).

34. *People v. Queen*, 108 Ill. App.3d 1088, 440 N.E.2d 126 (July 13, 1982).

35. *Commonwealth v. Maltais*, 387 Mass. 79, 438 N.E.2d 847 (Aug. 4. 1982).

36. *Commonwealth v. Graves*, 456A.2d 561 (Pa. Sup. 1983) (Feb. 4, 1983).

37. *State of Kansas v. Galloway*, Unpublished opinion filed March 26, 1983.

38. *People v. Jordan*, 114 Ill. App.3d 16, 448 N.E.2d 237 (Apr 14, 1983).

39. *Miller v. State*, 448 N.E.2d 293 (Ind. 1983) (May 6, 1983).

40. *State v. Stokes*, 433 So.2d 96 (La. 1983) (May 23, 1983).

41. *State v. Dixon*, 191 Cal. Rptr. 917 (Cal.App. 4th Dist, 1983) (June 7, 1983).

42. *People v. Columbo*, 118 Ill. App.3d 882, 455 N.E.2d 733 (June 24, 1983).

43. *State v. Sapsford*, 22 Ohio App.3d 1 (Nov. 9, 1983).

44. *Chase v. State*, 678 P.2d 1347 (Alaska App.) (Mar. 9, 1984).

45. *Marbley v. State*, 461 N.E.2d 1102 (Ind. 1984) (Apr. 19, 1984).

46. *State v. Welker*, 683 P.2d 1110 (Wash. App. 1984) (May 21, 1984).

47. *Bundy v. State*, 455 So.2d 330 (Florida Sup. Ct.) (June 21, 1984).

48. *People v. Smith*, 63 N.Y.2d 41, 468 N.E.2d 879 (July 2, 1984).

49. *State v. Asherman*, 193 Conn. 695, 478 A.2d 227 (July 17, 1984).

50. *People v. Schuning*, 125 Ill. App.3d 808, 466 N.E.2d 673 (July 19, 1984).

51. *State v. Adams*, 481 A.2d 218 (R.I. 1981) (Aug. 21, 1984).

52. *Southard v. State*, Slip opinion, 1st Court of Appeals of Arkansas (Aug. 29, 1984).

53. *Graves v. State*, Slip opinion, lst Court of Appeals, Houston (Aug. 30, 1984).

54. *Maynard v, State*, 455 So.2d 632 (Florida App.) (Sept. 13, 1984).

55. *People v. Jordan*, 103 Ill,2d 192, 469 N.F,.2d S69 (Ill. Sup. Ct.) (Sept. 20, 1984).

56. *People v. Williams*, 128 Ill. App.3d 384, 470 N.E.2d 1140 (Oct. 22, 1984).

57. *State v. Perea*, 142 Ariz. 352, 690 P.2d 71 (Nov. 1, 1984).

58. *State v. Bullard*, 312 N.C. 129, 322 S.E.2d 370 (Nov. 6, 1984).

59. *Smith v. State*, 253 Ga. 536, 322 S.E.2d 492 (Nov. 16, 1984).

60. *People v. McDonald*, 37 Cal. 3d 351, 690 P.2d 709 (Nov. 21, 1984).

61. *State v. Thornton*, 253 Ga. 524, 322 S.E.2d 711 (GA 1984) (Nov. 2l, 1984).

62. *Bradford v. State*, 460 So.2d 926 (Fla. App. 2d Dist. 1984) (Nov. 30, 1984).

63. *Tuggle v. Commonwealth*, 228 Va. 493, S.E.2d 539 (Nov. 30, 1984).

64. *People v. Bethune*, 484 N.Y.S. 2d 577, 105 A.D.2d 262 (Dec. 31, 1984).

65. *People v. Oueen*, 130 Ill. App.3d 523, 474 N.E.2d 786 (Jan. 11, 1985).

66. *Southard v. State*, Slip opinion, Supreme Court of Arkansas (Apr. 1, 1985).

67. *State v. Dickson*, 691 S.W.2d 334 (Mo. App. 1985) (Apr. 2, 1985).

68. *State v. Carter*, 74 N.C.App. 437, 328 S.E.2d 607 (May 7, 1985).

69. *Clemons v. State*, 470 So.2d 653 (Miss. 1985) (May 29, 1985).

70. *Standridge v. State*, 701 P.2d 761 (Okl. Cr. 1985) (June 6, 1985).

71. *Tuggle v. Comonwealth*, 230 Va. 99, 334 S.E.2d 838 (Sept. 6, 1985).

72. *State v. Ortiz*, 198 Conn. 220, 502 A.2d 40Q (Dec. 31, 1985).

73. *People v. Walkey*, 177 Cal. App. 3d 268, 223Cal. Rptr. 132 (Cal. App., 4th Dist) (Jan. 23, 1986).

74. *Thornton v. State*, 255 Ga. 434, 339 S.E.2d 240 (Feb. 13. 1986).

75. *Wade v. State*, 490 N.E.2d 1097 (Ind. 1986) (April 3, 1986).

76. *People v. Vigil*, 718 P.2d 496 (Colo. 1986) (April 14, 1986).

77. *Commonwealth v. Cifizzari*, 397 Mass. 560, 492 N.E.2d 357 (May 14, 1986).

78. *State v. Bingham*, 105 Wash. 2d 820, 719 P.2d 109 (Wash. 1986) (May 15, 1986).

79. *Rogers v. State*, 256 Ga, 140, 344 S.E.2d 644 (Ga. 1986) (June 25, 1986).

80. *State v. Johnson*, 317 N.C. 343, 346 S.E.2d 596 (Aug. 12, 1986).

81. *People v. Pante*, 147 Ill. App. 3d 1039, 498 N.E.2d 889 (Oct. 3, 1986).

82. *Smith v. State*, Unpublished opinion, Texas Ct. of Appeals (Oct. 9, 1986).

83. *State v. Johnson*, 721 S.W. 2d 23 (Mo. App.) (Oct. 14, 1986).

84. *State v. Stinson*, 134 Wis. 2d 224, 397 N.W.2d 136 (Oct. 28, 1986).

85. *In Re The Marriage of Rimer*, 395 N.W.2d 390 (Minn. App.) (Nov. 4, 1986).

86. *McCrory v. State*, 505 So.2d 1272 (Ala. Cr. App.) (Dec. 9, 1986).

87. *Marquez v. State*, 725 S.W.2d 217 (Tex. Cr. App.) (Jan. 14, 1987).

88. *Bundy v. Wainwright*, 808 F.2d 1410 (11th Cir.) (Jan. I5, 1987).

89. *DuBoise v State*, Slip opinion, Supreme Court of Florida (Feb. 19, 1987); (superseded by Case #110 below).

90. *People v. Davis*, 189 Cal. App. 3d 1177, 234 Cal. Rptr. 859 (Feb. 26, 1987).

91. *People v. Dace*, 153 Ill. App. 3d 891, 506 N.E.2d 332 (Mar. 23, 1987).

92. *People v. Drake*, 129 A.D.2d 963, 514 N.Y.S.2d 280 (Apr. 3 1987).

93. *State v. Vital*, 505 So.2d 1006 (La. App.) (Apr. 9, 1987).

94. *State v. Kendrick*, 47 Wash. App. 620, 736 P.2d 1079 (May 11, 1987).

95. *Ngoc Van Le v. State*, 733 S.W.2d 280 (Tex. App.) (May 14, 1987).

96. *People v. Wachal*, 156 Ill. App. 3d 331, 509 N.E.2d 648 (May 29, 1987).

97. *State v. Moen*, 86 Or. App. 87, 738 P.2d 228 (June 24, 1987).

98. *Handley v. State*, 515 So.2d 121, Court of Criminal Appeal of Alabama (June 30, 1987).

99. *Jackson v. State*, 511 So.2d 1047 (Fla. App.) (Aug. 7, 1987).

100. *State v. Crump*, Slip opinion, Ohio Court of Appeals (Aug. 11, 1987).

101. *People v. Perez*, 194 Cal. App. 3d 525, 239 Cal. Rptr. 569 (Aug. 26, 1987).

102. *Strickland v. State*, 184 Ga. App. 185, 361 S.E.2d 207 (Sept. 11, 1987).

103. *State v. McDaniel*, 515 So.2d 572 (La. App. 1 Cir) (Oct. 14, 1987).

104. *Inman v. State*, 515 So. 2d 1150 (Miss. Sup. Ct.) (Nov. 18, 1987).

105. *People v. Watson*, 521 N.Y.S.2d 548, 134 A.D.2d 729 (Nov. 19, 1987).

106. *People v. Hampton*, 746 P.2d 947 (Colo. Sup. Ct.) (Nov. 30, 1987).

107. *Busby v. State*, 741 S.W.2d 109 (Mo. App.) (Dec. 8, 1987).

108. *State v. Hasan*, 205 Conn. 485, 534 A.2d 877 (Dec. 15, 1987).

109. *Harward v. Commonwealth*, 5 Va. App. 468, 364 S.E.2d 5ll (Jan. 19, 1988).

110. *DuBoise v. State*, 520 So.2d 260 (Fla. Sup. Ct.) (Feb. 4, 1988) (supersedes #89 above).

111. *State v. Pierce*, Slip opinion not designated for publication, Supreme Court of Kansas (Feb. 19, 1988).

112. *Valenti v. Akron Police Dept.*, et al., Slip opinion, Court of Appeals of Ohio, 9th App.Dist. (Mar. 2, 1988).

113. *People v. Howard*, 529 N.Y.S.2d 51, 139 A.2d 927 (Apr. 8, 1988).

114. *State v. Armstrong*, 369 S.E.2d 870 (W.Va.) (Apr. 22, 1988).

115. *Mitchell v. State*, 527 So.2d 179 (Fla. Sup. Ct.) (May 19, 1988).

116. *State v. Jamison*, Slip opinion, not designated for publication, Supreme Court of Kansas (June 3, 1988).

117. *People v . Ferguson*, 172 Ill. App.3d 1, 526 N.E.2d 525 (June 30, 1988).

118. *People v. Rich*, 755 P.2d 960 (Cal. Sup. Ct.) (June 30, 1988).

119. *People v. Randt*, 530 N.Y.S.2d 266, 142 A.2d 611 (July 5, 1988).

120. *State v. Kirsch*, Unpublished opinion, Wis. Ct. of App. (July 20, 1988).

121. *Commonwealth v. Jones*, 403 Mass. 279, 526 N.E.2d 1288 (Aug. 18, 1988).

122. *Andrews v. State*, 533 So.2d 841 (Fla. App. 5 Dist) (Oct, 20, 1988).

123. *People v. Hernandez*, 253 Cal. Rptr. 199, 763 P.2d 1289 (Nov. 28, 1988).

124. *State v. Combs*, 1988 Ohio App. slip opinion (Dec. 2, 1988).

125. *Commonwealth v. Edwards*, 521 Pa. 134, 555 A.2d 818 (Mar. 6, 1989).

126. *State v. Turner*, Slip opinion, Tenn. Cr. App. (Mar. 20, 1989).

127. *People v. Marsh*, 441 N.W.2d 33 (Mich. App. 1989) (May 15, 1989).

128. *Commonwealth v. Thomas*, 561 A.2d 699 (Pa. 1989) (June 27, 1989).

129. *Bromley v. State*, 380 S.E.2d 694 (Ga. 1989) (June 30, 1989).

130. *Chaney v. State*, 775 S.W.2d 722 (Texas App. Dallas) (July 5, 1989).

131. *Green v. State*, 542 N.E.2d 977 (Ind. 1989) (Aug. 30, 1989).

132. *Fox v. State*, 779 P.2d 562 (Okl. Crim. App.) (Aug. 30, 1989).

133. *State v. Mebana*, 19 Conn. App. 618, 563 A.2d 1026 (Sept. 9, 1989).

134. *State v. Hill*, Slip Opinion. Ohio App. (Nov. 27, 1989).

135. *Cox v. State*, 555 So.2d 352 (Sup. Ct. of Florida) (Dec. 21, 1989).

136. *Commonwealth v. Henry*, 524 Pa, 135, 569 A.2d9 929 (Feb. 8, 1990).

137. *Litaker v. State*, 784 S.W. 2d 739 (Tex. App.) (Feb. 21, 1990).

138. *People v. Bass*, 553 N.Y.S.2d 794, 160 A.D.2d 715 (April 2, 1990).

139. *Bouie v. State*, 559 So.2d 1113 (Sup. Ct. of Florida) (April 5, 1990).

140. *Monk v. Zelez*, 901 S.2d 885 (l0th Cir.) (April 25, 1990); (Monk is also known as Martin of Case #'s 16 and 31).

141. *State v. Ford*, 301 S.C. 485, 392 S.E.2d 781 (May 7, 1990).

142. *People v. Calabro*, 555 N.Y.S.2d 321, 161 A.D.2d 375 (May 15, 1990).

143. *Williams v. State*, 790 S.W.2d 643 (Tex. Crim. App.) (June 6, 1990).

144. *Spence v. State*, 795 S.W.2d 743 (Tex. Crim. App.) (June 13, 1990).

145. *State v. Richards*, 166 Ariz. 576, 804 P.2d 109 (Aug. 7, 1990).

146. *Howard v. Kelly*, Slip opinion, (U.S. Dist. Ct. W.D. New York) (Sept. 18, 1990); (same defendant/same incident as in Case #113).

147. *Baker v. State*, 797 S.W.2d 406 (Tex. App.) (Oct. 19, 1990).

148. *State v. Gardner*, Slip opinion (Tenn. Crim. App.) (Oct. 25, 1990).

149. *State v. Jackson*, 570 So.2d 227 (La. App. 5 Cir.) (Nov, 14, 1991).

150. *Mallory v. State*, 563 N.E.2d 640 (Ind. App. 1 Dist.) (Dec. 10, 1990).

151. *Salazar v. State*, Slip opinion (Tex. App. Houston) (Jan. 10, 1991).

152. *People v. Cardenas*, 209 Ill. App. 3d 217, 568 N.E.2d 102 (Jan. 16, 1991).

153. *Harris v. State*, 260 Ga. 860, 401 S.E.2d 263 (Feb. 28, 1991).

154. *State v. Wimberly*, 467 N.W.2d 499 (Sup. Ct. of S. Dakota) (March 20, 1991).

155. *Wilhoit v. State*, 809 P.2d 1322 (Ct. of Crim. App. of Okla.) (April 16, 1991); 816 P.2d 545 (same opinion with appendix).

156. *Williams v. State*, 815 S.W.2d 743 (Tex. App. Waco) (May 30, 1991).

157. *People v. Perkins*, 216 Ill.App.3d 389, 576 N.E.2d 355 (June 28, 1991).

158. *State v. Edwards*, Slip opinion (Ohio App.) (July 3, 1991).

159. *Adams v. Peterson*, 939 F.2d 1369 (9th Cir.) (July 30, 1991); (opinion withdrawn March 27, 1992).

160. *People v. Case*, 218 Ill. App. 3d 146, 577 N.E.2d 1291 (July 30, 1991).

161. *State v. Thomas*, 329 N.C. 423, 407 S.E.2d 141 (Aug. 14, 1991).

162. *Deutscher v. Whitley*, 946 F.2d 1443 (9th Cir.) (Oct. 15, 1991); (same defendant/same incident as Case #18).

163. *Washington v. State*, 822 S.W.2d 110 (Tex. App. Waco) (Nov. 20, 1991) (Co-Defendant of #156).

164. *State v. Correia*, 600 A.2d 279 (Sup. Ct. of Rhode Island) (Dec. 5, 1991).

165. *People v. Stanciel*, 225 Ill. App. 3d 1082, 589 N.E. 2d 557 (Dec. 11, 1991).

166. *State v. Ukofia*, Unpublished opinion, Minn. Ct. of App. (Dec. 17, 1991).

167. *State v. Pearson*, 479 N.W.2d 401, Minn. Ct. of App. (Dec. 31, 1991).

168. *Davasher v. State*, 308 Ark. 154, 823 S.W. 2d 863 (Jan. 27, 1992).

169. *Mitchell v. State*, 595 So. 2d 938, Florida Supreme Court (Feb. 6, 1992); (another appeal of Case #115).

170. *State v. Joubert*, 603 A. 2d 861, Maine Supreme Court (Feb. 21, 1992).

171. *Williams v. State*, 829 S.W. 2d 216, (Tex. Crim. App. En Banc) (April 15, 1992); (same defendant/same incident as Cases #143 and 1561).

172. *State v. Williams*, 80 Ohio App. 3d 648, 610 N.E. 2d 545 (May 20, 1992).

173. *Adams v. Peterson*, 968 F.2d 835 (9th Cir.) (June 24, 1992); (same defendant/same incident as Case #159).

174. *State v. Hill*, 64 Ohio St. 3d 313, 595 N.E. 2d 884 (Aug. 12, 1992); (same defendant/same incident as Case #134).

175. *People v. Dunsworth*, 233 Ill. App. 3d 258, 599 N.E. 2d 29 (Aug. 19, 1992).

176. *People v. Holmes*, 234 Ill. App. 3d 931, 601 N.E. 2d 985 (Sept. 8, 1992).

177. *Freeman v. State*, Slip opinion (Alabama Crim. App.) (Sept. 18, 1992).

178. *U.S. ex rel. Milone v. Camp*, Slip opinion (U.S. Dist. Court, N.D. IL.) (Sept. 29, 1992); (same defendant/same incident as Cases #7 and #204).

179. *Williams v. State*, 838 S.W. 2d 952 (Tex. App. Waco) (Oct. 14, 1992); (same defendant/same incident as Cases #143, 156, and 171).

180. *Harris v. State*, Slip opinion (Arkansas App.) (Nov. 18, 1992).

181. *People v. Stanciel*, 153 Ill. 2d 218, 606 N.E. 2d 1201 (Nov. 19, 1992) (Same defendant/same incident as case #165).

182. *People v. Blommaert*, 237 Ill. App. 3d 811, 604 N.E. 2d 1054 (Nov. 30, 1992).

183. *State v. Jones*, 83 Ohio App. 3d 723, 615 N.E, 2d 713 (Dec. 2, 1992).

184. *Davis v. State*, 611 So. 2d 906 (Miss. Sup. Ct.) (Dec. 17, 1992).

185. *People v. Noguera*, 4 Cal. 4th 599, 842 P. 2d 1160 (Dec. 28, 1992).

186. *R.M. v, Dept. of Health and Rehabilitation Services*, 617 So. 2d 810 (Fla. App.) (April 30, 1993).

187. *State v. Bennett*, 503 N.W. 2d 42, (Iowa App.) (May 4, 1993).

188. *State v. Schaefer*, 855 S.W. 2d 504 (Mo. App.) (June 22, 1993).

189. *Spindle v. Barrong*, 996 F, 2d 311 (Table) Unpublished Disposition (U.S. Court of Appeals, l0th Circuit, Kan.) (June 24, 1993).

190. *U.S. v. Dia*, 826 F. Supp. 1237 (U.S. Dist. Ct. Ariz.) (July 8, 1993).

191. *Murphy v. State*, Slip opinion, not designated for publication (Tex. App. Dallas) (July 20, 1993).

192. *State v. Donnell*, 826 S.W. 2d 445 (Mo. App.) (Sept. 21, 1993).

193. *State v. Williams*, 865 S.W. 2d 794 (Mo. App.) (Oct. 13, 1993).

194. *Rodoussakis v. Hosey*, 8 F. 3d 820 (U.S. Ct. of Appeals 4th Cir. W.Va) (Oct. 20, 1993).

195. *State v. Lyons*, 124 Or. App. 598, 863 P.2d 1303 (Nov. 17, 1993).

196. *State v. Welburn*, Slip opinion (Ohio App.) (Nov. 17, 1993).

197. *Verdict v. State*, 315 Ark. 436, 868 S.W.2d 443 (Dec. 20, 1993).

198. *Kinney v. State*, 315 Ark. 481, 868 S.W.2d 463 (Jan. 10, 1994).

199. *State v. Hodgson*, 512 N.W.2d 95 (Minn. Sup. Ct.) (Feb. 11, 1994).

200. *State v. Cazes*, 875 S.W.2d 253 (Tenn. Sup. Ct.) (Feb. 14, 1994).

201. *Mobley v. State*, 212 Ga. App. 293, 441 S.E.2d 780 (Feb. 16, 1994).

202. *People v. Gallo*, 260 Ill. App. 3d 1032, 632 N.E.2d 99 (Mar. 18, 1994).

203. *Harrison v. State*, 635 So.2d 894 (Miss. Sup. Ct,) (Apr. 14, 1994).

204. *Milone v. Camp*, 22 F.3d 693 (7th Cir.) (Apr. 21, 1994); (same defendant/same incident as Cases #7 and #178).

205. *Morgan v. State*, 639 So.2d 6 (Flor.Sup.Ct.) (June 2, 1994).

206. *Commonwealth v. Alvardo*, 36 Mass. App. Ct. 604, 634 N.E.2d 132 (June 3, 1994.

207. *State v. Hummert*, Slip opinion (Ariz. App. Div. 1) (July 26, 1994).

208. *People v. Brown*, 162 Misc. 2d 555, 618 N.Y.S.2d 188 (N.Y. Co. Ct.) (Oct. 6, 1994).

209. *State v. Martin*, 645 So.2d 190, (La. Sup. Ct.) (Oct. 18, 1994).

210. *U.S. ex rel Dace v. Welborn*, Memorandum opinion,U.S. Dist. Court, N.D. IL; (same defendant/same incident as Case #9l) (Oct. 25, 1994).

211. *State v. Carpentier*, Unpublished opinion, Minn. Ct. of Apeals (Dec. 6, 1994).

212. *People v. Tripp*, 271 Ill.App.3d 194, 648 N.E.2d 241 (March 10, 1995).

213. *Brim v. State.*, 654 So.2d 184 (Flor. App. 2d Dist.) (April 12, 1995).

214. *State vs. Warness*, 77 Wash. App. 636, 893 P.2d 665 (May 1, 1995).

215. *Chaplin vs. McGrath and Donohue*, 626 N.Y.S.2d 294 (May 4, 1995).

216. *Bass v. Scully*, Memorandum Order, U.S. Dist. Court, Eastern Dist. N.Y.; (same defendant/same incident as Case #138) (May 25, 1995).

217. *People v. Rush*, 630 N.Y.S.2d 631 (N.Y. Sup. Ct. Kings Co.) (June 7, 1995).

218. *State v. Mann*, Slip opinion (Ohio App. 8th Dist.) (June 15, 1995).

219. *Purser v. State*, 902 S.W.2d 641 (Texas App. El Paso) (June 15, 1995).

220. *State v. Krone*, 182 Ariz. 319, 897 P.2d 621 (Ariz. Sup. Ct.) (June 22, 1995).

221. *Tuggle v. Thompson*, 57 F.3d 1356 (U.S. Ct. of Appeals, 4th Circuit, Virginia); (same defendant/same incident as Cases #63 and #71) (June 29, 1995).

222. *Seate v. Boles*, Slip opinion (Ariz. Ct. of Appeals) (Aug. 3, 1995).

223. *State v. Teasley*, Slip opinion (Ohio App. 8th Dist.) (Aug. 17, 1995).

224. *People v. Cumbee*, Unpublished, not precedential opinion, (Ill. App.Ct. 2nd Dist.) (Nov. 15, 1995).

225. *Franks v. State*, Slip opinion (Mississippi Sup. Ct.) (Nov. 30, 1995).

226. *Hodgson v. State*, 540 N.W.2d 515, (Minnesota Sup. Ct.) (Dec. 15, 1995); (same defendant/same incident as Case #199).

Law Review Articles

11 Santa Clara Computer and High Tech L.J. 269 (July 1995)

2 Health Matrix, Journal of Law-Medicine 303

Case Western Reserve University School of Law, Summer, 1992

24 American Criminal Law Review 983 (1987)

37 Florida Law Review 889 (1985)

16 Cumberland Law Review 127 (1985-86)

12 Westerm State University Law Review 519 (Spring, 1985)

61 North Carolina Law Review at 1149 (1983)

4 Campbell Law Review 179 (Fall, 1981)

32 So. Cal. Law Review 119 (October, 1980)

51 So. Cal. Law Review 309 (1978)

77 ALR 3d 1108 (1977 and 1995 Supp.)

Additional Articles

"Bite Mark Evidence: Making an Impression in Court", by Captain D. Ben Tesdahl, in *The Army Lawyer,* July, 1989.

"Bite Mark Evidence: Its Worth in the Eyes of the Expert", by Pamela Zarkowski, in *Journal of Law and Ethics in Dentistry,* Vol. 1, No. 1, 1988.

APPENDIX B:
Bite Mark Citation Photographs

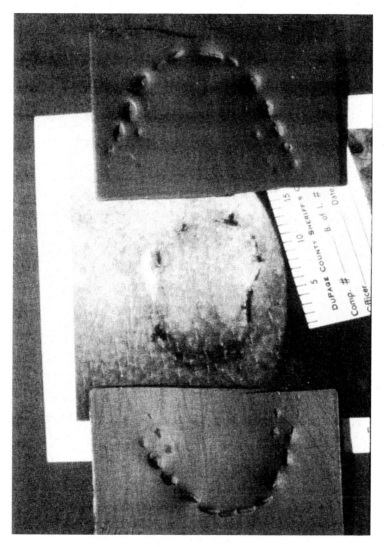

Figure 1 Aluwax impression of Milone's dental study models compared with bite mark on thigh of victim. Note T-shaped mark on upper-right portion of bite mark near ruler and "configuration to the right" on the same side near ruler which shows variation of bite mark compared to suspect's arch size. Ruler is placed toward genitalia of victim.

Figure 2 Bite mark on penis of deceased teenaged homicide victim.

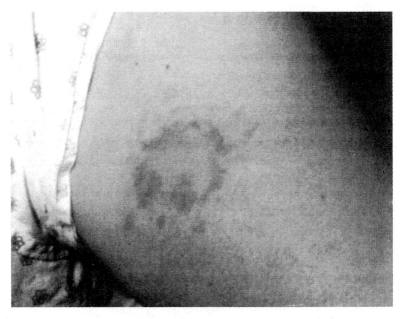

Figure 3 Recent (20-hour-old) bite mark on posterior surface of upper arm inflicted on a prisoner in a fight with another inmate.

Figure 4 Photograph of Theodore Bundy. (Photo courtesy of Dr. Richard R. Souviron.)

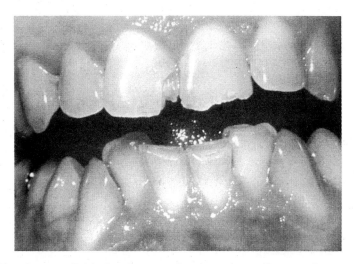

Figure 5 Photograph of Theodore Bundy's anterior teeth. Note fracture in maxillary right central and sharpness of incisal edge of left central. (Photo courtesy of Dr. Richard R. Souviron.)

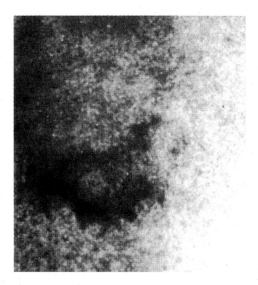

Figure 6 Photograph of "double bite" caused by Theodore Bundy's anterior teeth. Not all of bite mark is shown, but is illustrative of double bite. (Photo courtesy of Dr. Richard Souviron.)

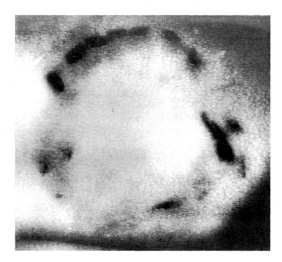

Figure 7 Bite mark on shoulder of abused child homicide victim.

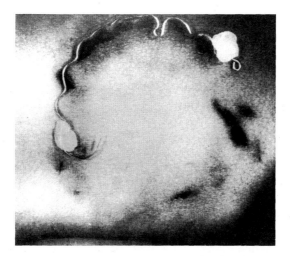

Figure 8 Bite mark on shoulder of abused child homicide victim, with orthodontic wire outlining mandibular teeth.

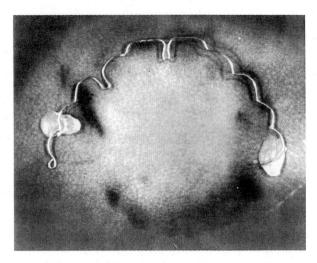

Figure 9 Bite mark on shoulder of abused child homicide victim, with orthodontic wire outlining maxillary teeth. Successfully introduced into trial proceedings.

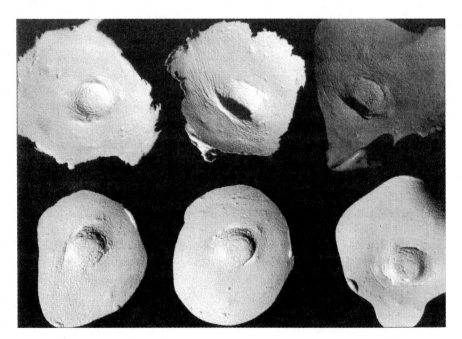

Figure 10 Impressions and models of bite mark on breast. Two different materials were used for the impressions.

Figure 11 Models of bite mark on breast, with cast metal templates of outer surfaces of upper and lower anterior teeth over the bite mark for court or jury use.

APPENDIX C:
Sample Exhumation Release and Retainer Agreement Forms

NOTE: THIS IS A SUGGESTED AGREEMENT ONLY. Advice and assistance of a competent council is necessary in each situation to insure proper procedure depending on state or territory.

Exhumation Authorization And Release

We (I) (insert name or names), the undersigned, nearest blood relatives and survivors of (insert name of deceased), Deceased, who died on (insert date), and was buried (insert date), in (insert name of cemetery, legal description of property, village or city, county, and state), do with this request, authorize and direct that (insert name and professional degrees), conduct an examination (or other assignment) of the body of (insert name of deceased) after disinterment from said cemetery (or grave, etc.). Said examination shall include (list exactly what is going to be done and the methods to be used) removal of the jaws and/or teeth from the body and transportation of same to an appropriate place where (list what kind of examination or tests, that are to be done) X-rays, radiographic studies, and/or photographs of same can be obtained and any and all other dental (medical, forensic, etc.) procedures deemed necessary. If, after examination, it is determined that the actual specimens should be retained, we hereby authorize retention of same.

We hereby certify that this request and authorization is made of our (my) own free will and accord.

We (I) hereby agree and bind ourselves (myself) to protect and indemnify (insert name, professional degrees), and any other person, firm, or corporation charged or chargeable with responsibility or liability, his (her) heirs, representatives, or assigns, from any and all claims, demands, damages, costs, expenses, loss of services, actions, and causes of action arising from any act or occurrence resulting from said examination as described above (make sure that the entire examination and tests you wish to perform as above are included).

We hereby also agree to release (insert name and degrees), from any and all claims of whatsoever kind arising from this authorization and release.

SIGNED this _____ (Insert date and year), signed by absolute legal next of kin, and have properly notarized.

NOTE: THIS IS A SUGGESTED MODEL OF A PROPOSAL ONLY. Prior to use, meet with a competent attorney and draft and agree to the type of retainer letter that will be used in pursuit of your own personal forensic or business matters.

RETAINER AGREEMENT

Attorney Name:

Address:

Regarding, Case Number, Client Name, etc.:

Date:

You have retained (insert name), to assist you in the above case (affair, matter).

You have furnished me with the facts and have agreed to pay a non-refundable initial retainer in the amount of (fill in according to the case). All expenses and the consultant's hourly fee will be drawn from the retainer on a regular basis for such activities as record review, interviews, research, site visits, out of office (or place of employment) appointments, telephone consultation, report writing, and preparation for deposition and testimony. When the deposited retainer fund reaches the amount of (insert amount) an additional payment will be required to replenish it. Any unused portion beyond the original retainer will be refunded to the attorney upon conclusion of services. It is further understood that while I cannot estimate the full charges regarding this matter, you will be required to pay fees at the rate of (insert) per hour. Failure to retain a positive current balance shall be grounds sufficient for the undersigned consultant at any point to proceed to withdraw from consulting with the attorney and/or releasing any work product created during the course of the consultancy.

In order to schedule a deposition in this matter it will be required that you furnish me with a payment in the amount of (fill in) for a full day or part thereof, at least one week in advance of the appearance date. Should the deposition be canceled due to settlement within 48 hours before the scheduled date, one half the amount will be retained as a cancellation fee.

In order to schedule testimony at a trial or an administrative hearing in this matter, it will be required that you furnish me with a payment in the amount of (fill in) for a full day or part thereof, at least one week in advance of the appearance date. Should the trial or administrative hearing be canceled due to a negotiated settlement within 48 hours prior to the scheduled date, one half the amount will be retained as a cancellation fee.

Invoices will be submitted prior to the end of each month. A detailed breakdown will be furnished itemizing all charges for the month. Payments are due upon receipt of statement. Late charges at the rate of (fill in percent) per month will be added to invoices not paid within 30 days. The payment of all fees and customary expenses are the responsibility of the attorney notwithstanding the attorney's relationship with third parties, contingency arrangements, subjugation, etc. As a convenience, we may agree to prepare separate billing for an attorney taking a discovery deposition, but the responsibility for Payment remains that of the original attorney. Failure to include a chargeable item in one billing shall not constitute a waiver of the right to assess the charges in a subsequent billing.

It is further understood that I make no promises to you as to the outcome of this matter except that I promise to execute and use my best professional skill possible. I will be available for every meeting, mediation session and/or court appearance, as necessary, to provide testimony and/or expert advice, consultation or advocacy if I am furnished proper notice as above.

Dated:

Signed (Attorney)   Signed (Name of Doctor or Forensic Scientist, etc.)

Index